Living Free

Finding freedom from habits that hurt

Why the Butterflies?

The butterfly is the national symbol of *freedom from addictions* because of the radical changes it experiences in its growth. Those changes teach three important lessons:

1. *The butterfly's transformation (metamorphosis) is complete.* Metamorphosis is defined as "a complete or marked change in appearance, form, or character." Butterflies go through complete metamorphosis—caterpillars and butterflies are as different as night and day, both in appearance and behavior. A metamorphosis must also take place in the life of a person struggling with addictions. The old life of addiction and the new life of living free are just as dramatically different!

2. *The old has to die in order for the new to take root.* Because the challenges faced by a caterpillar and an adult butterfly are totally different, there is a total restructuring of the caterpillar in order to equip the butterfly for its new life. That change involves a dramatic reorganization of the entire organism. Breaking free from addictions requires a restructuring of the thoughts, choices, actions, and associations.

3. *Transformation leads to a change in lifestyle.* The caterpillar's transformed nervous system initiates processes that lead to the emergence of a robust adult butterfly from the cocoon that lives life in a totally different way.

The principles outlined in *Living Free* will help you experience a new resiliency in mental, physical, and spiritual health. And that will help you form new habits, thoughts, and actions so the transformed you will soar to new heights of *Living Free*!

Adapted from: David N. Mbungu, PhD, Associate Professor, Biology, Andrews University, Berrien Springs, MI.

*A*cknowledgements:

The authors gratefully acknowledge the individuals that shared their stories of inspiration and hope for our readers. A special thanks also to Pier I Imports and JC Penney for props and clothing for models.

DESIGN STAFF:
Dexter Saddler,
Art Director
Eric Pletcher,
Layout and Design

COVER:
David Sherwin

PHOTOGRAPHY:
David Sherwin
Marc Ullom
Karen Hopkins

MODEL/FASHION COOR-DINATOR:
Patricia Stewart

FOOD STYLISTS:
Carol Corbin
Jo Ann Rachor

EDITOR:
Sandra Blackmer

TECHNICAL ASSISTANT:
Sheri Christie

PRINTING
The Hamblin Company
Tecumseh, Michigan 49286

———

The information in this book is not intended to replace medical intervention. Always work with your physician when making lifestyle changes.

I

$\mathcal{F}$oreword

Changing bad habits—for good! Is it possible to change bad habits, even addictions? How do bad habits develop in the first place? It all happens in the brain. And what amazing discoveries are emerging about the most amazing organ of the human body—the brain. *Living Free* is all about developing a healthy mind, body, and spirit. *Living Free* is about how the mind and body operate. *Living Free* is about developing good habits—and keeping them.

Human knowledge in the area of scientific discovery has advanced with great strides over the past 100 to 150 years. The decade of the 1990s witnessed a quantum leap forward toward understanding what has been called the final frontier … the brain. Amazing things have been revealed about the brain and its functioning at all levels, including molecular biology, especially pertaining to genetics and cell chemistry. This decade of the brain has caused us to make a paradigm shift toward accepting the fact that the brain is plastic; that is, the brain is highly flexible and can change and adapt to its environment well into old age.

Increased knowledge has affected every aspect of civilization, especially the numerous ways we can now communicate—also called information systems. Information technology has revolutionized our social environment, and it is no coincidence that the explosion of knowledge about computers has paralleled the quest to understand the greatest computer ever engineered—the brain. It is the biological information system which, of all organs, is the paramount instrument of human existence. Other tissues may be transplanted or exchanged, but it is the nervous system that forms the basis of our thinking. It determines who and what the person is. Without it, there is no personality and no perception.

The brain is the only structure in the body that produces an abstract product with no physical dimensions—the mind. The brain is physical but the mind is not. The mind cannot be measured by height, weight, or texture and has never been seen. It exists in the spiritual realm, in a limited sense, like the God who made it—intangible but nonetheless very real.

The mind is unique in that it is a product of brain function and so it is subject to the laws of cause and effect. A well-functioning brain results in a well-functioning mind. In addition, directed and willed mental activity results in changes that are embossed on our material selves—in the brain. It is God's plan for each individual to function at their best mentally and spiritually. The Bible refers to the harmonious blend of mind and spirit as "the heart—the whole personality."

Physically speaking, the brain is an amazing structure weighing about 3 pounds. Although it occupies less than 2 percent of the body weight of a 150-pound person, it receives about 15 percent of the heart's output of blood to the body; a disproportionate share relative to its weight in order to supply its "needy" sophisticated electrical generators and neurotransmitter systems.

The brain's influence is all-pervasive from within the skull, which houses it, to the tips of the toes, receiving and sending messages throughout of nerve pathways. In this manner its communication network is in contact with the entire body and commanding the body in achieving its ultimate quest—to enjoy vibrant health and freedom.

Unfortunately, disease, poor choices, and trauma can undermine this biological computer just as a computer virus can disrupt a man-made computer. An impaired brain often results in an impaired mind. What can be more important to a person than the proper functioning of the mind and the brain that produces it? There is a mutual relationship between the body, mind, and brain that forms the foundation of total health. This book examines how the physical, mental, and spiritual environment a person creates has a profound shaping affect on the brain.

In the pages that follow we shall outline these body-mind relationships and show how they are practically related to the success of a person's life. Physical and mental health imply a balance of forces in the body so that distress, disease, and premature death are minimized and delayed as much as our individual genes will allow. Destructive habits undermine physical, mental, and spiritual health. This book shows you how to develop good habits and overcome bad ones. These are well-researched volumes with practical information, explaining the rationale for good habits and, hence, laying out for you the road to personal success and freedom. May you receive to the fullest all that is offered within these pages.

David Gaston, M.D.
Assistant Clinical Professor
of Neurology,
Wayne State University
School of Medicine,
Detroit, MI

Preface

Habits. We all have them. When they are good ones, they help us. When they are bad ones, they hurt. Positive habits help a person perform multiple tasks with minimal mental effort, repeat safe and effective behaviors, and build consistency and security in his or her life.

Understanding how the brain works helps us to understand why habits are so important, and so critical for normal life. The brain is constantly mapping, categorizing, and condensing information, building associations and memories, and learning new ways to increase the efficiency with which people perceive and respond to the world. Some of those functions occur automatically and become habits.

But when habits become addictions or compulsions they suddenly put on another face, emerging as demanding tyrants, overriding and crushing the best of intentions and destroying hope in those who are victims of their vise-like grip.

Are certain people more prone to becoming addicted? Can lifestyle choices put someone at greater risk? How do addictions impact or change the way the brain works? Are there specific clues that indicate an addiction is present? Is it possible to become addicted to behaviors and activities, or only to drugs? Can the brain that has been affected by addiction be changed? Once a bad habit or addiction is formed, can it be broken?

It has been said that old habits die hard, and that is true. But the fact that they can and do die is the reason for *Living Free*. It is possible to change!

Living Free reveals how habits and addictions change brain chemistry and contribute to continued bad behaviors despite their negative impact in many areas of life. But *Living Free* shows that healing from addictions is possible.

You will learn simple, powerful strategies that can help you break free from enslaving habits. But more important, you will learn how to empower your life, enrich your environment, and enjoy new ways of thinking and living— and that's how people not only get free, but stay free.

Living Free includes the thrilling stories of people who have been delivered from varying addictions. You'll also find many practical nutrition and lifestyle inserts loaded with helpful, easy-to-follow information and tips. The information in this book can help you on your journey to breaking the chains of bad habits and addictions.

Living Free

Finding freedom from habits that hurt

Table of Contents

Chapter 1

The Addicted Brain

"Certain habits of men are like luxurious
vines: they destroy the trees they decorate."

Abraham Lincoln

Routine or Rut?

Habits—we all have them. American author Elbert Hubbard said: "Habit is the great economizer of energy." He was exactly right.

Habits are our friends—when they're good ones. Habits are routines that help us perform multiple tasks with minimal mental effort. They help us repeat safe and effective behaviors, and build consistency and security into our lives.

In mechanical fashion we drive a familiar route to work, brush our teeth from front to back, enjoy our daily walk with the dog, twist a certain lock of hair when we are nervous, or put the right shoe on before the left. Family habits such as enjoying mealtimes together and regular bedtime improve emotional well-being

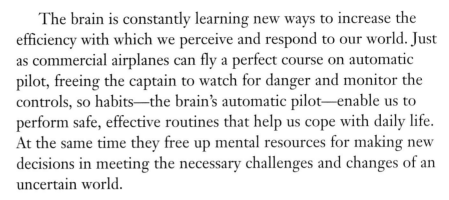

In mechanical fashion we drive a familiar route to work, brush our teeth from front to back, enjoy our daily walk with the dog, twist a certain lock of hair when we are nervous, or put the right shoe on before the left.

The brain is constantly learning new ways to increase the efficiency with which we perceive and respond to our world. Just as commercial airplanes can fly a perfect course on automatic pilot, freeing the captain to watch for danger and monitor the controls, so habits—the brain's automatic pilot—enable us to perform safe, effective routines that help us cope with daily life. At the same time they free up mental resources for making new decisions in meeting the necessary challenges and changes of an uncertain world.

Automation in planes and brains is great, but what happens when the automatic pilot becomes dysfunctional and gets stuck in the wrong routine? Every other control is weakened or rendered powerless with disaster looming on the horizon unless the renegade routine is righted. Instead of being tame servants, dysfunctional habits can become ruthless tyrants—relentless, illogical, expensive, depressing, isolating, and destructive. They weave themselves around us like silken cobwebs but soon become iron chains that squeeze us more tightly the more we struggle to get free.

It has been said that old habits die hard, and that is true. But the fact that they can and *do* die is the reason for this book. It *is* possible to change—because life is all about change. The brain is more than just "a device for recording change"[2]; because as we change, *the brain* changes right along with us!

Habit Forming

Forming new habits—or breaking old ones—is one way that the brain changes. Habits can range in intensity from mildly annoying, such as the nervous accountant who keeps his fingernails bitten, to the illogical and uncontrollable, such as the compulsive bulimic who engages in food bingeing and purging many times a day.

Bad habits can sometimes become addictions. Addiction is viewed in many and varied ways. In the past, the term *addiction* was used only to refer to the compulsive need for and use of a habit-forming substance (such as heroin, nicotine, or alcohol). Addictions were characterized by drug tolerance and the withdrawal symptoms a user experienced when not using the drug.

Sigmund Freud's use of tobacco provides a good example of serious addiction to a substance: nicotine. Smoking about 20 cigars a day caused Freud to have a serious heart arrhythmia, and upon the advice of a friend he tried to stop. But Freud found the subsequent depression during periods of abstinence almost unbearable. He continued to smoke heavily despite admitting that it hindered his analytic studies.

He later developed sores on his palate and jaw that failed to heal, so he had surgery—the first of 33 for cancer. He complained that he was out of work and could not swallow, yet he continued to smoke. His heart condition forced him to retire, and he eventually had to have his entire jaw removed and an artificial jaw substituted. In constant pain, often he could not speak, chew, or swallow. Yet Freud continued to smoke what a friend termed "an endless series of cigars."[3]

Sigmund Freud

However, drugs are not the only factor in addiction. Freud's long-term compulsive, destructive drug behavior, even after months of abstinence, is truly remarkable, since it takes only 30 hours for nicotine to clear the system. Clearly, a failure to stop cannot be linked to the discomfort of withdrawal symptoms alone. Such conclusions have triggered a broader understanding of the meaning of addiction, and what it encompasses.

Today, addiction has been more broadly defined to include not only the use of drugs but also persistent compulsive behaviors that are harmful or destructive, characterized by an inability to stop. It is recognized that structural changes take place in the brain when any addiction occurs, whether or not drugs are involved.

While most people are aware of the acute, short-term withdrawal symptoms with some addictions, they are not aware that there are long-term effects that can last for years. To hope that a recovering addict will be "back to normal" within a couple of months after treatment is neither realistic nor fair for the addict. Nestler and Landsman (2001) affirm that a major feature of addiction is its chronicity. A person can experience intense cravings for the substance, activity, or behavior and remain at increased risk for relapse even after years of abstinence, especially if they don't develop proper strategies for long-term success.

Expanding Addictions

The addiction picture is bigger than drugs. Howard Shaffer, who heads the Division of Addictions at Harvard University, asserts that drug use "is not a necessary and sufficient cause of addiction. It is improper to consider drugs as the necessary precondition for addiction."[4] "A lot of addiction is the result of experience: repetitive, high-emotion, high-frequency experience."[5]

Stanford University psychologist Brian Knutson agrees: "It stands to reason if you can derange these circuits with pharmacology (drugs), you can do it with natural rewards too."[6] "What is coming up fast as being the central core issue…is continued engagement in self-destructive behavior despite adverse consequences," says Steven Grant of the National Institute on Drug Abuse.[7] The development of an addiction is a process that involves more than drugs, and can take place even in the absence of drugs.

With this expanded definition, addictions can take the form of not only drugs but food, gambling, shopping, overwork, sex,

The development of an addiction is a process that involves more than drugs, and can take place even in the absence of drugs.

television, or any other activity that becomes excessive, destructive, or compulsive. This does not mean that all addictions have the same results.

Substance addictions involve the introduction of a chemical agent that has varied consequences. Behavioral addictions may involve activities that are in and of themselves normal and even necessary, such as eating or using the Internet. In this case, total abstinence is impossible, but rather remodeling the behavior and thinking concerning the activity, is essential. In fact, all addictive tendencies require vigilance and remodeling of thinking and behavior.

One example of a nondrug addiction is food. Notice how similar the behavior and thinking of this psychologist and former food addict compare with a typical drug addict: "I knew from my own internal experience just how compelling a food craving can be, how powerful and irresistible. My food addiction had seemed like a curse, preventing me from feeling like a normal person. I knew my relationship with certain foods was not normal. I knew that my thinking and obsessing, planning and hoarding, sneaking and hiding resembled the behavior of an addict."[8]

There are profoundly different physical, emotional, social, and personal effects of addictions, and they will vary widely with each addiction and person. Addictive disorders can also be related to underlying disease processes or head injury. Always work with your physician and get a complete evaluation.

While new research points to the marvelous ability of the brain to change, there *are* points of no return for some brain changes impacted by addiction, especially those involving substances. These changes will vary with each individual. However, the *Delivered* stories throughout this book show that the hope of recovery can become reality.

The Process of Addiction

The process of addiction involves four stages: (1) experimental and/or social engagement in the substance, activity, or behavior; (2) problem use (abuse of the substance, activity, or behavior); (3) addiction; and (4) recovery/relapse.

■ Stage 1 involves occasional engagement—perhaps a few times monthly, maybe on weekends. Reasons for entering stage 1 are to satisfy curiosity, peer pressure, to be accepted socially, to defy parents, to take a risk or seek a thrill, to relieve boredom, to produce pleasurable feelings, and/or to be entertained. A person in stage 1 feels little or no physical or psychological change in the absence of his or her addictive substance or behavior.

■ Stage 2 involves regular participation in the activity or behavior, either alone or with others. Reasons for stage 2 involvement may include: to manipulate one's emotions; to experience pleasure; to cope with stress and uncomfortable feelings, such as pain, guilt, anxiety, sadness, depression, etc.; to overcome feelings of inadequacy; to keep from feeling down because of not engaging in the activity or behavior.

In stage 2 a person may experience a decline in performance at work, church, school, or in other settings. There may be mood swings, personality changes, dishonesty, changes in friendships, intimacy problems, or decreased interest in other activities. More "acting out" behaviors may be seen, and all interest is focused on engaging in the activity or behavior.

■ Stage 3 involves frequent, continuous use. Reasons here may include: avoiding pain and depression, escaping the realities of daily living, and loss of control over the frequency of engaging in the activity or behavior (the behavior or substance now controls them).

When an addiction develops, what is happening in the brain? For one thing, the pleasure circuits in the brain become "hijacked"

7

In stage 3, changes may include physical deterioration, poor appearance, or volatile mood swings such as aggression, irritation, depression, and apathy. If alcohol and drug use are involved, there may be memory loss, flashbacks, and/or paranoia.

In this stage, an addict's most frequent state is pain or discomfort and engaging in the addictive activity in an attempt to achieve normalcy. Because they are more focused on escaping the pain of withdrawal than on the pleasure of a "high," addicts are unlikely to experience euphoria at this stage. But they do experience deteriorated relationships, guilt, shame, remorse, and may even consider suicide.

■ In stage 4, the recovery process, a person may experience a relapse into an old behavior. But that does not mean he or she is doomed to fail. It means that person needs to develop watchfulness, new thinking patterns, and a new supportive lifestyle. This is a growing process that helps the brain, body, and spirit to grow in resolve and to develop new habits. Mistakes can be turned into victories when you refuse to give up and continue to practice those positive choices.

Haywire or Hot-wired?

When an addiction develops, what is happening in the brain? For one thing, the pleasure circuits in the brain become "hijacked" by the addictive substance or behavior and stop functioning in harmonious concert with other brain circuits. Judgment and reason take a back seat to habits that have taken over the pleasure and motivational centers of the brain, making them repeatedly produce intense cravings. This is followed by a "reward cascade" of pleasure neurotransmitters (chemicals that transmit information from one brain cell to another), including dopamine, serotonin, enkephalin, and GABA[9] when that craving is satisfied. These repeated quick fixes for

pleasure paralyze the regulatory mechanisms of the brain that put the brakes on pleasure neurotransmitters with their messages that say, "Stop! I am satisfied!"

When the process happens enough times, the normal pleasures of life may become blurred or even of no interest to the addict. Why? One reason is that with repeated abuse the amount of neurotransmitter released in response to normal stimuli is reduced. Now the feelings of satisfaction that were produced by these neurotransmitters (especially dopamine) under normal pleasurable circumstances (such as eating a cookie) are not felt with the same intensity. Bigger sensations and surging rushes of pleasure are required to get the "lift" that provides a feeling of well-being and normalcy. And the addict will do anything to get it—even if it lasts only for a moment.

Another reason is that the brain records information about what produced pleasurable responses in the past. In the normally

functioning brain, these memories are used to help the individual decide what needs to be done next. Thus, we are able to order our lives and decide when is the appropriate time to eat, go for a walk, read a book, or enjoy the company of friends. For the addict, the only motivation that exists is to obtain the source of the addiction—all other motivations and goals, whether short-or long-term, are overwhelmed by addiction-generated cravings.

In other words, addiction is a form of learning. But it is learning wrong routines or habits that destroy rather than promote well-being and block normal desires and habits (such as eating and spending time with loved ones). Addictive drugs in particular enhance the action of a brain neurotransmitter called glutamate, one of the most common neurotransmitters in the brain. Glutamate interacts with dopamine in the pleasure circuits, but also is involved in memory centers that strongly "fix" the habit in the brain as a learned behavior.[10]

Examining how glutamate is used in the brain helps us understand why cravings are so powerful in the addict. Because glutamate is involved in memory and learning, it helps to store the information that can lead to cravings and relapse after abstinence from drug use.[11] Later on, cues in the environment (a place, a smell, or a person, for example) can "trigger" addiction memories that can then prompt relapse-prone thinking.

While that may sound like a large dose of bad news, here's the good news. An understanding of how glutamate influences learning suggests that behavioral therapy is one of the most promising treatments for overcoming addictions. Molecular biologist and addiction specialist Eric Nestler explains that people can "unlearn aspects of addiction and relearn new things to do in life" by establishing new behaviors that provide an alternative focus.[12]

Like a house with circuits that link switches to lights in the rooms, the brain has circuits, too, and they can become dysfunctional.[13] But circuitry in houses and brains can be improved, rewired, and restored. New experiences, thoughts, actions, and behaviors affect the structure and function of the brain. The ongoing process of learning new, positive behaviors and ways of thinking can help any person overcome the tangled roots of addiction.

The Tangled Roots of Addiction

Addiction of any kind has many possible roots, including emotional, physical, environmental, and genetic. It is important to understand the strength of the enemy in order to develop a strategy for decided victory. Addictions can creep into the lives of the vulnerable or unwary in many forms, crossing all racial, class, social, educational, and economic boundaries with cold impartiality. Emotional, behavioral, spiritual, and lifestyle factors are involved in addictions. Finding lasting freedom requires positive change in every one of these areas.

Are there environmental or genetic factors that increase the risk of developing addictions? Anything that lives and grows responds to its environment. Environmental factors and genes can influence a person's vulnerability to addiction. Studies of juvenile offenders consistently reveal three prominent features they share: drug involvement, a history of family violence, and neurological or cognitive vulnerabilities.[14] The more of these features they possess, the more likely they are to struggle with addiction, crime, and violence.

In other words, addiction is a form of learning. But it is learning wrong routines or habits that destroy rather than promote well-being and block normal desires and habits.

Why? For several reasons. Drug involvement affects the ability of the brain to experience normal pleasure when the user is off the drug. Because a drug user often experiences depression when not using the drug, drug addiction lends itself to increased drug taking, risk taking, and other addictive behaviors. Addictive drugs have a profound impact on the brain's reward circuits and increase the likelihood of crime, addiction, and long-term mood disorders. While a person may begin using drugs for many reasons, addictive drugs can create problems where none may have existed before because of what they do to the brain.

11

Second, crime, especially violent crime,[15] is associated with drug use. One study of 85 adolescent criminals showed that 82 percent were drug dependent.[16] Surprisingly, adolescents comprise only 8 percent of the population but commit more than 50 percent of the nation's crimes.[17]

Just experiencing or witnessing violence has an emotional and physiological impact on body and brain function.[18] Especially in a child, in the area of the brain where the emotional networks are being formed, changes occur in neural patterns and gene expression that may put the child at higher risk for addictions, sensation-seeking behavior, and violence later in life.

Witnessing or experiencing trauma can also produce changes in brain and body chemistry that foster the inclination toward violence, depression, and addiction.[19] It is not uncommon for emotionally or physically traumatized individuals to attempt to control rage, depression, nightmares, and intrusive thoughts by using heroin, cocaine, or alcohol. We could expand that list to include tobacco, food, television, gambling, pornography, compulsive overexercising, or any number of mind-numbing, health-destroying habits.

Third, prolonged exposure to stress affects how efficiently glands and nerve cell circuits respond to stress over time. Early exposure to profound stress actually influences which genes in the brain are activated and the way brain hormone and neural systems are developed.[20] Early exposure to traumatic events not only predisposes a person to illness later in life but also increases hormone responses to stress in adulthood, increasing the likelihood of depression.[21]

Just experiencing or witnessing violence has an emotional and physiological impact on body and brain function.

For various reasons, some infants' brains are more vulnerable to addiction, such as children born to drug-addicted mothers or alcohol abusers, or who have other inborn cognitive impairments. Babies of mothers who are chronically stressed are more likely to suffer from anxiety and depression as adults.[22] This is partly because the mother's chronic stress alters the development of the baby's stress system,[23] leaving the baby more sensitive to environmental stressors.[24] Fortunately, the brain is resilient in childhood as well as adulthood, and recovery, restoration, and renewal is possible, even when inheritance and environment have dealt a hard blow.

Winning any war depends on knowing the strength of the enemy and also having a powerful cache of weapons to win a decided victory.

13

We have seen the strength of the enemy, and that the tangled roots of addiction can have genetic, environmental, and behavioral elements. But the weapons available to win the war against addiction are mighty. They include creating an environment, both internal and external; creating a lifestyle; creating a community; and creating a spiritual Connection. These weapons, used together, play a powerful role in overcoming liabilities, amending weaknesses, building strength, coping with stress, and experiencing permanent recovery from addiction.

Damaged But Not Doomed

Any time a food, drug, or activity (such as using pornography or excessive television viewing) is persistently used to avoid dealing with life's pain and challenges, or is used as a substitute for unmet needs, addiction may loom dangerously near.

But there is a wide difference between vulnerability and destiny—a significant distinction between risk and predetermined fate. There are many who are at high risk for addiction who overcome the odds and become stellar citizens; we see others who have many of life's advantages but nonetheless become helpless victims of addictions, not realizing the potency of the addictive substance or activity. Studies may reveal certain links, and understanding those links is important for intervention and therapy, but they do not predict success or failure. It is important to understand where we have come from, but it is equally important to know that we do not have to remain stuck there; we can go on.

Brain structure is not predetermined and fixed—even when early experience has not been good. According to neuropsychiatrist John Ratey, "We can alter the ongoing development of our brains and thus our capabilities. Poverty, alienation, drugs, hormonal imbalances, and depression don't dictate failure. Wealth, acceptance, vegetables, and exercise don't guarantee success. Our own free will may be the strongest force directing the development of our brains, and therefore our lives.

It is important to understand where we have come from, but it is equally important to know that we do not have to remain stuck there; we can go on.

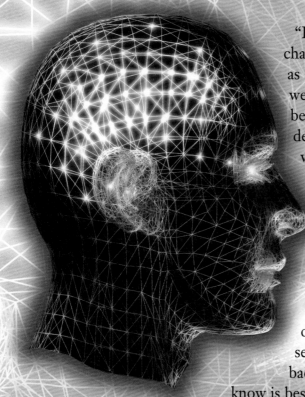

"Experiences, thoughts, actions, and emotions actually change the structure of our brains. By viewing the brain as a muscle that can be weakened or strengthened, we can exercise our ability to determine who we become. Indeed, once we understand how the brain develops, we can train our brains for health, vibrancy, and longevity."[25]

Addicted people feel they have lost their will-power—the power to choose what they rationally know is right. There is a loss of a sense of self-control. Once a person has experienced addiction, changes have taken place in the brain that involve multiple brain circuits, especially circuits involving reward, motivation, drive, memory, conditioning, stress, and self-control.[26] This book outlines how to take back the brain—and the power to choose what you know is best for you—in every area of your life.

Dispelling Myths About Addiction

For years, ignorance of the facts regarding addiction has led many to not be treated and/or to be mistreated by family, friends, health care providers, or fellow church members. The following facts outlined on pages 17 and 18 are from the United States Department of Labor (2004) and help clear up some of that ignorance.

Experiences, thoughts, actions, and emotions actually change the structure of our brains. By viewing the brain as a muscle that can be weakened or strengthened, we can exercise our ability to determine who we become.

Addiction Facts

1. Addiction can be a life-threatening condition, with roots in genetic susceptibility, social circumstance, and personal behavior. Research by the National Institute on Drug Abuse suggests that long-term exposure to the substance, activity, or behavior produces addiction by eliciting changes in specific neurons in the central nervous system.

2. Most people with an addiction cannot simply stop, no matter how strong their resolve. Most need one or more courses of structured treatment to reduce or end their addiction.

3. One of the most disturbing and confusing aspects of addiction is that it is often characterized by denial: "I'm not out of control"; "This isn't affecting my family or my job."

4. Enabling behavior by family and friends can worsen the addictive process in the victim. Examples of enabling behavior include covering up for the addict, excusing his or her behavior as acceptable, avoiding the addict, blaming the person for lack of self-control, or attempts to control addicts them by threats or coercion.

5. Many factors can lead to developing a problem with substances, activities, and/or behaviors. While accurate predictions of addiction risk is not possible, certain factors such as a family history of addictions, self-destructive lifestyle, stress or trauma, violence, or prior addictions can increase the likelihood of addiction.

6. Addiction is a treatable disorder. Every day thousands are making changes in their lives, grasping the keys for living free and shedding the burden of addiction.

What is available to help an addict to recover? There are four ways to weaken the hold of an addiction: (1) reduce the reward value of the drug or behavior; (2) increase the rewarding experience of positive choices; (3) reduce the power of addiction triggers; and (4) strengthen the brain by learning new habits.

Addictions have many faces and many causes. They have their roots in our inheritance; the social, emotional, and spiritual environment we have grown up in; the lifestyle choices we have made; and the way we relate to all of the above. All these powerful factors have a profound shaping influence on the brain. But what we have learned, we can unlearn. New and positive experiences can override old, negative ones. Brain changes occur in response to experience. This book is about learning how to activate new and positive experiences that override the old negative ones. And that is good news indeed for those who have become tangled in the iron meshes of addiction—but are determined to find freedom from habits that hurt!

Addiction is a treatable disorder. Every day thousands are making changes in their lives, grasping the keys for living free and shedding the burden of addiction.

10 Signs of an Addicted Brain

1. Spending a lot of time with it.*

2. Using it more than intended.

3. Repeated failure to reduce time with it.*

4. Lying, sneaking, hiding regarding it.*

5. Inability to enjoy other pleasures.

6. Obsessing, planning, and hoarding of it.*

7. Underlying depression, anxiety.

8. Work, school, and family deterioration because of it.*

9. Giving up useful activities for it.*

10. Withdrawal symptoms when use stops.

* "It" is the addiction, whether it is food, drugs, an activity, or a behavior.

19

8 Common Symptoms of Withdrawal

Withdrawal from addictions of any kind can produce symptoms that range from temporary and frustrating to prolonged and serious. It takes time for the brain and body to readjust to the absence of the repeated, habitual stimulation of any addiction.

In the same way that it takes time and patience to regain energy and focus after fighting a bodily ailment such as the flu, it also takes time and patience to regain brain health, bodily strength, and emotional energy after fighting an addiction.

The lifestyle tools in chapters 7-9 can help you develop the resources you need to cope with temporary "brain flu" and guide you in the restoration of your body, mind, and spirit.

1. Depression

2. Restlessness, tension

3. Fatigue

4. Aggression

5. Poor concentration

6. Cravings

7. Suicidal thoughts

8. Insomnia

* This list does not include the physiological symptoms associated with withdrawal from specific substances, such as drugs, alcohol, or nicotine. For physical symptoms associated with various substance addictions, see insert in the back of this book. Work with your healthcare provider if symptoms are uncontrollable.

Tony
HALL

Delivered

Drugs, Dealing, and Death

I was the oldest of seven children with six different absentee fathers. Without a male to model in my home, I chose the negative role models of the older guys in my neighborhood. I was drinking cheap bottled wine and smoking every day before I was a teenager. On my eleventh birthday I was locked in Juvenile Court for stealing and selling bicycles. By the time I was 14, I had been arrested again, had left home and dropped out of school, and was using drugs regularly.

Before I turned 18 I had overdosed three times. Twice the doctors entered into the records that I was clinically dead.

By the time I was 19, I had been arrested 14 times in eight different states. I must have committed a thousand or more drug-related felonies, including murders, stealing, gambling, and running prostitution houses, although I was never arrested for any of these crimes.

Early in life I felt doomed. I had decided that no matter what I did, nothing would change the bad hand life had dealt me. I enjoyed my lifestyle and counted the dangers and arrests as occupational hazards. I was surrounded by those who were totally unconcerned about their future.

In a dream I had when I was 12, I was flying with a group of eagles and would swoop down to feed my younger brothers and sisters. Even with the lifestyle I had chosen, I felt a desire to learn as much as I could so that one day I could teach my younger brothers and sisters a better way. But at that time, I was traveling alone through the United States, briefly contacting relatives on rare occasions.

Eventually, I joined the Marines, went AWOL (absent without leave), and wound up in Massachusetts running houses of gambling and prostitution. One day while robbing a senior citizens' complex, I realized for the first time I had a conscience. I remembered my great aunt who raised me and took me to church, where I developed a respect for senior citizens. While robbing that complex, I prayed for the first time. My prayer was, "Please, God, make Yourself known to me. Speak to me in a language I can understand." It was at this point that I realized I wasn't a hundred percent evil, but also knew that I wasn't all that saintly either!

Delivered
Tony Hall – Drugs, Dealing, and Death

I soon left Massachusetts and headed for Alabama in a stolen Cadillac—with a trunk full of weapons, drugs, and cash. While passing through New York City, I was arrested and sent to the Rikers Island Correctional Facility. That's where I picked up a Bible for the first time, which I read for three weeks straight. I was released from Rikers Island to spend 18 months in a rehabilitation program. By then I was a serious Bible student, filled with hope and a determination to change my ways so I could leave and fulfill my dream of helping my siblings. The foundation for freedom I found includes three simple steps. **Step 1: Accept.** I cannot overcome without the power of the Word guiding me (John 15:5, last part). **Step 2: Believe.** I can overcome all things with the power of the Word supporting me (Philippians 4:13). When I accepted those two principles, I had no more excuses for failure. If and when I found myself off track, I'd go to **Step 3: Confess.** God is right and I'm wrong; the power of the Word is faithful and just to forgive me and cleanse me from all unrighteousness (1 John 1:9). That's what kept me free for 30 years!

There was a time when I hated the law of God and I hated people. Today my favorite scripture is John 14:15: "If you love me, you will keep my commandments." The Lord has written His commandments in my heart.

I have been married for more than 25 years and have one son, three daughters, and five grandchildren. I have served as an elder in my local church for 20 years, a prison chaplain for more than 20 years, and am a prison ministries coordinator in my area. Today, I am living my dream—flying free as an eagle and helping others to do the same.

Richard
CONSTANTINESCU

Delivered

Smoking and Drugs

I was diagnosed with serious food allergies when I was very young. Those allergies, and the medications I took to combat them, made it very difficult for me to feel normal or to focus on simple tasks. I didn't handle the medications or the condition well. To combat my feelings of failure, I started to experiment with drugs, beginning with cigarettes. In my quest to feel good and gain control of my emotions and my environment, I progressed to heavier drugs, spending all my money, time, and energy on getting high. The "party" lasted for almost three years.

My sister, who lived close by noticed my deteriorating condition. Through a series of events she got me into a rehabilitation program. I began eating a healthful diet, getting lots of fresh air and exercise, and forming new friendships. I also found a connection with God.

It wasn't until two months later while praying to God one day that I realized the extent to which I had been wasting my money, time, and health. I had also made those around me miserable. In all, it took me six months to realize my drug habit was destroying me.

Two years after my rehabilitation, I was still having hallucinations regularly and my memory was worse than before I started taking drugs. Fearful that the heavy drug use had permanently damaged my brain, I visited a local pastor and asked him his advice since he also used to be an addict. He counseled me to do what he had done—read and memorize portions of the Bible.

I had never been able to memorize and retain verses, but I took his advice. What did I have to lose? Amazingly, after just 2 months, I noticed that my brain was much clearer and that I could learn and remember the Bible passages. I was retaining other information better as well! I was thrilled! I had more joy, peace, and confidence than ever before! I had finally found what the drugs could not give—competence and confidence!

Delivered
Richard Constantinescu – Smoking and Drugs

I've been free for 8 years now. Yes, I tried some of my old habits again, but the results were so horrible, and I missed my "new life" so much, I went right back to my new ways! Scripture memorization played an essential part in my realizing that God forgives and empowers those who are sorry for their mistakes.

Things are so much better now. I see a horizon of opportunity and freedom. I am no longer dependent on any addictive substances to have happiness because I know a Creator God who wants me to feel good and treat myself with respect and dignity. I'm no longer abusing my relationships with people and especially those who care about me! For me, drugs and other addictions represent failure and bondage while a temperate lifestyle ensures genuine peace and true strength.

Personal Worksheet 1

The Addicted Brain

1. What is the value of learning "good" habits?* What makes them good? How do people learn positive habits? _____

_____

_____

2. True or false: Addictions can involve either substances or behaviors.** How do you know if you have an addiction? Review *Ten Signs of an Addicted Brain* on page 19.* What withdrawal symptoms occur when you stop an addictive activity? Review *Eight Symptoms of Withdrawal* on page 20.*_____

_____

_____

3. Can anyone develop an addiction? Look up Romans 6:16 and Hebrews 2:14, 15. How do these passages describe the basic condition of all humankind? _____

_____

_____

4. How do addictions develop? How can attitudes, lifestyle or environment help me to avoid developing destructive habits? _____

_____

5. How can I gain strength when I am weak? Look up Luke 4:18; Romans 5:6; and Isaiah 40:29. What do these verses say about the help available to me? _____

_____

_____

Answers located on page 342 in the back of book.

* If you are working in a group, review the sections before you meet.
** It is important to rule out other medical conditions. Always work with your physician or healthcare provider. Serious mood disorders or physical symptoms require clinical intervention.

Chapter 2

The Learning Brain

"What we learn to do, we learn by doing."

Aristotle

Small Beginnings—the Road to Personhood

Who are you? What makes you, you? You came into this world as a unique, special, human being. Your brain began its marvelous development shortly after conception, influenced by the genes you inherited and the hidden environment of your mother's womb.

Out of these small beginnings emerge the human body and the human brain— marvelous, mysterious, and surprisingly malleable, or *plastic*. *Plastic* simply means that brain cells have an amazing capability of being influenced and changed. Although this capability is greater in childhood, we will see that the brain retains this *plastic*, or changeable, potential throughout life and is central to our ability to learn, to grow, and to change.

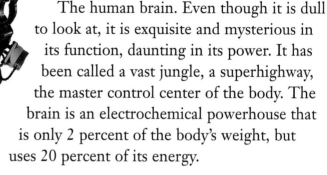

The human brain. Even though it is dull to look at, it is exquisite and mysterious in its function, daunting in its power. It has been called a vast jungle, a superhighway, the master control center of the body. The brain is an electrochemical powerhouse that is only 2 percent of the body's weight, but uses 20 percent of its energy.

The brain generates 20 watts of power during waking hours, rocketing thought messages at speeds of up to 250 miles an hour! Even terms such as awesome don't begin to do justice to this internal wonder which is more complex than our entire solar system.

The brain can soar to the heights of brilliance or hold its inhabitant in the cruel tyranny of mental illness. But how is the brain fashioned, and when is its fashioning complete? Is what each brain finally becomes helplessly fastened in the grip of our genes, or do the environment and our individual choices help to mold this marvelous machine?

It's in Your Head!

Consider the power of the human brain. It is responsible for the painting of the Mona Lisa, the designing of a suspension bridge, the forming of a democracy, the memory of an early childhood experience, the drive to accomplish a difficult task, the virtue of honesty, and the ability to taste a succulent peach. In short, the brain not only supervises the nervous system, it is also the site of emotions, memory, learning, self-awareness, spirituality, and thought.

How does the brain achieve such incredible diversity? One reason is that although humans share with other species the same control mechanisms for developing the brain, the human cortex, the outer layer of tissue that covers the two hemispheres (brain halves), makes up an enormous 80 percent of the brain.

We all start out with a unique set of genes, or hereditary instructions. But we also have different experiences, or environmental influences, that can impact our brain's development. And people relate to their experiences differently.

There has been considerable debate as to which has a more powerful influence on who we are and why we do what we do—nature (genes) or nurture (environment). For instance, do genes determine a child's interest in reading, or do a rich learning environment and a nightly family reading circle have the greater influence? Are we hardwired by inheritance or influenced by environment and choice, or both, and to what extent?

Reading the popular press, one could draw the conclusion that genes hold ominous sway over environmental factors in a wide variety of areas. Scientists report that they have found the genes for alcoholism, anxiety, bedwetting, violence, happiness, dementia, and obesity. But actually, many genes are involved in these traits. So, are faulty genes responsible for all of society's ills? Just how much do they influence who we are and the choices we make?

Synaptic Self—Connections to Reality

In his book *Synaptic Self*, Joseph Le Doux explains how genes and the environment work together to achieve their mental and behavioral effects by shaping the synaptic organization of the brain.[1] What exactly is *synaptic organization*? There are about a hundred billion neurons (nerve cells) in the brain that transmit electrical and chemical signals to one another. They have projections called axons, which carry the electrical signals within the cell, and then send chemical signals to other cells and branching, treelike projections called dendrites, which receive the chemical signals. The chemicals used in signaling are the neurotransmitters discussed in Chapter 1.

One way that axons and dendrites communicate is through nerve cell junctions, or gaps, called synapses. These are the meeting places of neurons, much like a patio adjoining two buildings where employees can meet to deliver important messages.

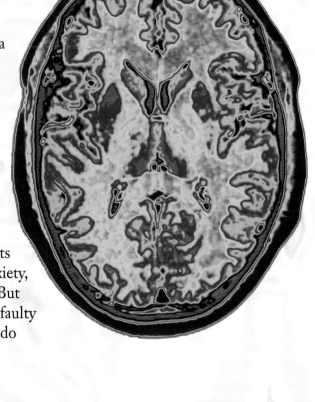

The human brain. Even though it is dull to look at, it is exquisite and mysterious in its function, daunting in its power.

The synaptic "patio talk" represents neuronal activity in the brain and is very important. With increased nerve cell activity, more synapses are created. Interestingly, neurons and synapses (patios) that are not activated early in life do not usually survive. Animals raised in the dark, for example, have fewer synapses and fewer dendritic branches in certain vision centers of the brain.[2] On the other hand, rats that interact with other rats have thicker cortexes with greater dendritic branches, and therefore more efficient mental function.[3] Those extra synapses and dendritic branches require a greater network of life-sustaining blood vessels, all of which enable quicker and more efficient communication and a greater ability to "bounce back" when stress or damage occurs.

Dr. John Ratey, a neuropsychiatrist at Harvard University, further explains: "It is believed that most learning and development occur in the brain through the process of strengthening or weakening these connections (synapses). Each one of our one hundred billion neurons may have anywhere from 1 to 10,000 synaptic connections to other neurons.

"This means that the theoretical number of different patterns of connections possible in a single brain is approximately 40,000,000,000,000,000—forty quadrillion. If changes in synaptic strengths are the primary mechanism behind the brain's ability to represent the world, and if each synapse has, say, ten different strengths, then the different electrochemical configurations in a single brain come to a staggering number: ten to the trillionth power (That's 10 with ten trillion zeroes behind it!). Happily, this dynamic complexity is actually the solution to many people's fears that our nature is genetically 'hard-wired.' The brain is so complex, and so plastic, that it is virtually impossible, except in the broadest fashion, to predict how a given factor will influence its state."[4] This wonderful complexity of the brain reveals its amazing capacity to adapt, change, and recover from negative influences.

As we learn, make choices, exhibit various behaviors, and store memories, changes occur at brain synapses. But it is still a

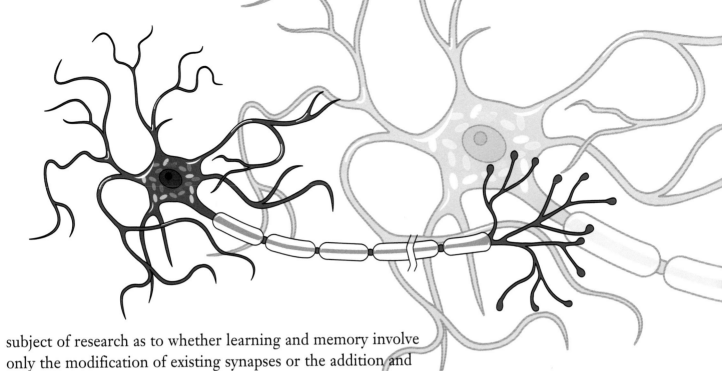

subject of research as to whether learning and memory involve only the modification of existing synapses or the addition and elimination of them.[5]

Animal studies have shown that a stimulating environment not only influences the strength of brain connections but may also encourage the growth of new brain cells.[6] [7] [8] [9] In commenting on this and other similar research showing that certain, but not all, neurons can replicate, geneticist Fred Gage remarked: "A milestone is marked in our understanding of the brain with the recent acceptance, contrary to early dogma, that the adult nervous system can generate new neurons."[10] [11] The full implication of this phenomenon is still under investigation.

Other exciting research shows that older people who engage in stimulating mental activities are less likely to develop Alzheimer's disease than those who were less active.[12] Mental challenges stimulate the brain to produce new connections, which may prevent or delay the onset of dementia in individuals prone to the disease.

While research is ongoing, one thing is certain: The brain is capable of almost innumerable forms of learning and memory, and potentially as many ways for neurons to change their function. Neuroscientist Mary Kennedy describes the brain's wonderful range of activity and subtlety of function as being based on "highly tunable" properties of each neuron during development and also in adults, which ultimately influence behavior.[13]

A milestone is marked in our understanding of the brain with the recent acceptance, contrary to early dogma, that the adult nervous system can generate new neurons.

Built-ins or Add-ons?

Each one of us has a unique genetic makeup that contributes to our individuality. Genetic factors can influence tendencies to aggression, depression, insomnia, and mental illness. To a certain extent, even such traits as shyness versus gregariousness are influenced by genes.[14] Genes may bend us in a certain direction, but many other factors influence how those genes are expressed.[15] Le Doux makes this important point: "We hear a lot these days about how identical twins, reared apart by separate adoptive parents, can have similar habits and traits. We hear less about the many ways they differ. Genes are important, but not all-important."[16]

Genes *do* contribute to personality traits but do not entirely determine them or dictate who we are. According to biopsychologist John Pinel: "Life's experiences, in the form of learning and memory, shape how one's genotype is expressed."[17] Activity influences how cells grow and cluster, and thus how the brain grows and functions, as well as which traits and tendencies are strengthened or weakened. An example is shyness, which is often reinforced by the teasing of peers, the reaction of parents, and pressure by teachers.

John Ratey explains it this way: "The point to remember is that genes can be active or inactive and that everything we do affects the activity of our genes. For example, genes activate the exploratory network in a child's brain, and the more enriched the child's environment, the more these genes turn on, and the more the child explores. Adults experience many similar effects: Learning increases the activation of genes that turn on the production of proteins in the brain needed to strengthen memory."[18]

Ratey makes the point that the environment and our choices have a profound effect on genetic tendencies for conditions we have long considered "fixed" such as obesity, homosexuality, and even personal traits such as leadership or optimism. He continues: "We humans are not prisoners of our genes or our environment. We have free will. Genes are overruled every time an angry man restrains his temper, a fat man diets, and an alcoholic refuses to take a drink. It may be harder for people

with certain genes or surroundings, but harder is a long way from predetermination."[19]

People make dramatic mid life career changes, master new skills, adopt healthful lifestyles after years of wrong habits, make positive changes in the way they relate to people after years of dysfunctional relationships, and learn to enjoy new activities, hobbies, foods, and friends. All this human dynamism involves change—genetic, neuronal, and hormonal. These changes are involved in the ongoing formation of new brain circuits—and a new you!

Sometimes, however, genes exert a stronger influence over a person than environmental factors do, such as in diseases like cystic fibrosis or color blindness. But many times the environment wins over genes, such as a heart disease-prone person who avoids the disease by living a healthful lifestyle, or the shy person who speaks up for an important cause.

We have all heard the expression "practice makes perfect." That is, the performance of a given task or behavior improves or strengthens with repetition. This is because the brain is wonderfully plastic, or changeable, throughout life. The processes of thinking, learning, and memory are dynamic and ongoing.

What we learn, we become. The ability of the nervous system to wire and rewire itself in response to life changes is known as *experience-dependent plasticity*.[20] This includes the learning of new physical[21] [22] as well as mental and behavioral tasks.[23] The fact that neurons can forge new connections and blaze new pathways means that the adult brain can change, and change in profound ways.[24]

37

The brain also has an amazing ability to adapt when damage from disease or injury occurs. Even when serious damage has occurred, in many cases the brain can recover, or at least compensate for lost function.

For instance, monkeys that experienced brain lesions in the important brain center that controls their ability to pick up food pellets were clumsy at first, but with practice they learned to retrieve their tasty treats with almost the same ease as before the damage.[25] Analysis of their brains showed extensive neuronal remodeling in response to their determined effort to achieve their goal.

Changes also occur in the brain in response to the thousands of behavioral and lifestyle choices that we make. Such choices include drugs we take or the food choices we make, or whether we spend our time reading and exercising versus sitting and watching television. Even how we choose to respond to an irritating person makes changes in the brain.

We have to pay attention in order to make a choice, and what we pay attention to changes us! "Attention is a mental state that allows us, moment by moment, to choose and sculpt how our ever-changing minds will work, to choose who we will be the next moment in a very real sense. These choices are left embossed in physical form on our material selves."[26] As was mentioned in Chapter 1, people with addictions feel they have lost the power to choose what they rationally know is right. There is a loss of a sense of self-control. This is because changes have taken place in the brain that involve multiple brain circuits, especially circuits involving reward, conditioning, and self-control.[27] But once that power is reharnessed, amazing changes can take place.

So what happens to our brain when we have new experiences? For one thing, experience promotes the development of active neural circuits,[28] which help embed in our memory the things we do frequently.

Changes also occur in the brain in response to the thousands of behavioral and lifestyle choices that we make.

38

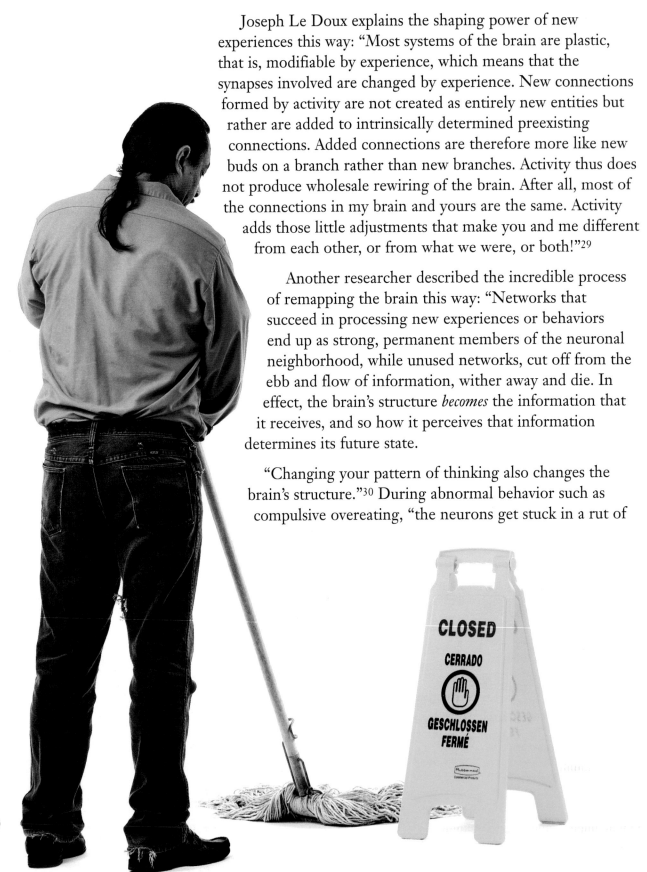

Joseph Le Doux explains the shaping power of new experiences this way: "Most systems of the brain are plastic, that is, modifiable by experience, which means that the synapses involved are changed by experience. New connections formed by activity are not created as entirely new entities but rather are added to intrinsically determined preexisting connections. Added connections are therefore more like new buds on a branch rather than new branches. Activity thus does not produce wholesale rewiring of the brain. After all, most of the connections in my brain and yours are the same. Activity adds those little adjustments that make you and me different from each other, or from what we were, or both!"[29]

Another researcher described the incredible process of remapping the brain this way: "Networks that succeed in processing new experiences or behaviors end up as strong, permanent members of the neuronal neighborhood, while unused networks, cut off from the ebb and flow of information, wither away and die. In effect, the brain's structure *becomes* the information that it receives, and so how it perceives that information determines its future state.

"Changing your pattern of thinking also changes the brain's structure."[30] During abnormal behavior such as compulsive overeating, "the neurons get stuck in a rut of abnormal patterns of activity, becoming underactive or overactive or just nonperforming, it being either too easy or too hard for them to fire. A person who forcibly changes his behavior can break the deadlock by requiring neurons to change connections to enact the new behavior. Changing the brain's firing patterns through repeated thought and action is also what is responsible for the initiation of self-choice, freedom, will, and discipline. We always have the ability to remodel our brains."[31]

Neuropsychiatrist Jeffrey Schwartz puts it this way: "The time has come for science to confront the serious implications of the fact that directed, willed mental activity can clearly and systematically alter brain function."[32] Individual choices cause "one brain state to be activated rather than another."[33] That is, mental action can alter brain chemistry. Or, to put it another way: Choices make changes!

Another way to remodel the brain is by getting exercise. We know that physical exercise exerts its influence on many body systems, strengthening muscles, increasing immunity to infection and cancer, and lowering the risk of many diseases. It also improves brain activity and mood by remodeling synaptic structure and function.

The time has come for science to confront the serious implications of the fact that directed, willed mental activity can clearly and systematically alter brain function.

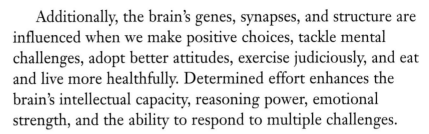

Additionally, the brain's genes, synapses, and structure are influenced when we make positive choices, tackle mental challenges, adopt better attitudes, exercise judiciously, and eat and live more healthfully. Determined effort enhances the brain's intellectual capacity, reasoning power, emotional strength, and the ability to respond to multiple challenges.

Learning how to cultivate these resources is of great benefit to those who have habits that hurt, and those who are caught in the clutches of guilt, shame, and discouragement. Knowing that the brain can recover from addictions and learn new habits is exciting. As Dr. Schwartz puts it, "With the ability to shape our brains comes the power to shape our destiny."[34]

If you have a habit that hurts—this book is about how to tap into some wonderful resources—and into the Creator, who can give you power to start *Living Free!*

Susan
KOLLENBERG

43

Delivered

Molestation and Multiple Drugs

When I was very young I was sexually molested, which left me feeling unlovable, ugly, abandoned, and different from others. I felt like I was walking around with this big black hole inside of me.

The first time I smoked a cigarette, at age 10, it made me feel good and filled up a little bit of the emptiness inside me. But the cigarettes weren't quite enough to fill me up, and I moved on to alcohol and then marijuana. By age 13 I had tried cocaine, and by age 15 I was using it on a regular basis.

By the time I was 19, I was using crack cocaine, heroin, pot, and other drugs, and I was arrested for selling an ounce of cocaine to an undercover police officer. It was the first of several arrests and stays in institutions and drug-rehabilitation programs. I did whatever I had to do to get drugs and stay high, but it got to the point that nothing was strong enough to satisfy me. Drugs took me to places and made me do things I swore I would never do.

When I was 31 years old I was arrested in the home where I grew up. It was probably the biggest drug arrest in the town of Lincoln, where my father was the mayor. I had been through a lot and had done many things that humiliated my family and myself, but nothing could stop me from using the drugs.

After three years of abusing the recovery opportunities the courts made available, my probation officer had had enough. Facing certain prison time, I knew I couldn't live like this anymore. But I also knew I couldn't stay clean on my own. The night before I turned myself in, I knew that if things didn't change, I was going to die. I cried and asked God to help me. I still used many drugs that night, but I was unable to get high. Somehow I still ended up getting myself to jail the next day. I was extremely underweight, my hair and teeth were falling out, and I had sores all over my skin.

Susan Kollenberg – Molestation and Multiple Drugs

After being transferred from the main jail to minimum security, I met a woman who asked me why I kept doing what I was doing. I told her I didn't have a choice in the matter. It was the only life I knew. I was hopeless. She asked me if she could pray with me and ask God to deliver me from this addiction. I didn't think it would help, but I didn't think it would hurt either. I don't remember exactly what she said. All I know is that God heard her prayer, and I have never had an obsession to use drugs since! I began to pray simple prayers like, "God, please help me!" From that point I knew it was only by the power of God that I was able to stay clean.

I also knew I had to be as determined in my search to know God and to do His will as I had been in getting my drugs. I knew that if I didn't take an active part in a relationship with God every day, then I would never make it. Now, rather than blaming others for what I do, I know that I am the one who decides how to react to the things of this world.

I look back at my past and am amazed at who I used to be and what my life was like. I never dreamed I would be able to live without drugs. After 25 years of drug abuse, I have been clean for seven years, and each day is incredible. Life is still difficult. I have done a lot of damage to my body because of the drug use, but God is so good. It is as if the former things have passed away and have been forgotten, and I am a new creature. I work for a Bible correspondence school and love my work. The most important thing for me today is to continue to share my story of God's power, because, as the saying goes, "You can't keep it unless you give it away."

Visit the Kollenbergs at their Web site: www.justasiamministries.com.

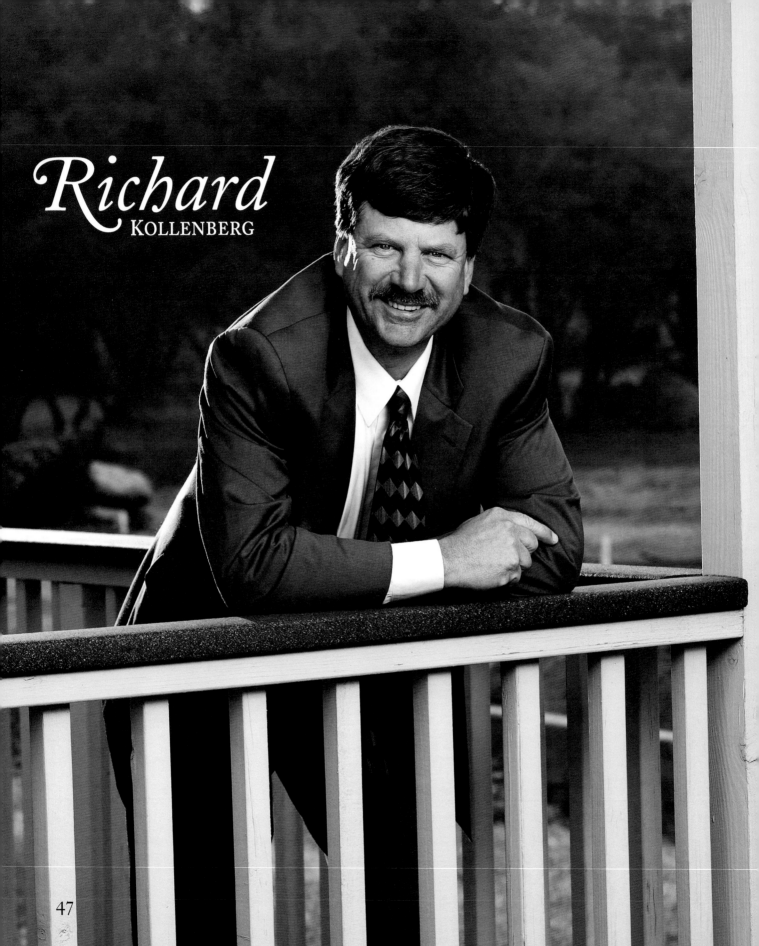

Richard
KOLLENBERG

47

Delivered

Cocaine and Alcohol

I wasn't born with a tag stapled to my ear that read, "If you add drugs or alcohol to this one he will continue doing so until he ruins his life and the lives of everyone around him." There were no warnings. I didn't use drugs or alcohol during high school, and I was very driven in everything I did. I excelled in music, sports, and academics, graduating as valedictorian, class president, and earning other numerous awards.

I didn't go on to college, however, but worked as a mechanic and started drinking and smoking with the guys. This became the norm because my conscience was silenced with alcohol. Smoking and drinking became a routine, a ritual— something I did every afternoon and evening, like eating breakfast. I felt so bad about my behavior that every morning I swore I wasn't going to do it again that afternoon—but I always did.

About this time I got into construction. The combination of rock music, which I loved, and construction allowed me access to an unlimited supply of every drug imaginable. I was now doing that which I had assured myself I would never do when I was in high school.

My new friends were different from those of my high school days; I was impressing them with new "talents," such as using cocaine. I fell in love with it, and my life began to revolve around the drug. I cared about nothing but cocaine and alcohol, and was addicted to both. I maintained, however, that I wasn't addicted to anything.

During this period of time I began dealing large quantities of drugs, storing weapons, and growing marijuana. Having guns held to my head or stuck in my face was a daily event in my quest to get drugs. Drugs came first, before family, girlfriends, and work. I lived in a one-room garage and slept on the floor with a beer keg as a fireplace. There was no one left in my life. Even my girlfriend, Susan, had left me.

Rich Kollenberg – Cocaine and Alcohol

In a fog, I reflected on my life, and somehow, without hurting me too much, God showed me what I had done. I realized I had tried living life my way for 41 years—23 of them in alcohol or drug abuse—and it hadn't worked. I cried out to Him for help at the top of my lungs, and instantly the obsession to use drugs and alcohol was gone. My life then became a diligent search for the truth. I realized I needed to surrender to win, to stop fighting everything and simply search for God. He had already helped me to stop using drugs. So I clung to Him and the hope that He would fix my life which I had ruined by all those years of abuse.

Susan and I got back together and were married shortly after we both got clean. We knew we had to make right choices or we would end up back where we had been. We understood that God's ways are different from the world's. We had seen how seemingly small choices and compromises took us down a road that led us to do things we swore we would never do.

The Lord has been so good to us. He has given us a wonderful church family, a new home, and great jobs with great employers. He has also given me back a relationship with my family which I had unknowingly worked so hard to destroy. There are continuous trials and challenges that come our way, but if we continue to rely on God, claim His promises, and rely on His strength, we are OK. We tend to associate God's miracles with a Man who walked this earth 2000 years ago, but believe me—Christ still works miracles today!

Visit the Kollenbergs at their Web site: www.justasiamministries.com.

Personal Worksheet 2

1. The human brain is amazingly "plastic," or malleable. What does this mean?*

   _____

   _____

   _____

2. Behavior and habits are learned. What are some positive habits I have in my life? What habits do I have that are causing me problems? _____

   _____

   _____

3. Is it possible to change bad habits? What help is available? Look up Psalm 119:73; Isaiah 1:16, 17; and Matthew 11:28, 29. _____

   _____

   _____

4. How can a positive, stimulating environment improve learning, memory, mood, and mental function? In what ways can I improve my environment to encourage a positive mood and better mental processing?

   _____

   _____

   _____

5. How do brain neurons get "stuck in a rut" during abnormal behavior?** Look up Isaiah 14:3; John 8:36. What promises are given to me when I find myself in this trap? _____

   _____

   _____

Answers located on page 342 in the back of book.

* If you are working in a group, review the sections before you meet.
** It is important to rule out other medical conditions. Always work with your physician or healthcare provider. Serious mood disorders or physical symptoms require clinical intervention.

Chapter 3

Junk Food Junkie

"The belly talks but doesn't listen."

Anonymous

The junk-food junkie. Who doesn't know one? We all have heard people who laughingly refer to themselves as "junk-food junkies" as they dip into a plate of brownies for the third time at a party. But for many it is no joke. To the serious food addict those brownies can be more irresistible than gold.

The food addict is awed by the person who pushes back his or her plate with a portion of cake remaining on it with the remark, "It's just too rich to finish!" Such a feat is beyond their comprehension. If a desired food item is in the house, whether it be fried cheese curls, chocolate kisses, or sugar-laden soda pop, the food addict knows exactly how much is left, where it is, and cannot stop thinking about it until it is gone—"down the hatch," that is.

Many food addicts have a Jekyll and Hyde relationship with food. They make many rules to avoid overeating the rich dainties they constantly crave; rules that they cannot keep. As the old Larry Groce song "Junk Food Junkie" teased:

> In the daytime I'm Mr. Natural
> Just as healthy as I can be
> But at night I'm a junk food junkie
> [Oh] have pity on me![1]

Not everyone who overeats is a food addict. Food addictions involve the compulsive use of food to improve mood and the loss of control over the amount consumed despite adverse effects. Food addicts are often obsessed with food, preoccupied with weight and appearance, and progressively lose interest in other activities because of their preoccupation with food.[2]

Psychological and Behavioral Aspects of Food Addiction

The following illustration depicts a typical behavior associated with food addiction—that of setting rules about food and eating and then breaking those rules only to set new ones, which are, in turn, also broken.

Rule 1. Before you enter the store, you decide you definitely will not buy a bag of your favorite binge food.

Rule 2. In the store, you find yourself in front of your binge-food section. You decide to buy the bag. (Rule 1 broken.) But you compensate by making a new rule: "I'll eat only three pieces."

Rule 3. You tell yourself you will not open the bag and eat those three pieces until you get home. But you watch the clerk to see which sack he puts your special bag in. When you get into the car you rummage through the sack, find the bag, and hold it in your lap as you start the car. You open the bag. (Rule 3 broken.) As you drive out of the parking lot, you eat three pieces. You stop at the light.

Rule 4. You decide to eat just three more pieces. (Rule 2 broken again.) You eat four more pieces. (Rule 4 broken.)

Rules 5 through 11. You keep making new rules and breaking them until the bag is empty.[3]

Not everyone who overeats is a food addict. Food addictions involve the compulsive use of food to improve mood and the loss of control over the amount consumed despite adverse effects.

53

Food addicts are in a strange predicament. They generally are not seen as *real* addicts, and often they themselves don't understand they have a real addiction that causes very real changes in the brain.

Food addicts can be as isolated, driven, and controlled by their addiction as are drug abusers. Indeed, it is hard to imagine how anyone could develop an obsession over something as commonplace as a cinnamon swirl donut or a triple fudge sundae. People who relate normally to food often send subtle but demoralizing messages such as, "Why can't you eat just one of those—your sister does." "You would be so pretty if you would just lose weight." The food addict is obsessively preoccupied with certain foods and often does not understand the problem as an addiction. Like a drug addict fixated on narcotics, the food addict's hopes, dreams, and goals are often overruled by a relentless obsession to eat compulsively, secretly, and excessively, often until it hurts.

Licensed therapist Anne Katherine tells of her compelling personal struggle with food in her book *Anatomy of a Food Addiction*: "I knew from my own internal experience just how compelling a food craving can be, how powerful and irresistible… I knew that my thinking and obsessing, planning and hoarding, sneaking and hiding resembled the behavior of an addict. I also knew that only when I stopped eating the foods in quantities that kept me in a hazy prison, could I develop a normal relationship with food. Till then, foods acted just as addictive drugs do; they stimulated the desire for more. Finally, I knew that if I was food addicted, then others probably were, too."[4]

While not all people who have emotional problems become addicts, addictions destroy normal brain functioning, and for that reason all addicts either have or develop emotional problems as a result of their addiction. Addictions occur more readily in individuals who have unmet needs for love, security, or happiness that they have not learned to deal with in constructive ways. And once those addictions occur, emotional problems are on the way, because addictions are isolating, disabling, and destructive by their very nature.

Although separate disorders, overweight and food addictions are overlapping and related.[5] All food addicts are not overweight, nor are all overweight people food addicts. But poor eating habits become just that—habits. And bad food habits are hard to kick, even though they make you feel bad, drain energy, and cause weight gain. Many overweight people are enslaved by habits they know are harmful to their health, and many food addicts suffer from overweight or other eating disorders such as bulimia or compulsive overeating.

Globesity!

An alarming 64.5 percent of the U.S. population are overweight, and of that number 30.5 percent are obese and 4.7 percent are severely obese. That translates to 127 million overweight adults, 60 million obese adults, and 9 million severely obese adults.[6] About one third of U. S. children are either overweight or obese. But the problem of overeating and food addiction is not just a problem in the U.S., as is reflected in burgeoning *globesity* statistics.

An alarming 64.5 percent of the U.S. population are overweight, and of that number 30.5 percent are obese and 4.7 percent are severely obese. That translates to 127 million overweight adults, 60 million obese adults, and 9 million severely obese adults.

55

Half the adult populations of Brazil, Chile, Columbia, Peru, Uruguay, and Russia are overweight or obese.[7] Nearly one in five Chinese is overweight.[8] On some South Pacific islands more than 7 out of 10 adults are dangerously obese.[9] According to the International Association for the Study of Obesity, almost one third of the people in the European Union are overweight, and one in 10 is obese. Around the globe, 300 million people are obese, and 750 million are overweight.

According to the World Health Organization (WHO), "Obesity is becoming one of the most important contributors to ill health."[10] In fact, it is the second leading cause of preventable death in the United States.[11]

Unfortunately, these weighty problems are not confined to adults. It is estimated that 22 million of the world's children under age 5 are overweight or obese.[12] In Africa overweight and obesity coexist with malnutrition. In fact, there are regions where obesity afflicts more children than malnutrition does—up to four times as many.[13]

In Britain, youth obesity rates have increased 70 percent in just 10 years.[14] One third of Italian children are overweight as a result of a cultural shift away from the Mediterranean-type diet combined with a decline in physical activity.

Obesity is associated with more than 30 serious medical conditions. New research shows that obese children rate their quality of life with scores as low as those reported by young cancer patients undergoing chemotherapy.[15]

A study conducted by Dr. Jeffrey Schwimmer indicates that "the likelihood of significant quality-of-life impairment was profound for obese children."[16]

Clearly, obesity is a complex, multifactor chronic disorder involving environmental, genetic, metabolic, behavioral, and psychological components. Many researchers, including John Hewitt of the Institute for Behavioral Genetics at the University of Colorado, believe there is a strong genetic link to childhood and adult obesity.[17] But Dr. Hewitt also states that "changes in energy expenditure have brought about a significant increase in the prevalence of obesity."[18]

Scientists believe that those with a genetic inclination to obesity have a constitution that is more susceptible to environmental triggers. Some of those triggers are easy access to calorie-dense food, and energy-saving technologies such as TV, Internet, remote-control gadgets that discourage movement, and the sedentary lifestyle they may promote.

Excessive intake of highly refined foods over-develops brain circuitry involved with the sensory processing of food, especially the mouth, lips, and tongue. This enhanced sensitivity tends to make the taste experience of eating these foods even more rewarding, and may be a factor in excess food consumption among the obese or binge eaters.[19] Calorie-dense refined foods such as fries and fudge may be tasty, but they do not fill you up and keep you satisfied because of their low fiber content.[20] Replacing junk foods with satisfying high-fiber plant foods can help tame over-stimulated palates, curb cravings, control weight, and train taste buds to enjoy the natural flavor of fresh fruits, vegetables, and whole grains.

Food Fixations

Charles Billington, a professor of medicine and the former president of the North American Association for the Study of Obesity, believes that many have become "habituated" to the consumption of high-calorie refined foods. "As we develop full understanding of the neuroregulation of appetite, I think the addictive nature of foods will become clear. And I think we will

Replacing junk foods with satisfying high-fiber plant foods can help tame over-stimulated palates, curb cravings, control weight, and train taste buds to enjoy the natural flavor of fresh fruits, vegetables, and whole grains.

58

learn that these addictions can develop at various stages of life, in adulthood as well as in childhood. And I think we will learn that they are very, very powerful."[21]

Dr. Mark Gold, a researcher and psychiatry professor, says mounting evidence suggests that chronic overeating may be a substance disorder and should be considered an addiction.[22] "What's the difference between someone who's lost control over alcohol and someone who's lost control over good food?" Dr. Gold asks. "When you look at their brains and brain responses, the differences are not very significant."[23] He says overlapping syndromes of emotional disorders and appetite-control signaling hormones that no longer function properly are major mechanisms of addiction.[24]

Dr. Gold concludes: "We've taken the position that overeating is, in part, due to food becoming more refined, more palatable, more hedonic [pleasurable]. Food might be the substance in a substance abuse disorder that we see today as obesity."

Indeed, research suggests that large concentrations of sweet and fatty processed foods have powerful effects on hormone signals that control appetite. According to Peter Havel, an endocrinologist at the University of California, Davis, the more fat- and fructose-laden processed foods you eat, the less effect certain long-term appetite stabilizing hormones such as leptin, insulin, and ghrelin have on the body.[25] Havel gives one example: "These hormones help keep your body weight stable. When you drink beverages with lots of fructose the body continues to take in calories, but the hormones are not able to tell the body it is full and to stop eating. Many fast food meals are washed down with a large beverage."[26]

How much fructose is in a soft drink? A large 64-oz. soda contains 130 grams of fructose. By contrast, you would have to eat 32 peaches to get that amount of fructose.

How much fructose is in a soft drink? A large 64-oz. soda contains 130 grams of fructose. By contrast, an apple contains 13 grams of fructose, a banana has 7, and a peach contains 4.[27] But fruits are not only significantly lower in fructose, they are loaded with phytochemicals, nutrients, and fiber.

Ignorant Gains?

Our creeping corpulence may have as much to do with ignorance about what we are eating as any other factor. In his documentary, *Super Size Me*, Morgan Spurlock ate nothing but McDonald's food for 30 days. He also cut his exercise to match that of the typical American. In just 30 days his muscle mass plunged and his body fat soared from 11 to 18 percent. He gained 25 pounds and developed obesity-related liver disease. One month of binging caused a weight gain and liver disease that took 14 months to reverse.

"I look at my film as a snapshot of your life," Spurlock says. "This 30 days is what could happen to you in 20, 30, 40 years if you continue to eat the way most Americans eat. You can develop all these health problems—that can be stopped if you change the way you eat and start exercising.

"There's no thought about what we're eating and what's going to happen to our bodies next week, next month, next year. The last thing they [the fast food industry] want you to do is think about what you're eating because they're making millions by you not [thinking about it]. When you go to the doctor, what you eat is one of the last questions asked. The impact of food on your body, your well-being, is so immense. But there's no money in people eating broccoli. There's money in people eating pills."[28]

60

Fortunately, what we learn, we can unlearn. New habits, new associations, and new choices help reroute neural pathways and establish new connections. Forming positive habits can establish new neural neighborhoods to counteract and override dysfunctional ones.

As Spurlock's experience shows all too clearly, obesity can not only be the price of overeating rich food but can also lead to food addiction. Although research is still in its infancy, there is some indication that binging on foods high in fat and sugar can not only hijack hormones that govern appetite but also cause changes in the brain that promote addiction in susceptible individuals.[29]

Sugar addiction, for instance, has been documented in rats.[30] Scientists studying this commented that "because palatable food stimulates neural systems that are implicated in drug addiction, intermittent, excessive sugar intake might create dependency, as indicated by withdrawal signs."[31]

John Hoebel, a Princeton University psychologist who led the research, showed that rats fed a diet containing 25 percent sugar were thrown into a state of anxiety when the sugar was removed. "The implication is that some animals—and by extension some people—can become overly dependent on sweet food. The brain is getting addicted to its own opioids as it would morphine or heroin. Drugs give a bigger effect, but it's essentially the same process. Highly palatable foods and highly potent sexual stimuli are the only stimuli capable of activating the dopamine system with anywhere near the potency of addictive drugs."[32]

Dr. Gene-Jack Wang, clinical head of the PET imaging program at the

61

Brookhaven National Laboratory in New York, specializes in working with obese patients. He has found that overweight people have decreased dopamine receptors in the pleasure centers of the brain, similar to what happens in a drug addict's brain.[33]

Addiction researcher Dr. Prem Srivastava confirms these findings: "The findings have been proven again and again in studies of addictions to drugs and food/overeating," although it is unclear whether preexisting dopamine abnormality leads to addiction, or vice versa.[34]

Anne Kelley, a neuroscientist at the University of Wisconsin Medical School in Madison, found similar results in her studies. She also found that rats who chronically overindulge in highly refined foods show marked, long-lasting changes in their brain circuitry similar to changes caused by extended heroin or morphine use. "This says that mere exposure to pleasurable, tasty foods is enough to change gene expression, and that suggests that you could be addicted to food," says Kelly.[35]

Fortunately, what we learn, we can unlearn. New habits, new associations, and new choices help reroute neural pathways and establish new connections. Forming positive habits can establish new neural neighborhoods to counteract and override dysfunctional ones.[36]

Diets and Deprivation

Is it possible... to change bad eating habits—for good? ...The answer is Yes!

While many overweight people have spent much of their lives dieting, at the other end of the spectrum is the obsession with achieving super-thinness. Extreme dieting decreases dopamine concentrations in the pleasure center of the brain, and actually increases the risk for drug abuse.[37] Studies show that animals increase drug intake when they are underweight.[38]

More than five million Americans, mostly women, suffer from eating disorders—anorexia nervosa, bulimia nervosa, and binge eating disorder.[39] Millions more periodically display symptoms of eating disorders or constantly worry about their weight.[40]

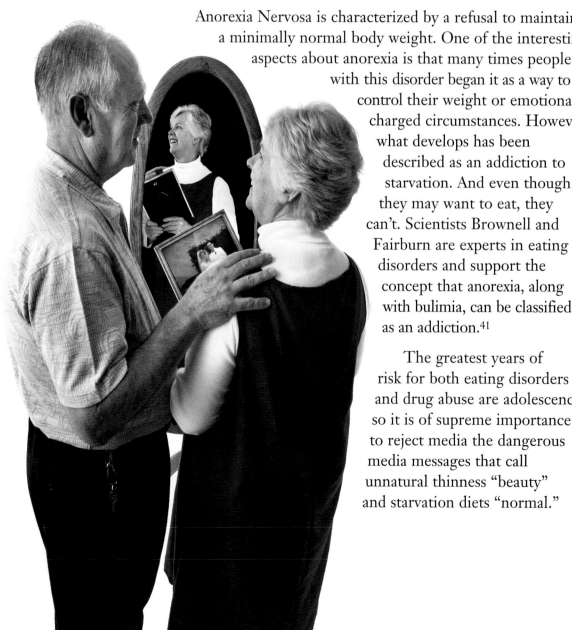

Anorexia Nervosa is characterized by a refusal to maintain a minimally normal body weight. One of the interesting aspects about anorexia is that many times people with this disorder began it as a way to control their weight or emotionally charged circumstances. However, what develops has been described as an addiction to starvation. And even though they may want to eat, they can't. Scientists Brownell and Fairburn are experts in eating disorders and support the concept that anorexia, along with bulimia, can be classified as an addiction.[41]

The greatest years of risk for both eating disorders and drug abuse are adolescence, so it is of supreme importance to reject media the dangerous media messages that call unnatural thinness "beauty" and starvation diets "normal."

It is essential to teach children and adolescents that fitness, vitality, and health are the result of long-term sensible choices, not crash exercise and diet plans. True attractiveness is available to everyone, both young and old. But attractiveness is not the same as natural beauty. Natural beauty fades and is incapable, alone, of holding a relationship together. But true attractiveness is a quality of personality combined with a true sense of self-worth that never fades. It is what makes a person more beautiful over time.

Those who have severe conditions such as anorexia nervosa need clinical intervention by a licensed, professional healthcare provider. Other mental health conditions may coexist with any abnormal eating behavior, so a thorough clinical evaluation is advisable.

The Satiety Factor

Is it possible for a junk-food junkie to change bad eating habits—for good? Is it possible to curb those cravings and cut those calories and still feel satisfied? The answer is Yes!

Before he got out of bed in the morning he would eat a handful of candy he kept stashed by his bedside.

64

If you are hooked on fast foods, sweets, and high-fat snacks, start by eating more high-fiber foods, sugar from whole fruits, and healthful plant fats.

Simple changes can produce profound results. Fred[42] is a prime example. He could not get through the day without frequently consuming hard candy and soda pop. Before he got out of bed in the morning he would eat a handful of candy he kept stashed by his bedside. He suffered from fatigue, irritability, and had trouble sleeping. The doctors ruled out any specific disorder, so he began to examine his habits, and decided to try just *one* change.

"I became convinced," Fred said, "that my problems were due to sugar addiction, and I decided to try something new. I prayed for courage, and rather than reaching for candy first thing in the morning, I grabbed a fresh, crisp apple or a peach. When tempted to snack on candy and soda, I chose fresh fruit and water instead. It was hard at first, but very soon I began incorporating fresh fruits and vegetables, salads and whole grains into my meals. I began to enjoy the food and even look forward to it. Before long I no longer had the urge to snack. I feel better, sleep better, and am free from my addiction."

A better understanding of your biology, a cache of lifestyle tools to implement lasting change, and trust in the God who gives the power to change can help you make lasting changes. It is also important to replace negative thinking with an attitude of hope, otherwise there is no energy for the journey. A vital tool for lasting change in overcoming food addictions is adopting new food choices. As Fred's story illustrates, plant foods are satisfying and reduce hunger between meals.[43]

When you eat plant foods, you feel full before you eat too many calories. Plant foods are also lower in calories and high in long-term satisfaction, so you don't crave high-calorie snacks.

Fiber: Your Fabulous Friend

The advantages of fiber foods are truly impressive. Fiber foods can help you reach and maintain a healthful weight. They are low in calories, high in fill-up value, and may also increase metabolism. A large study of middle-age women found that those who ate more fiber-rich grains, such as oatmeal and whole grain breakfast cereals, gained less weight over time than women who got the least fiber in their diets.[44] Intake of three types of fruit a day has also been shown to help with weight loss.[45]

Perhaps this is why vegetarians tend to have less overweight and obesity.[46] Fiber foods can be a tremendous aid in weight loss.[47] Instead of a quick, greasy pizza slice for dinner, why not enjoy a bowl of black beans, fresh cucumber and tomato slices, corn bread, and a slice of fresh pineapple?

When you eat plant foods, you feel full before you eat too many calories. Plant foods are also lower in calories and high in long-term satisfaction, so you don't crave high-calorie snacks. See *Understanding Carbohydrates* and *Easy Ways to Reduce Your Sugar Intake* (pages 74-80). Instead of a donut and coffee for breakfast, try a half grapefruit, some fresh strawberries, whole wheat toast with peanut butter and applesauce, and a cup of fortified soy milk.

The slow-release energy from plant foods also helps maintain consistent serotonin levels, which help control your mood, appetite, and cravings through the day. Severely calorie-restricted diets and very high-protein, low-carbohydrate diets cause a drop in brain serotonin. If your serotonin level drops, you may feel down, which may cause a craving for sweets. So, help keep your serotonin levels balanced by eating complex carbohydrate-rich, high-fiber foods, such as beans, legumes, whole grains, pasta, leafy vegetables, fresh fruits, and nuts.

For most people, meals that are not excessively high in fat or carbohydrates but contain a good balance of both, will be most conducive to sustained alertness and energy, especially in the afternoon.[48] Refined carbohydrates such as white bread and pastries cause a sharp elevation of blood sugar, which is followed by

It is essential to teach children and adolescents that fitness, vitality, and health are the result of long-term sensible choices, not crash exercise and diet plans.

a fairly rapid decline. That rapid decline can drop blood sugar levels below normal, resulting in tension, fatigue, and irritability.

Conversely, whole grains and other complex carbohydrates bring a more gradual, steady rise in blood sugar and serotonin, higher-sustained levels, and a slower decline. That's why complex carbohydrates are the best "octane" fuel for the brain. Instead of skipping meals and fueling up on chocolate to keep going, take time for a wholesome, satisfying meal. Such meals will release energy over the next 4 to 6 hours. Consuming high-fiber foods, especially high-fiber cereals, may be one simple method of reducing fatigue.[49]

Fiber foods may also help reduce emotional distress.[50] One group of researchers wrote: "Can what we eat influence mental function? The answer is certainly affirmative; we ingest each day any number of compounds that we know alter mental function. . . . We also think that dietary macronutrients [those nutrients that the body needs in larger amounts] can have an impact on brain function."[51] "Over the past 40 years, several lines of investigation have shown that the chemistry and function of both the developing and the mature brain are influenced by diet."[52]

High-fiber foods may also improve brain function because they provide a steady release of glucose, the optimal fuel for your brain. Children who eat breakfast perform better in school, and adults who eat high-fiber foods for breakfast are more productive and think more clearly. Individuals on high-fiber diets also reported fewer cognitive difficulties overall.[53]

Why? One reason may be that brain cells are damaged by free radicals. The antioxidants and phytochemicals found in fiber foods can help protect cells from free-radical damage and repair damage when it is done. Foods high in plant fiber are also rich in complex carbohydrates that provide energy.

A special benefit of consuming a wide variety of fiber-rich green and yellow vegetables is that they contain many different types of

Fiber foods can be a tremendous aid in weight loss. Instead of a quick, greasy pizza slice for dinner, why not enjoy a bowl of black beans, fresh cucumber and tomato slices, corn bread, and a slice of fresh pineapple?

carotenoids. An interesting study revealed that some of these carotenoids, such as beta-carotene, actually have a stress hormone-lowering effect when consumed on a regular basis. They have also been associated with lower levels of irritation and insomnia.[54] In one study, participants who had high blood levels of carotenoids had less irritability and sleeplessness.[55]

In a discussion of nutrition on stress management, researchers Ali Waladkhani and Michael Clemens noted that "plant foods have a wide variety of phytochemicals that have the potential to modulate stress, e.g., carotinoids, flavonoids, and sulfides."[56]

In Waladkhani and Clemens' study, monkeys who were switched from their customary vegetarian diet to a typical Western diet showed altered testosterone levels. The researchers remarked: "Changes in nutritional behavior could cause changes in endocrine balance and eventually in stress response."[57]

The conclusion of these two researchers is that "modification of the diet and changes in frequency of the diet intake may be helpful in stress management. It is of great importance to eat properly. A large part of the diet has to be of complex carbohydrates. In general, foods of plant origin have to be preferred. Reduction and modification of dietary fat may be helpful. In particular, a diet rich in monounsaturated and omega-3 fatty acids is advisable. These modifications can produce consistent changes in concentrations of cortisol [a stress hormone]. Further, plant foods are rich in phytochemicals, trace elements, and vitamins, which show a variety of positive effects on health."[58]

The antioxidants and phytochemicals found in fiber foods can help protect cells from free-radical damage and repair damage when it is done.

68

According to research…
it is possible that
fats, especially the
omega-3 fats, have an
effect on mood by
influencing serotonin.

Whatever you do, be on the offensive by planning meals that will curb cravings later in the day. High-fiber foods provide a powerful package of healthful benefits such as vitamins, minerals, phytochemicals, and antioxidants to keep your appetite satisfied and enhance your physical and mental health.

Brain-Healthy Fats

Fat in the diet is important for many reasons. Fats increase meal satisfaction and slow digestion. Dietary fat is important because it aids the body's absorption of fat-soluble vitamins and phytochemicals, and is involved in the production of important hormones. (See *Fat: Essential for Life on pages 81-84*.)

Lipids (fatty acids) are found in cell membranes and are highly concentrated in the brain and nervous system. They are vital to the electrical insulation of nerves and influence how efficiently chemical messengers are transmitted. Increasing evidence suggests that the type of fat we consume can actually alter the makeup of the cells themselves and influence properties such as membrane fluidity and flexibility, and cell receptor sensitivity.[59]

One expert on brain function put it this way: "If the diet is largely junk food with large amounts of highly saturated animal fat, the membranes will reflect that diet by being less flexible—stiffer, and more restrictive to normal enzyme function of those membranes."[60] So enjoy more healthful plant fats. Choose nuts, seeds, olives, olive oil, and avocados instead of hydrogenated fat and animal saturated fat.

According to research by Dr. Joseph Hibbeln and others, it is possible that fats, especially the omega-3 fats, have an effect on mood by influencing serotonin.[61]

69

While results are tentative, his studies with omega-3 fatty acid levels and serotonin "suggest that dietary intake of these fatty acids might influence the serotonin process and that altering this process may possibly reduce depressive, suicidal, and violent behavior."[62]

Dr. Hibbeln's work was with fish as a source of omega-3 fatty acid. Plant sources include nuts, especially walnuts, flax seed, whole soy, canola oil, and soy oil. Trace amounts of omega-3 fats are even in leafy green vegetables.

Besides adding a brain-health component to your meals, plant fats also add satisfaction and flavor. For a real taste treat, start putting nuts or seeds on your cereal or salad, or olives and avocado on your salad or sandwich. For breakfast, eat whole grain cereal and fresh fruit, then add fruit and/or vegetables to your lunch and supper. Enjoy whole grains and beans in your meals many times during the week. Do this, and before you know it, you'll prefer healthful, tasty high-fiber choices. And once they become a part of your regular eating habits, you will find that eating healthfully is easy and enjoyable.

Finally, don't underestimate the power of small choices. Neuropsychiatrist and addiction specialist Dr. John Ratey states it this way: "Critics sometimes claim that a focus on 'ordinary' measures like exercise and diet is too simplistic to affect unordinary behavior. Not so. The brilliantly simple evidence from exciting new areas of physical and social science shows how powerful such universal factors can be in affecting the brain-body system. There are many tools right at our fingertips for changing our mental health, both in correcting our problems and simply in becoming the kind of person we want to be."[63]

Eating right is a powerful tool in any health-building program. Breaking free from food addictions and overweight is not about deprivation—it's really about *expansion*! Expand your food choices to include plenty of delicious plant foods

If the diet is largely junk food with large amounts of highly saturated animal fat, the membranes will reflect that diet by being less flexible—stiffer, and more restrictive to normal enzyme function of those membranes.

70

Eating right is a powerful tool in any health-building program. Breaking free from food addictions and overweight is not about deprivation—it's really about expansion!

and you will become a *successful* loser—you will lose unwanted pounds and lose cravings. But you will also gain needed body muscle and mass if you are too thin. You will *gain* many food choices that you had never before considered. Special nutrition, meal planning, and recipe inserts have been provided in this book for you to enjoy. Chapters 7-9 provide the keys to a balanced life. By following these guidelines, you will gain energy, gain freedom, and regain health. And that's a gain that will move you closer to your goal of *Living Free*!

73

Understanding
Carbs

There are two forms of Carbohydrates

1. Complex carbohydrates (whole grains, vegetables, beans, and fruits):

- are long chains of glucose units;
- provide fiber to slowly release energy over next 4-6 hours;
- provide long-lasting energy;
- increase serotonin level to help you feel good;
- satisfy appetite;
- are rich in vitamins, minerals, antioxidants, and phytochemicals;
- reduce the risk of disease.

2. Simple carbohydrates (sugar, desserts, candy):

- are short units of sugar;
- go into the system very quickly;
- do not promote satiety in high intakes, and they can:
  - ➤ compromise nutrition and health,
  - ➤ provide calories without many nutrients,
  - ➤ promote insulin resistance,
  - ➤ turn off appetite-control mechanisms,
  - ➤ increase appetite for more sugar,
  - ➤ increase tension and fatigue.

Be Sure to

- eat high-fiber, complex carbohydrates.
- reduce your sugar cravings by eating adequate complex carbohydrates.
- satisfy your sweet tooth with:
  - ➤ fresh fruits and
  - ➤ cereal sweetened with dried fruit such as cherries, apples, apricots, and raisins instead of refined sugar.
- Limit sugar intake to 30 grams or less of added sugars per day. (This does not include fresh fruits that provide natural sugars.)

Remember: 1 teaspoon of sugar = 4 grams of sugar

To find out how many teaspoons of sugar are in a product:

- Read the label.
- How many grams of sugar are listed per serving?
- Divide the number of grams by 4.
- This number equals the teaspoons of sugar in a serving.
- How many servings are you planning on consuming from the food or drink? The average soda contains 2.5 servings, but we rarely share it!

76

Easy ways to Reduce Your Sugar Intake

Easy ways to Reduce Your Sugar Intake

1. Be Aware.

- What are you eating and drinking?

2. Eat more.

- Eat more meals on time. Stay with a schedule for meals.

- Eat more fiber—Fiber helps reduce sugar cravings, gives long-lasting energy, and raises serotonin levels.

- Eat more vegetables and fruits—These provide fiber, vitamins, and minerals for a satisfied appetite.

- Eat more breakfast—A high-fiber breakfast will help control your appetite and desire for sweets.

- Eat a high-fiber lunch—You will be less likely to need an afternoon candy bar.

3. Keep fresh
fruit available.

- Stock plenty of fresh fruits.
- Eat fruits to satisfy your sweet tooth.
- Serve fruit for dessert. Few desserts can match the flavor or benefits of some fresh, crisp apple slices, or a few red strawberries.
- Take fresh fruit to work with you to add to lunch or for your snack.

4. Drink water.

- Drink water instead of high-sugar drinks.

5. Go for a walk.

- Get plenty of exercise to give you energy so you will not need a pick-me-up from a sugar snack. When you get the urge for sweets, take a 10-minute brisk walk.

6. Modify your recipes.

- You would be amazed at how much sugar you can cut out of many recipes without anyone ever noticing! Many dessert recipes can actually have the sugar cut in half. Experiment with your recipes; the first time you may want to reduce the sugar by one third. If all is well, the next time cut the sugar by one-half.

80

FAT:
Essential for Life

FAT:
Essential for Life

Fats are essential for life and health. Choose plant fats for optimal health.

Why You Need Fat

- Fats are essential for the absorption of phytochemicals and fat-soluble vitamins.
- They are important components of hormones and cell membranes.
- They are critical to healthy heart, vessel, nerve, and brain function.
- They insulate us and help keep a stable body temperature.
- They taste good and provide food satisfaction.

Three Intake Guidelines

1. Eat fat and high-fat foods in moderation, according to your age and activity level.
2. Select "good fats".
3. Even if you are overweight, you need some fats.

Fat: What Kind Is Best?

Plant fats contain mostly unsaturated fats, which include omega-3, omega-6, and monounsaturated fatty acids. Here are some delicious sources to include in your diet:

- Monounsaturated: nuts (walnuts, pecans, almonds, etc); seeds (sesame, sunflower); avocados; olives; some oils (olive, soy, sesame, canola).
- Omega-3: ground flax seed, walnuts; other nuts, whole soy bean products, canola oil, soy oil.

Fat: How Much Is Enough?

When looking at labels, look for grams of fat:

  5 grams of fat = 1 teaspoon of fat
 15 grams of fat = 1 tablespoon of fat (3 teaspoons = 1 tablespoon)
  1 gram of fat = 9 calories
  2 tablespoons of nuts = approximately 10 grams of fat

- Your fat allowance depends on how many calories you need, which is reflected in age, gender, and activity level. Preventive recommendations suggest 20 to 35 percent of your calories from fat. If you need 2,000 calories per day, your fat allowance is between 50 to 78 grams of fat per day. Active children and teenagers who need more calories will have a higher fat allowance. Sedentary older adults require fewer calories, therefore fewer fats.

83

Avoid Unhealthful Fats

Unhealthful fats contribute to heart disease, cancer, stress, and overweight.

Reduce intake of:

■ Saturated fats: meat, whole-fat dairy, fast food, refined snack foods.

■ Trans fatty acids: partially hydrogenated fats found in many snack foods such as microwave popcorn, cookies, crackers, and chips; margarine; and fast foods such as French fries and donuts.

High-fat Food	Approx. Grams of Fat
Chips—8 oz. bag	88
Large burger and fries	60
Steak—8 oz.	50

Making the Switch [2]

Here are some tips for switching to more healthful fats as you make your daily food choices.

■ Eat regular meals to cut down the urge to snack.

■ Fill up on fresh fruits, vegetables, whole-grain breads and cereals, beans, nuts, and seeds instead of calorie-dense snacks and fast foods.

■ Bake or steam potatoes instead of frying them.

■ Enjoy salads with mixed dark greens with olive oil and lemon instead of heavy cheese dressings. Top your salads with a healthful variety of olives, avocado, and a sprinkling of walnuts for a real taste treat.

■ Enjoy spreads such as hummus and nut butter instead of dairy butter. Enjoy trans-fat free margarines.

■ Choose fresh pineapple, kiwi, or a few strawberries in place of rich desserts.

■ Choose fortified soy, almond, rice, or other milk alternatives, to high-fat dairy products.

■ Use olive oil and garlic on vegetables in place of butter.

■ Edge out fatty meats by eating more plant-based foods, especially beans and legumes, whole-grain pastas, brown rice, and meat alternatives such as gluten- or soy-based entrees.

■ Limit high-fat baked products and desserts.

■ Limit commercial baked goods; make your own baked goods using healthful fats.

■ Avoid fried foods.

[1] Calgary Health Region Hypertension and Cholesterol Centre website: www.calgaryhealthregion.ca.
[2] Adapted from Donald R. Hall, Dr.PH, CHES. *Choose healthy fats*. Wellsource, Inc. Clakamas, OR

Dolly
DIMPLES

85

Delivered

Obesity, Dieting, and Binge Eating

For almost fifty years I was caught in the clutches of my own jaws. I was addicted to food! I was a 555-pound freak, the sideshow fat lady at the circus. Curiosity seekers came from all around to see me and poke fun at me. One woman asked me if my beefy legs were really mine. With my tongue-in-cheek I told her that they were phony, that I had an intake valve on my big toe, and each morning my legs were inflated for effect.

"Why don't you run away some night when they let the air out?" she suggested sympathetically. I wish it had been that easy.

For all those years that I lived to eat, I existed in a kind of hazy buffer state between uncertain happiness and certain heartbreak. Despite my weight I tried to be active but my activities were extremely limited. During all those years I lived very much on the sidelines of life—just observing, just wishing, just being watched!

I was finally able to "kick" my habit because I was faced with a tremendous decision that gave me one simple choice: "Diet or die." That's what my doctor told me in April of 1950. I had been brought to the Orange Memorial Hospital in

Orlando, Florida. I labored for every breath, and my blood pressure was 240 over 132. My heart seemed to be in a frantic race for life. As I lay there I suddenly realized that life was more than eating. I had to make a life or death decision.

I promised God that I would follow the doctor's orders if only I survived. "Dear God," I prayed, "let me live through this night." I did. And I dieted. And I lost 433 pounds—four-fifths of my body! Today, as a 122-pound normal woman, I have a phenomenally new outlook. I'm a totally different person living an entirely different life. It's like being reborn. I lived a miserable existence that, fortunately, came to an end.

Dolly Dimples – Obesity, Dieting, and Binge Eating

I never realized that millions of men and women suffer from the same malady I did. Like most people, I always pitied the dope addict and the alcoholic. But when I started getting thousands of letters from obese people, I realized they're hooked, too—to food. I never considered that the outcome of overindulgence is the same for the victims of alcohol, drugs, and food alike. The habit grows because of some psychological reason, and there is a steady line of destruction in the social, moral, and physical composition of the person until death ends it all.

With the miracles of modern medicine and our social developments, cures and treatments have been devised to break the habit of alcoholism and drug addiction. Perhaps food addicts will get equal attention one day, and this problem can be solved for many who have been unable to cope with their own individual, insurmountable disorder. Living free is possible—just look at me!

Reprinted and adapted with permission from *The Greatest Diet in the World*, Geyer C. (Chateau Publishing, 1600 Hull Circle Orlando Fl 32806) pp. 13-15.

Eric
PLETCHER

89

Delivered

Obesity, Anorexia, and Bulimia

I do not remember a time when I was not overweight; but I do remember the first time I realized it was a problem. School was difficult because of the teasing and bullying that go along with being overweight. Even the teachers viewed me as different, and few students wanted me for a friend. I hated school and hated my teachers because they could not protect me. I felt isolated and lonely, wishing someone would be my friend.

As I became older these feelings became a thick blanket of dark depression. I could not separate hating my condition from hating myself; in my mind they were one and the same. My time at home after school was the best time of my day. Because both my parents worked, I would raid the cabinets of the chips, pop, cookies, and ice cream and plop myself in front of the TV to watch 3 to 4 hours of cartoons until my parents came home. Mom would then make a wonderful supper, and I would eat again.

This vicious cycle swirled until I became older, fatter, and felt an overwhelming desperation. I saw my peers dating and socializing, and I wanted to be a part of this type of behavior. I knew in my mind that if I could only lose my excess weight people would like me and I would fit in.

Nobody understood how I felt, so I decided if nobody would help me, I would help myself. Armed only with ignorance, I decided that I would do the only logical thing—I would stop eating altogether. In no time, my clothes felt looser, which only confirmed me in my folly.

My parents were alarmed over my refusal to eat and tried to reason with me, but I would not listen. I determined I would never go back to being fat. But I did not see my pale, haggard face; nor did I see my increasingly bony frame. I didn't understand that I was losing more than the fat. My parents, desperate for help, called my nurse cousin, who convinced me to eat again. But I gained weight very quickly, and, in a desperate attempt to control my weight, I developed bulimia. But I never escaped from the battle of weight gain, depression, or need for acceptance.

Eric Pletcher – Obesity, Anorexia, and Bulimia

It was after this that I turned to drugs, alcohol, and smoking, which led me further down the road to deeper troubles.

While in college, I found myself staring out my seven-story apartment window wishing I had the courage to throw myself out. I will never forget that day because it is the day my life changed.

As I stared out the window, I heard a man on the radio tell a woman her opinion of herself was based on what others thought of her, not on what God thought of her. He said: "God's opinion of you will never change because you are worth everything to God." His statement shook me into reality, and for the first time in my life I realized that my opinion of myself was based on what others thought and what I thought, not on what God thought.

I decided then and there that if God thought I was special, and He will never think any different of me, then I would turn my life over to Him. The blanket of depression that darkened my life left me that day and God began to change me on the inside as well as the outside. Rather than quick fixes, I began to look for intelligent ways to control my weight. I tried many different diets, but they were not very satisfying or successful over the long-term. Then I learned about the benefits of a wholesome, well-rounded plant-based diet and exercise.

I had many struggles with food cravings that only prayer could help me with, but each time I yielded my will to God's will I got the victory.

The health principles I live by now are true and accurate, but balanced—and I don't have to starve to maintain a good body weight. I lost 60 pounds and have been able to keep it off for six years. I have more energy, and a host of health problems—including my allergies—have vanished. I make mistakes and am still learning—but God is good, and the praise and glory go to Him. He is my closest and dearest Friend. I am thankful for my new life.

Toby
PAWSON

Delivered

Obesity, Dieting, and Binge Eating

It all started with my first diet at 12 years old. The sad thing was, I wasn't even overweight. I just had this obsession that I needed to lose ten pounds. But the first diet set me up for the second diet, and then the third, and then the fourth, and then the …

My life became an almost unbroken chain of chronic dieting for the next 20 years. I would lose five pounds and gain ten. Obsessed to lose that weight, I would try another diet and lose the ten, only to soon find myself 20 pounds heavier. After many "diet cycles," I had found 120 extra pounds—along with severe depression and anxiety!

My life revolved around trivial things such as my current diet, the clothes I couldn't wear, how much I weighed, and how big I looked in pictures. As a result of all the years of yo-yo dieting, I developed a compulsive eating disorder as well. So, when I wasn't on a diet, all I could think of was what foods I could binge on.

As I entered my late 20s and early 30s, I should have been experiencing the happiest times of my life. I had a wonderful husband and three beautiful children. But, sadly, those were the years I was feeling the most desperate and despondent about my weight. That was also the time my binge eating became the worst.

My favorite time to binge was at night when my family was sleeping. I would stay up until midnight, sometimes even 2:00 in the morning, and eat nonstop, trying to lose all the pain I was carrying from the excessive weight—and anything else that was bothering me.

Needless to say, my life was absolutely miserable. I lived in a constant state of numbness and pain, feeling hopeless about ever finding any joy in my life. I tortured myself with a mental list that I would run through my mind all day long. I call it my *as soon as* list:

"My life will be perfect *as soon as* I can fit into my skinny clothes."
"I'll never be depressed *as soon as* I stop binging on peanut-butter cups."
"I'll be a better wife and mom *as soon as* I stick to my diet."
My list was endless, but there was one "*as soon as*" I really needed now, and not later:
"I will finally be **happy** *as soon as* I lose all this weight."

Toby Pawson – Obesity, Dieting, and Binge Eating

After years of battling my bulge, I finally found the way to escape my addiction. It happened one evening when I was, ironically, searching for yet another diet. But, strangely enough, it wasn't a diet that delivered me. In fact, there isn't anything powerful enough on this earth that could have pulled me out of the dark pit I was living in. I was rescued by a Savior who asked if He could come into my heart. I had a knowledge of religion, but now I felt impressed that God wanted to heal the dysfunctional relationship I had with food and help me fill my needs in a healthful way. He showed me Isaiah 55:1-5; inviting me to come to Him, not the diet industry, for help. God pulled me out of that dark, lonely pit, and I have never turned back to dieting again.

I have stayed off the dieting "roller coaster" for three years because God is showing me how to see food through His eyes. Now, I see that food is simply for nourishment and enjoyment, and that it can never be a substitute for unmet emotional needs. He made food to strengthen my body and mind so I can live a healthy, blessed life and feel good about myself, too. While on this new journey, I found it takes a daily commitment on my part; I constantly rely on Him to come with me to the table and impress me what to eat and how much to eat. Daily exercise is also a new part of my life.

I eat lots of fresh fruit, vegetables, beans, and whole grains. I don't feel deprived or starved anymore!

I have to admit, at times it's very painful to work on things that I had stuffed inside for many years. However, I know God wants to show me how to have a more fulfilling life and teach me how to be the wife and mother that He wants me to be—how to solve problems without running to food to "fix" my troubles.

I thought I would be happy—*as soon as* I lost all my weight. I have lost 75 pounds, and I have some to go, but that doesn't matter to me anymore. My present happiness is no longer based on wish lists of future accomplishments. What matters to me now is that my life has completely changed, and I have finally found happiness—*today*. And it all happened *as soon as* I found the help that only a Savior can give!

Personal Worksheet 3

1. How would you describe the basic characteristics of a person who suffers from food addiction?* What is the good news for those who suffer from food addictions? _____
_____

2. How does food marketing affect consumer food choices? How do fast foods affect eating behavior?** What healthful convenience foods are available to substitute unhealthful junk food? _____
_____
_____

3. What promises can help me when I suffer from restless cravings of heart, mind, and body? Look up Psalm 103:5; Psalm 107:9, 10; and Isaiah 58:11. _____
_____

4. What are some strategies for overcoming food addictions and cravings, especially the addition of high-fiber plant foods? _____
_____
_____

List some positive, realistic goals for:

Breakfast: _____

Lunch: _____

Supper: _____

Exercise: _____

TV habits: _____

Attitude: _____

5. What encouragement and power are available to me? Look up Isaiah 59:1, 19 and Philippians 4:7, 13, 19. What do I do with guilt? Look up Psalm 103:8-12. _____
_____
_____

Answers located on page 342 in the back of book.

* If you are working in a group, review the sections before you meet.
** It is important to rule out other medical conditions. Always work with your physician or healthcare provider. Serious mood disorders or other clinical disorders such as anorexia nervosa require clinical intervention.

Chapter 4

Substance Addictions

Drugs, Alcohol, Nicotine, and Caffeine

"Insanity is doing the same thing over and over and expecting different results."

Anonymous

Addictive Drugs: Brain on a Binge

Roger[1], a registered nurse who worked in a burn unit, drank socially and smoked marijuana from the time he was 17. Over time he experimented with small doses of highly addictive pain killers he took from patients on the unit. Before long, he began supplementing his hospital highs with street heroin.

Although now recovered, drugs consumed Roger's life for more than 25 years, cutting a devastating path through his manhood, vitality, and productivity. Roger is not alone. There are several classes of commonly abused drugs, and millions of people who abuse them. They include opiates such as morphine and heroin, stimulants such as cocaine and amphetamines, and other drugs such as marijuana, alcohol, and tobacco. There are many other drugs of abuse including steroids, inhalants, Ecstasy, Ritalin, OxyContin, and numerous other prescription drugs.

According to a 2003 survey, an estimated 19.5 million Americans—8.2 percent of the population 12 and older—were illicit drug users. Marijuana is still the most commonly used illicit drug, used by 6.2 percent of those surveyed; while 2.3 million Americans, or 1 percent, were cocaine users.[2] One million people admitted to using hallucinogens, and 119,000 were heroin users.[3]

Prescription and Over the Counter Drugs: The Hidden Addiction

While the statistics for illicit drug use are startling, the prevalence of prescription drug use and addiction is even more startling. It has been dubbed "the *other* drug problem" by experts in the field, often going unrecognized and untreated.

The November 2004 DASIS (Drug and Alcohol Services Information System) report stated that prescription and over-the-counter-drugs were the primary substances of abuse for 4 percent of the 1.9 million treatment admissions reported in 2002. An additional 100,000 admissions listed these drugs as their second and third substances of abuse.

According to the 2003 National Survey on Drug Use and Health, there was a significant increase in pain killer use for nonmedical reasons, increasing to 31.2 million Americans who use pain killers for nonmedical reasons.

Sales of nonprescription drugs have skyrocketed 60 percent since 1990, with sales topping $20 billion. Supplement sales have also dramatically increased, topping $17 billion in the year 2000.[4] Such explosive access to and use of multiple medications has resulted in an alarming increase of drug *misuse*—taking a drug incorrectly or in a dangerous mix with other drugs. Worse yet, users combine them with alcohol, a potentially deadly mix.

But prescription and over-the-counter drugs are not only *misused*, they are often *abused*. These accidental addicts begin by taking drugs to alleviate uncomfortable physical or mental symptoms—and become unwitting slaves to drugs, often within a matter of weeks.

According to a 2003 survey, an estimated 19.5 million Americans—8.2 percent of the population 12 and older—were illicit drug users.

Radio commentator Rush Limbaugh became a victim of the addiction trap when he used a powerful painkiller, OxyContin, for chronic back pain. After five weeks of intensive therapy and detoxification at a treatment center, he said: "I detoxed myself twice and tried to do it by force of will, which is not possible. This is something someone cannot do alone."[5]

The challenge Limbaugh referred to is that no matter how well a pill works on the brain, it can never fix complex life issues. That requires mental, spiritual, and emotional tools that are eclipsed by addictions. Fortunately, these tools can be recovered. Addictions are no respecter of race, class, or economic status. In fact, the risk that any teen will smoke, drink, or use illegal drugs rises sharply if he or she is highly stressed, frequently bored, or has plenty of spending money.[6] Understanding risk and developing a protective, watchful lifestyle are key ingredients to avoiding addiction in the first place and escaping relapse in the future.

The Three Domains of Addiction

Perhaps the biggest question about drug addiction is, What makes a person seek drugs when the rewarding high is no longer there? Why does a person continue the abuse when disease, degradation, and discomfort increase with use, and quality of life is devastated?

To answer those questions, we must understand what happens in the brain when a person becomes addicted to drugs and how drug-seeking and drug-taking become compulsive and overwhelming—regardless of the outcome.

There are three domains associated with drug addiction:[7] First, genetics does play a role. Increased vulnerability to addiction does exist within certain families.[8] Second, the environment plays a role in vulnerability to addiction. Chronic pain, depression, violence, and abuse are settings where

Laboratory animals that are given free access to cocaine will use it until they kill themselves.

100

susceptibilities to risk-taking behavior are greater. But genetics and the environment are not *causes* of addiction, they are only *associated* with increased risk—an important distinction.

The third domain may be the major reason why addicts continue the use of drugs long after the pleasure is gone. Repeated drug exposure causes changes in brain function that affect behavior. Drugs of abuse alter brain physiology at the molecular, biochemical, neurochemical, and structural level. This means that anyone with enough exposure to an addictive drug is a candidate for addiction. And the larger the quantity of drug used and the longer the drug-taking lasts, the longer it takes for the brain to recover—an important issue in relapse.

Drug-induced brain changes can take place quickly and can be persistent.[9] For instance, laboratory animals that are given free access to cocaine will use it until they kill themselves.[10] Drugs of abuse profoundly alter multiple brain systems, although often in subtly different ways. Precisely how addictive drugs rearrange brain chemistry is poorly understood, and is still the subject of much study. But it *is* known that drugs alter important chemical messengers in the brain, such as cortisol, serotonin, endorphins, enkephalins, and dopamine.[11] Under normal circumstances, these messengers work together to balance such characteristics as drive, appetite, pleasure, depression, stress sensitivity, mental processing, aggression, pain, movement, and motivation.[12] [13]

Drugs affect several of these messengers, known as neurotransmitters, and how they interact with one another. The result is that drug effects may "cascade," or create a domino effect, which then causes dysregulation or impairment of several neurotransmitter systems at once. When this happens, the brain can either overproduce or underproduce these important hormones, or just become nonfunctioning.

Of particular interest is dopamine, a chemical messenger linked to pleasure, reward, motivation, and elation. Drugs of abuse increase the concentration of dopamine in the brain's reward circuits, leading to feelings of euphoria or, in some cases, just preventing feelings of depression. But chronic use produces long-term changes, the most important change being the reduction of dopamine receptors. Receptors are the attachment sites on nerve cells that receive dopamine and allow it to enter into the cell. This reduction of receptors is the brain's attempt to quiet down an overly noisy pleasure circuit with too much dopamine activity.

Having fewer receptors means dopamine is less available to the cells, so more of the drug is needed to produce the desired effect. As a result, experiences that used to bring pleasure, such as a good meal or a friendly chat, no longer ignite the same feelings of happiness. The result can be chronic depression, anxiety, and irritability. But abnormal dopamine activity is also associated with disruption of brain circuits involved with drive, repetitive behavior, and compulsion.[14] Drug addicts, the obese, and those suffering from other addictions are known to have fewer dopamine receptors in key areas of the brain.

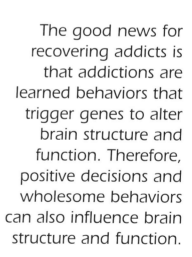

Although addictive behavior is involved in the loss of dopamine receptors, it is also probable that some people have fewer receptors to begin with, putting them at greater risk for addictions. Gary[15] is a prime example of this scenario. He comes from a family with a strong history of alcoholism, gambling, and obesity. Early in his adult life Gary realized that he had addictive tendencies in his personality with a bent toward depression. After some dangerous brushes with alcohol and marijuana at age 19, Gary realized he was well on his way to serious addiction. He made a conscious decision to develop a circle of friends who were involved in activities such as skiing, hiking, school, humanitarian activities, church, and work, and not involved with alcohol or marijuana.

Gary is now 50 and has led a fulfilled, happy, addiction-free life. When asked recently if he felt safe and free from his addictive tendencies, he answered without hesitation: "I refuse

The good news for recovering addicts is that addictions are learned behaviors that trigger genes to alter brain structure and function. Therefore, positive decisions and wholesome behaviors can also influence brain structure and function.

to give myself the chance to find out." Gary has developed a protective lifestyle as a hedge against his vulnerable tendencies, a vital key to staying free from addictions or avoiding relapse. He also carefully avoids situations that might weaken his resolve to remain committed to his chosen lifestyle. Many of these important lifestyle keys are covered in chapters 7-9.

The good news for recovering addicts is that addictions are learned behaviors that trigger genes to alter brain structure and function. Therefore, positive decisions and wholesome behaviors can also influence brain structure and function, so that dopamine receptors are replenished after a period of being drug free.

According to neuroscientist Jeffrey Schwartz, consciously adopting positive attitudes and choices results not only in "remarkable effects on mental and physical function—but also in the wholesale remodeling of neural networks."[16]

Harvard neuroscientist John Ratey puts it this way: "Although the brain's flexibility may decrease with age, it remains plastic [responsive] throughout life, restructuring itself according to what it learns."[17]

Alcohol: Why Not?

Many who can't understand how anyone could abuse drugs are unwittingly flirting with an addiction of another stripe: alcohol. Approximately two thirds of the American population consumes alcoholic beverages.[18] Alcoholism affects about 15 million Americans,[19] a staggering number even when comparing illegal drug and prescription drug abuse combined. Perhaps one reason is that people don't stop to think that they are taking a drug when they drink a beverage containing alcohol. But how can a drink be a drug?

Alcoholic beverages are legal, socially accepted, and relatively inexpensive—but they are not harmless. Alcohol abuse costs this country an amazing $185 billion a year directly in lost workdays, drunken-driver accidents, and medical expenses—more than all illegal drug abuse combined.[20] And that doesn't include the indirect costs. According to Donna Shalala, former secretary of United States Health and Human Services:

Although the brain's flexibility may decrease with age, it remains plastic [responsive] throughout life, restructuring itself according to what it learns.

103

"Alcohol problems, both those of individuals and those that affect society at large, continue to impose a staggering burden on our nation. Domestic violence, child abuse, fires and other accidents, falls, rape, and other crimes against individuals such as robbery and assault—all are linked to alcohol misuse. Alcohol misuse also is implicated in diseases such as cancer, liver disease, and heart disease. Although often not aware of it, everyone shares a portion of this burden."[21]

People like to think that when they drink alcohol they are gaining a great health benefit, whether they drink wine, beer, malt liquor, tequila, whisky, or some other liquor. Advertisers spend more than $1 billion a year to convince us that those who drink alcohol are healthier, friendlier, more cultured, better looking, sexier, and even more successful. Some clergy even get biblical about alcohol consumption: Jesus, they say, drank wine. And they're partially right. Jesus *did* drink wine, the "pure blood of the grape," or fresh grape juice.[22] It was no tailgate party at the wedding feast in Cana, where He turned hundreds of gallons of water into sweet, fresh juice.[23] Such succulent beverages were highly prized among the ancients and had the blessing of God. "As the new wine is found in the cluster do not destroy it, for a blessing is in it."[24]

Our word for wine always means a *fermented beverage*. But the Greek word for wine *(oinos)* can mean either fermented or unfermented juice. The Bible doesn't contradict itself, and there is nothing biblical about a beverage that the Bible warns us not to even look at when it is active, or fermented.[25] The Scriptures warn us that alcohol attacks the user with a vengeance and "at the last" has the death bite of a poisonous viper.[26]

Alarm abuse costs this country an amazing $185 billion a year directly in lost work-days, drunken-driver accidents, and medical expenses—more than all illegal drug abuse combined.

Body and Brain Effects

So, what makes alcohol so insidiously harmful? For one thing, alcohol molecules are very small and are soluble in both fat and water. This enables them to easily permeate almost all parts of the body. As a result, alcohol attacks numerous body tissues, especially fatty tissues. Alcohol irritates the lining of the digestive tract, and increases the risk of oral and liver cancer, stomach ulcers, pancreatitis, and gastritis.[27] And chronic alcohol consumption can cause extensive brain damage.

In light of these facts, it shouldn't surprise anyone that alcohol is listed by the U.S. National Toxicology Program and the International Agency for Research on Cancer as a known human cancer-causing agent.[28] Just one drink a day increases a woman's risk of breast cancer by 9 percent, independent of other risk factors.[29]

At low doses alcohol acts to stimulate firing of nerve cells and lessen inhibition, but it is classified as a depressant because at moderate to high doses it actually depresses, or hinders, proper nerve cell operation.[30] But Dutch researchers found that even one drink could cause reactions to slow, causing people to make more mistakes with less ability to perceive that they are making them.[31]

Like other addictive drugs, alcohol acts on numerous brain circuits, including the reward and compulsion centers of the brain, and produces tolerance and physical dependence. In addition to free radical damage, alcohol causes the actual death of brain cells, resulting in brain shrinkage. According to Kenneth Mukamal, an instructor at Harvard Medical School, every drink is associated with greater brain shrinkage, which itself is linked to dementia.[32] He remarked: "It's been clear that alcoholics have shrunken brains; it was a bit of a surprise that it wasn't just alcoholics."[33]

What about those "shrunken brains"? Is it possible for someone who quits drinking to recover motor and mental function lost through a long period of alcohol abuse? Thankfully, giving up alcohol can reverse much of the structural brain damage that occurs with chronic alcohol abuse.[34] The brain's frontal lobes, the centers for emotions and planning, are especially susceptible to alcohol damage. But after an average of two years of abstinence, this part of the brain recovers some of its lost weight. According to one study author, "These results suggest reversal of structural abnormalities in some brain regions of abstinent alcoholics."[35]

Abstaining alcoholics had a greater volume of white matter, the fibers connecting cells, in the frontal lobes. They also had less scarring of white matter in most areas of the brain, and a higher average volume of gray matter. Dr. Edith Sullivan, associate professor of psychiatry at Stanford University in California, commented on the study: "Taken together, these findings present hopeful data for recovering alcoholics and should provide encouragement for continued sobriety."[36]

The French Paradox

It is clear that alcohol, even in socially acceptable amounts, can damage brain tissue. But does alcohol really reduce heart attack risk? Some studies do indicate that light to moderate amounts of red wine consumption lower the risk of heart attack and fatal heart disease. However, the studies that question the extent of red wine's benefits, or if the benefits outweigh the risk, seem to receive very little publicity.

One analysis of 42 published studies on the effects of alcohol on the heart came to this conclusion: "This analysis found that consumption of up to two drinks per day can promote changes in the levels of molecules that *reduce* the risk of heart disease while also increasing the level of certain molecules that *promote* heart disease."[37] In other words, there is no real benefit.

Alcohol acts as a mild blood thinner, thus possibly reducing the risk of strokes caused by clots. But lowering saturated animal fat intake and increasing fruit, whole grain, and vegetable intake do the same thing—and much more—without the risk of brain and organ damage, cancer, and addiction to alcohol.

Thankfully, giving up alcohol can reverse much of the structural brain damage that occurs with chronic alcohol abuse.

For optimum heart health, you may want to grab the grapes or the grape juice instead of the wine bottle.

Articles on the so-called "French Paradox" have been widely published, which indicate that in France and other countries where saturated fat consumption and wine drinking is high, heart disease is lower than in countries such as Britain, where fat consumption is high and wine intake is low. But the conclusion that wine is the beneficial component of the French lifestyle has come under increasing fire.

British research has found no evidence that drinking red wine provides any protection against heart disease.[38] Researchers found that death rates from ischemic heart disease in the French were linked to their low consumption of saturated fat in the past, and high consumption of more healthful fats for more than 30 years. In addition, some illnesses considered to be cardiovascular in Britain are not considered to be cardiovascular diseases in France, thus seriously skewing study results. There was no difference between wine and other forms of spirits on heart disease deaths according to this and other reports.[39] [40]

A 21-year study of nearly 6,000 Scottish drinking men showed that there was no clear relation between alcohol consumption and death from coronary heart disease, but there was double the risk of stroke when moderate drinkers were compared with non-drinkers.[41] In addition, researchers concluded that drinking even small amounts had no increased health benefit.[42] In fact, at levels commonly seen in social drinking, even levels deemed safe for driving, alcohol prompts a sharp increase in destructive free radical activity, linked to a wide array of chronic diseases, including liver and heart disease.[43]

Finally, according to Dr. Robert Superko, director of the Cholesterol, Genetics, and Heart Disease Institute in Berkeley, California, the cardiovascular benefits of alcohol have been greatly overstated. At a recent conference held by the American College of Cardiology, he stated the strong possibility that the studies favoring alcohol consumption for heart health are "quite biased."[44] "Add that insight to the considerable role alcohol plays in the alarming obesity epidemic in the United States," Dr. Superko says, "and a highly unflattering picture of alcohol's cardiovascular effects emerges. Indeed, *alcohol avoidance*, along with increased physical activity and the elimination of simple sugars from the diet, ought to be at the core of any strategy to reduce the obesity problems. Alcohol is very calorie dense. One glass of wine contains as many calories as a Snickers candy bar—about as many as are burned in a one-mile walk."[45]

Grab Those Grapes!

For optimum heart health, you may want to grab the grapes or the grape juice instead of the wine bottle. In an animal model study, dark grape juice was "much more effective" than alcohol-containing wine in its ability to inhibit plaque buildup in the arteries, improve lipids, and raise blood levels of antioxidants that help fight heart disease.[46]

Plant compounds in grapes called polyphenols are thought to be the main source of benefit because they may dilate blood vessels, apart from the alcohol. In fact, wine without alcohol had the benefit of dilating vessels more quickly, while alcohol actually delayed the beneficial response, although it did occur.[47]

Here's the latest from the grapevine: The "pure blood of the grape," the unfermented juice, with its "blessing" in the wholesome cluster is undoubtedly the safest, wisest, and most wholesome way to receive the health-promoting benefits of grapes.

Nicotine: The Taxable Addiction

Tobacco addiction tops all drugs in terms of sheer numbers of people addicted. In 2001, 45.2 million Americans smoked tobacco, and 32 million of them wanted to quit.[48] In 1997, 42.7 percent of students used cigarettes, smokeless tobacco, or cigars within 30 days of being surveyed.[49] More than 4 million American adolescents currently smoke,[50] with 13 being the average age for youth to begin smoking.[51]

Smoking costs the United States almost $160 billion each year in healthcare costs.[52] Smoking-related deaths surpass 400,000 per year, more than twice the death toll for AIDS, alcohol, auto accidents, murder, suicide, and drug-induced deaths combined.[53] Income generated from taxes on tobacco products pales in comparison with the billions consumed in healthcare costs, lost productivity, and death due to tobacco use.[54] [55]

Worldwide, one billion cigarettes are produced a day, and there are almost 5 million reported smoking-related deaths every year. If trends remain the same, that figure is expected to double by the year 2030.[56] Children who smoke in China typically begin by age 6. If present patterns persist, tobacco will kill nearly a third of China's young men during the next few decades.[57] Worldwide, one of every seven youth ages 13 to 15 smokes, with nearly a quarter of them having tried their first cigarette by age 10.[58]

Why do so many people smoke? Like alcohol, tobacco is widely available, relatively inexpensive, and legal. Its initial drug effects include elevated stress hormone production, which increases energy and induces a pleasant mood.[59] But most significant, it is highly addictive.

Worldwide, one of every seven youth ages 13 to 15 smokes, with nearly a quarter of them having tried their first cigarette by age 10.

109

Former Phillip Morris tobacco company researcher Dr. Victor DeNoble was an expert witness at special congressional hearings when the news broke that cigarette companies were researching ways to make cigarettes more addictive. According to Dr. DeNoble's testimony, tobacco delivers 4,700 chemicals to the lungs, 3,000 of which are absorbed into the bloodstream.[60] It takes 7 seconds for nicotine, a main addictive compound, to go from the lungs, to the heart, and then to the brain. The average smoker takes a puff every 30 seconds, and smokes 10 to 15 cigarettes a day.

Safe Smokes, Snuff, and Stogies?

Is there a "safe" cigarette? Vegetable-based cigarettes produce hefty amounts of the poison carbon monoxide—even more than conventional cigarettes.[61] Smokers who use "addictive-free" cigarettes, hand-rolled Indian bidis, or other specialty cigarettes may find they are actually more toxic than conventional ones, with some being higher in nicotine.[62] The consumption of low-tar brands is behind a surge in cancers called adenocarcinomas, which attack the deepest part of the lungs.[63] Why? The users smoke more of them, take deeper drags, and hold the smoke in their lungs longer to get the drug effect.

Perhaps in an effort to get the nicotine high without the risks, some people switch to chewing tobacco, snuff, or cigars with the idea that since they are not inhaling smoke, it is "more healthful" or even less addicting. But nothing could be farther from the truth. People who smoke cigars have twice the incidence of cancer of the mouth, throat, and lungs as nonsmokers.[64] Cigars are associated with serious impairment of vessel dilation which robs blood from the heart and other body tissues.[65] Cigar smokers also have double the risk of heart disease compared to nonsmokers.[66]

In reality, cigars deliver a heavy nicotine punch and are very addicting. It is a myth that expensive cigars are less damaging than cheap ones. But despite these facts, cigar sales have risen 44 percent since 1993.

Tobacco delivers 4,700 chemicals to the lungs, 3,000 of which are absorbed into the bloodstream.

A writer with a 10-year chewing tobacco addiction describes his struggle with a daily two-tin "dipping" habit: "When I dip into the tin nicotine pours through my mucous membrane and into my bloodstream. Then I sit and work, knowing I have this ritual to thank for these paragraphs and the ones that follow. I do think about the possibility of cancer, of having my tongue amputated, or losing my jaw. Usually such thoughts come after a day's writing is complete and I've dipped so much tobacco that my mouth's interior feels Brilloed, the cores of my teeth throb with a deep, radioactive ache, and my brain roils with the neat lightening of nicotine. Afterward, I pull my lips away from my mouth to scan for tumors and observe my receding, sometimes bleeding, gum line. I again resolve to quit, which generates anxiety, and soon I want nothing more than to dip, and dip, and dip, and really get cancer, because only then will I be able to answer the question that burns in every addict's brain: What is it going to take to make me stop?"[67]

Nicotine and Dopamine

Nicotine, like other addictive drugs, changes the way the brain works by altering neurotransmitter function, especially dopamine. Nicotine causes dopamine to flood the communication sites at nerve endings, which causes receiving neurons to "down regulate," or reduce, the amount of dopamine they are able take up, or respond to. This could be likened to putting on cellular "earplugs" because of too much neurotransmitter "noise." Because dopamine is a pleasure transmitter linked to feelings of joy and happiness, the resulting inability of neurons to "hear" dopamine messages when they are at normal levels is translated as depression or lack of happiness. Normal activities no longer kindle the same pleasant feelings. Soon, once-normal levels of nicotine no longer bring pleasure, so tobacco users increase their intake.

According to Dr. DeNoble, it takes six to nine months of smoking to alter brain circuitry, but it can take 10 years for those circuits to restabilize and return to normal after someone kicks the smoking habit. This could explain why even though it

Exercise, for example, increases levels of dopamine, serotonin, and norepinephrine, all neurotransmitters associated with motivation, reward, learning, and behavior.

takes only 30 hours for nicotine to leave the body completely, relapse is common for ex-smokers.

Fortunately, an aggressive recovery program that stimulates dopamine circuits in other parts of the brain can greatly aid recovery, improve mood, and reduce the risk of relapse. Exercise, for example, increases levels of dopamine, serotonin, and norepinephrine, all neurotransmitters associated with motivation, reward, learning, and behavior.[68] Exercise also reduces withdrawal symptoms and the desire to smoke.[69] While many people smoke because they are stressed, quitting smoking measurably lowers stress levels in one month and cuts them in half in six months.[70]

The body, as well as the brain, responds to healthful lifestyle changes, which is why hundreds of thousands have quit tobacco forever! And for most people who stop smoking before irreversible damage is done, heart attack risk declines, nerve cells begin to regroup and repair, lung health and capacity improve, cancer risk declines, and stroke risk is reduced.

If you use tobacco, see chapters 7-9 for important keys to recovery that will help you kick the habit—for good!

Caffeine: Are the Perks Worth the Price?

Caffeine is nicotine's close chemical cousin and is the most widely used stimulant in the world. According to one researcher: "Caffeine is probably the world's most popular drug. It is taken regularly by most of the population from childhood onwards."[71] Five million tons of coffee are produced annually, making it second only to oil in international commerce.[72] Worldwide, coffee drinkers consume more than 400 billion cups per year.

The body, as well as the brain, responds to healthful lifestyle changes, which is why hundreds of thousands have quit tobacco forever!

Worldwide, coffee drinkers consume more than 400 billion cups per year.

Estimates vary, but approximately 90 percent of Americans consume caffeine in some form every day. It is found in varying amounts in coffee, tea, chocolate, cocoa, soft drinks, and caffeinated juice drinks. Now even caffeine-spiked water is available. It is also found in many drugs, especially weight-control aids, alertness tablets, pain relief medications, diuretics, and cold/allergy remedies.

More than half of Americans consume more than 300 milligrams (mg) of caffeine every day. Seventy-five percent of caffeine intake is generally in the form of coffee, although caffeinated soft drink consumption is dramatically increasing. More than 108 million Americans consume coffee, spending $18 billion a year for their favorite brew. American coffee drinkers average about 3 cups a day per person, or close to 1,100 cups per person yearly.[73] By conservative estimates, up to 30 percent of adult Americans have a daily caffeine intake of more than 500 mg.[74]

But are caffeine's perks worth the price? Does caffeine's broad usage create *grounds* for concern? There is much more to coffee than caffeine. It contains hundreds of chemicals that have biologic effects.[75] [76] Decaffeinated coffee has been linked to increased risk for rheumatoid arthritis in older women[77] and elevated blood pressure in occasional drinkers, presumably because they have not built a tolerance to its effects.[78]

Occasionally studies surface that suggest coffee consumption can have a medicinal benefit with certain disorders such as Parkinson's disease. But these studies must be weighed against the backdrop of other studies that link coffee use with heart disease, several cancers, and bone loss. Studies on either side of the question are inconclusive, but two things are certain: Tolerance to caffeine occurs quickly, and caffeine can be addictive.

Eight expert substance abuse clinicians randomly sampled 162 caffeine users for clinical measures of dependence and abuse. They found that 91 percent of the respondents exhibited dependence-like behavior to caffeine, with 56 percent reporting a "strong desire or unsuccessful attempt to stop" using it.[79] They concluded: "Our results replicate earlier work and suggest that a substantial proportion of caffeine users exhibit dependence-like behaviors."[80]

Caffeine causes metabolic mayhem in the body's stress system. Among its many actions, caffeine stimulates the brain in a similar way as drugs of abuse by increasing dopamine in its pleasure centers, although to a lesser degree. Caffeine works on every system of the body affected by the central nervous system. Caffeine also blocks major energy-braking chemicals in the body (phosphodiesterase) and brain (adenosine) that regulate excitement, wakefulness, and alertness. In short, caffeine's blockage of these two chemicals causes adenosine receptors in the brain to make you feel alert, injects stress hormones into the body to make you feel energetic, and manipulates dopamine to make you feel good.

But caffeine's quick pick-me-up has its let downs, too. Caffeine tolerance and dependence can occur quickly, sometimes within days. The long-term effects of repeated

Caffeine is nicotine's close chemical cousin and is the most widely used stimulant in the world.

Caffeine addiction is a habit that can form early in life, usually in the form of caffeinated soda pop.

caffeine stimulation are fatigue, depression, irritability, mental fog, and loss of quality sleep, which leave you craving more caffeine, quickly creating a vicious cycle of dependence. People use caffeine for energy and alertness, but healthful energy and alertness come from good nutrition and wise lifestyle choices, not a drug. And remember, like any other chemical stimulant, caffeine contains no nutritive elements, or fuel, your body can assimilate to create energy—which means its perceived energy and brain boost have to come from chemical tricks caffeine plays on the body.

As little as a single cup of coffee a day can produce a habit severe enough to produce withdrawal symptoms, according to new research from Johns Hopkins University.[81] "Caffeine is the world's most commonly used stimulant, and it's cheap and readily available so people can maintain their use of caffeine quite easily."[82] Withdrawal symptoms from this drug include headache, fatigue, difficulty concentrating, nausea, muscle pain, and other flu-like symptoms.[83]

Janice Keller Phelps, MD, who ran a drug detoxification center in Seattle, Washington, and authored the book *The Hidden Addiction*, shares this story: "A funny thing happened at a medical meeting I attended recently. The topic of the conference was 'Addictive Behavior,' and I was one of four or five people scheduled to speak. The organizers of the meeting had decided to change a practice usual at such functions: they would substitute fresh fruit, cheese, and fruit juice for coffee that is almost always offered in the morning before the day's program begins.

"The doctors were furious. Some of the most virulent reactions came from three of the speakers scheduled to deliver addresses. They flatly refused to start the program until they had their morning cup of coffee. They couldn't possibly go on, they insisted. The sponsors had to order up a special urn of coffee on the double, and we all had to sit around and wait until it was made and brought out before we could get on with the meeting. The program finally began an hour and twenty minutes late. I was supposed to talk about addictions that day, but the scene we had just witnessed said more about it than I could have if I had talked all day."[84]

Caffeine addiction is a habit that can form early in life, usually in the form of caffeinated soda pop. Carbonated soft drinks, many of them containing caffeine, account for more than 27 percent of Americans' beverage consumption.[85] In 1997, Americans spent more than $54 billion to buy 14 billion gallons of soft drinks, which translates to about 576 12-ounce servings per year for every man, woman, and child.[86] One-fifth of toddlers consume soft drinks every day. Almost half of children ages 6-11 drink about 15 ounces of soda pop a day. Teen consumption is the highest with one-fourth of teens drinking almost three cans a day.[87]

This high intake of sugar, phosphoric acid, and caffeine from soft drinks is not good for bones, brain, or body—and addiction is just as real in the young as in older people.

Research has shown that over time caffeine may increase stress sensitivity, anxiety, and depression. It can also encourage the loss of nutrients such as calcium, magnesium, and B vitamins.[88] [89]

The long-term effects of repeated caffeine stimulation are fatigue, depression, irritability, mental fog, and loss of quality sleep.

116

No artificial stimulant can provide what consistent healthful choices impart to the mind and body.

But the most subtle and devastating long-term effect of caffeine may be its slow erosion of vital nerve centers in the brain that balance stress hormone levels. This can eventually affect memory and risk for depression. How? Caffeine causes an elevation of a stress hormone called cortisol, which can accumulate in a brain memory center called the hippocampus.[90] The hippocampus is essential for short-term memory and is also a key player in regulation of your body's stress system.

When cortisol levels remain too high for too long from exposure to chronic stress or chemical stimulation such as caffeine, cell death can occur in the hippocampus, as well as other vital areas of the brain.[91] The result can include memory impairment, chronic depression, and chronic "dysregulation" of the stress system.

Caffeine has been called "bad habit glue" because it reinforces the effects of other drugs. In fact, caffeine increases the effects of nicotine, so it becomes a powerful factor that can hamper a person's attempt to quit smoking.[92]

Coffee, tea, and soft drink consumption also tend to cause vitamin and mineral loss and dehydration. According to the American Dietetic Association, dehydration of as little as 2 percent loss of body weight can reduce your mental and physical abilities. Plentiful water intake (about eight glasses a day for a typical adult) reduces sluggishness by enhancing and enables your blood to carry life- and energy-giving nutrients to your body's cells!

On the other hand, drug-induced energy and alertness have an expensive price tag of side effects such as dependence, tolerance, fatigue, jitters, sleeplessness, and depression. Eating right, exercising, getting plenty of rest, stress management, and drinking plenty of fresh water increase mental strength and overall energy, improve mood and mental processing, and enhance immune function and emotional health. No artificial stimulant can provide what consistent healthful choices impart to the mind and body.

117

Brew a New You!

While alcohol, nicotine, and caffeine are socially accepted drugs, they can be powerfully addicting. Many have found better success in eliminating all three substances than trying to avoid just one. Replacing these stimulants with food and lifestyle choices that generate real strength yields long-term benefits that no drug can top. Chapters 7-9 will provide you with the essential tools for building better habits that will help you beat the caffeine, nicotine, and alcohol habit and keep you on the road to living free!

Replacing these stimulants with food and lifestyle choices that generate real strength yields long-term benefits that no drug can top.

118

Under the Influence

"Water taken in moderation cannot hurt anybody."

Mark Twain

Alcohol's effects on the brain:

Under the influence of alcohol the brain can experience long-term overall shrinkage and impairment in the regions shown:

- *Frontal Lobe (A):* Loss of reason, caution, inhibitions, sociability, talkativeness, and intelligence.

- *Parietal Lobe (B):* Loss of fine motor skills, slower reaction time, shaking.

- *Temporal Lobe (C):* Slurred speech, impaired hearing.

- *Occipital Lobe (D):* Blurred vision, poor distance judgment.

- *Cerebellum (E):* Lack of muscle coordination and balance.

- *Brain Stem (F):* Loss of vital functions.

Used by permission of the Alcohol and Drug Awareness Project.

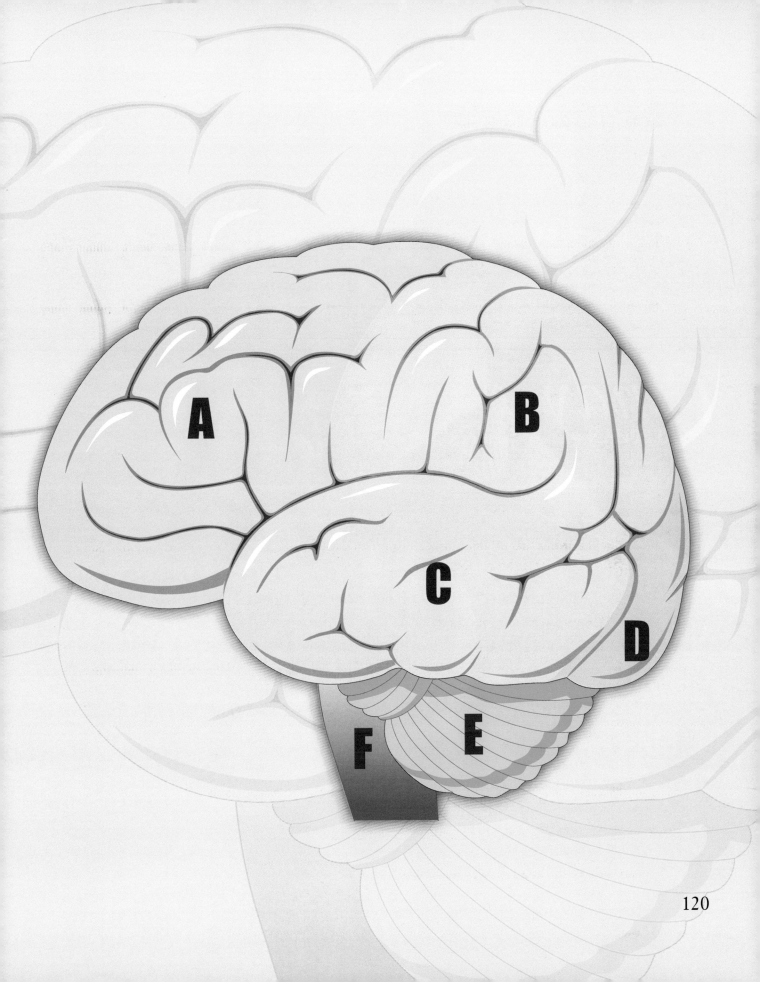

Cindy
STEPHAN

121

Delivered

Smoking

I smoked for 14 years. When I look at my past, it's easy to understand why. As a child, I intently watched my mom as she smoked. She smoked in the morning with her coffee. She smoked all day. She would wake up in the middle of the night just to have a cigarette. When my family went out to eat we had to stay after the meal so Mom could have her cigarette.

Then someone let me try their cigarette. I coughed terribly and I recall how horrible it was. But because of what I had seen with my mom, smoking had become a priority for me.

As a teenager I wanted friends so much that I started smoking and drinking, thinking that would help me fit in. I still didn't like the taste of cigarettes, but I thought I looked cool when I smoked and that I would never become addicted. Gradually the taste of cigarettes became more acceptable, and before I knew it, I was addicted, just like my mom was!

As an adult I tried to quit, but couldn't. The slightest annoyance would make me very tense and anxious, so I would cave in and have a cigarette just to keep my nerves at bay. It relaxed me, or so I thought. Three months after my wedding I found out I was pregnant. I quit smoking for those nine months, but started up again after the baby was born because I thought it would help me lose the extra weight I had gained during my pregnancy.

One year later, two days before Christmas, I received a call telling me that my mom had a near-fatal heart attack. I was so devastated I couldn't think straight. I smoked constantly. With my marriage falling apart, the news about Mom was too much for me. My cravings and stress were at an all-time high.

During my annual physical the doctor asked if I was still smoking, and I said yes. When he asked why I hadn't quit, I told him I had tried to quit many times but that I always caved in when I got angry or upset. Cigarettes kept me calm, I said. He told me to try deep breathing rather than the cigarettes. He said that cigarettes are stimulants and they don't relax you, the breathing does. But what he said next really hit home.

Delivered
Cindy Stephan – Smoking

"Why don't you quit smoking so you don't put your son through what your mom put you through?" With my marriage in pieces, my son was my life. I didn't want him to go through what I had been through with my mom's heart attack. The next day I quit smoking.

During my divorce I wanted so much to have a cigarette, but I remembered what my doctor said to me. So I did deep breathing—something like inhaling a cigarette and remembered that nicotine is a stimulant. After about five minutes the cravings would go away. I was delivered from my addiction in the midst of the most stressful point in my life.

I have been smoke free since 1999, and the smell of cigarettes or even the thought of smoking disgusts me. It took several years and a lot of prayer, but now I can walk outside and smell the pine scent of the trees, or walk by a flower bed and smell the roses in the air. I never used to be able to do that! Today I am living free, and by setting the right example for my son, he can more easily follow in my footsteps.

Jan
SYLVESTER

125

Delivered

Heroin and Alcohol

I come from a family with a long history of addictions on both sides. I believe my addictive tendency surfaced when I was 10 years old. My mother gave me codeine cough syrup for my cough on a regular basis. I remember my body being drawn to the warm sensation of it. This tendency surfaced again in 1981 when my divorce brought on feelings of rejection—the "I'm-not-good-enough" feeling. The loneliness, the strain of raising two children by myself, and the fear of life were tremendous burdens! Because I didn't know God, my days and nights were very dark. I started drinking alcohol to numb my feelings.

It wasn't long before I started using drugs, and eventually I turned to heroin. During the next 14 years my life became a nightmarish free fall. I was looking for fulfillment with external things, but on the inside I was losing all feelings and emotion. I was an empty shell.

I lived every day afraid of dying but also afraid of living. I trusted no one. I learned how to use people and manipulate them to get what I wanted. I was filled with anger and I hated people. Like a tornado I pulled everyone into the destructive path of my addiction. I made sure that my children, family, friends, and coworkers all felt my pain. I was a very selfish and self-centered person.

My 19-year-old daughter continually begged me to get help. She told me about God, but I could not get away from my feelings of self-pity. One day she told God that she had to give me up to Him.

She saw me slowly dying and felt that there was no hope for me. She wrote me a letter pleading with me not to leave her alone. Somehow that letter pulled me into reality, and I was ready to get help. Finally, on March 7, 1995, I entered a rehabilitation program.

126

Delivered
Jan Sylvester – Heroin and Alcohol

Today I have victory as I stay close to God. Every day I surrender my will and my life to His care, and I put all my trust in Him. I "clean house" every day by taking a good look at myself. I also examine the character traits that I no longer want to have in my life. This process helps me to be willing for God to work in my life and bring about the changes that I need for growth.

I will celebrate ten years of sobriety on March 7. Today God is working through me to help other recovering people. Helping others gives my life meaning and purpose. He saved me from dying a terrible and lonely death. He also taught me to love others and to receive love from them in return. I am daily discovering the good gifts He has given me to share with others. What keeps me sober? Every day when I wake up my heart is filled with gratitude and thanksgiving that I don't have to live like I used to anymore.

Personal Worksheet 4

Substance Addictions

1. How would you describe the basic characteristics of a person who suffers from substance abuse?* Review *Ten Signs of an Addicted Brain* on page 19.** What is the good news for those who suffer from substance addictions? (See page 103.) _____

   _____

   _____

2. What emotional, lifestyle, or environmental triggers can set off substance addiction? What positive steps can be taken to eliminate or reduce exposure to those triggers? What alternatives can replace them?

   _____

   _____

3. What promises can help me when I suffer from restless cravings of heart, mind, and body? Look up Psalm 91 and Isaiah 57:18. _____

   _____

   _____

4. What are some strategies and activities that can help me overcome cravings and addictive behavior? What is the value of refocusing attention on other things? What affect will nutrition, exercise, and rest have on this process? _____

   _____

   _____

5. What encouragement and power are available to me? Look up Psalm 50:15 and Psalm 46:1-3. What do I do with guilt? Look up Micah 7:18, 19._____

   _____

   _____

Answers located on page 342 in the back of book.

* If you are working in a group, review the sections before you meet.
** It is important to rule out other medical conditions. Always work with your physician or healthcare provider. Serious mood disorders or physical symptoms require clinical intervention.

Chapter 5

The Entertainment Trap

"I find television very educational. Every time someone switches it on, I go into another room and read a good book."

Groucho Marx

The Stats Tell the Story

In the mid-1800s the average work week was about 70 hours, or about six 12-hour days. At the turn of the twentieth century that figure dropped to about 60 hours per week, and by the mid-1900s, 50 hours were the norm. Today people work an average of 40 hours or fewer a week. But, ironically, with more leisure time than ever, we have collectively turned to television to satisfy our increasing appetite for novelty, news, and entertainment.

Americans spend half their free time in front of the television. Ninety-nine percent of households in America own at least one television—more than have refrigerators or indoor plumbing. Thirty-two percent of households have two television sets, and 66 percent have three. The average time that television is on each day in the typical U.S. home is seven hours, with individual viewing for adults topping four hours. That is 28 hours per week, or two months of nonstop television viewing per year.[1]

In a 65-year lifespan, the average person will have spent nine years glued to the television, enough time to obtain at least two university degrees.[2] American youngsters, on average, spend more time watching television than any other activity besides sleeping.[3] Psychologist Dr. Jane Healy notes that: "By ages three to five—the height of the brain's critical period for cognitive development—estimates place viewing time of the average child at twenty-eight hours a week. Average time for elementary students runs at about twenty-five hours a week, and for high-schoolers, twenty-eight hours a week, approximately six times the hours spent doing homework."[4] When television time is combined with playing video games, many teens are spending 35 to 55 hours in front of the television or game station every week, according to a study by the American Academy of Pediatrics.[5]

Retired award-winning news analyst Robert MacNeil asks: "When before in human history has so much humanity collectively surrendered so much of its leisure to one toy, one mass diversion? When before has virtually an entire nation surrendered itself wholesale to a medium for selling?"[6]

Watching television has become a major leisure activity; but, ironically, sitting in front of the tube is more likely than other leisure activities to leave people passive, tense, and unable to concentrate.[7] In fact, sitting in front of the television for long periods of time leaves people in a worse mood than when they started watching.[8]

Creative thinking, socializing, and individual or group reflection have been replaced by scripted reality in many homes. But meaningful mental and social activities produce a wiser, more productive, and fulfilled people, ultimately creating a safer society.

Plug-in Drug?

With those stats before us, it's sobering to consider that television can have a hypnotic, and possibly addictive, effect on the brain. The term *television addict* has become proverbial in our society, and even a subject of commentary by researchers: "Excessive cravings do not necessarily involve physical substances. Gambling can become compulsive; sex can become obsessive. One activity, however, stands out for its prominence and ubiquity—the world's most popular leisure pastime, television. Most of the criteria of substance dependence can apply to people who watch a lot of television."[9]

And what are the criteria of substance dependence? Spending a lot of time with the substance; using it more than intended; thinking about reducing use or making repeated unsuccessful attempts to reduce use; giving up important social, family, or occupational activities for it; and reporting withdrawal symptoms when one stops using it.[10]

One 32-year-old police officer has one wife, two children, and three TV sets. He watches 71 hours of television a week. "I rarely go out anymore," he admits.

Howard Shaffer, who heads the Division of Addictions at Harvard University, supports that, maintaining that drug use "is not a necessary and sufficient cause of addiction. It is improper to consider drugs as the necessary precondition for addiction."[11]

The effects of compulsive TV viewing can be devastating to home life, social relations, and even work. One 32-year-old police officer has one wife, two children, and three TV sets. He watches 71 hours of television a week. "I rarely go out anymore," he admits.[12]

Such uncontrolled television exposure seems to create an increased but unsatisfying thirst for more stimulation. Worse yet, the culture created by the entertainment industry provides a fantasy world that makes ordinary life boring. Media critic Neal Gabler notes how, as a result of media saturation and stimulation, everything is judged by its entertainment value.[13] Every experience has to be highly entertaining, whether it is work, school, church, or leisure time.

People report feeling more relaxed and passive while watching television, but their sense of relaxation ends when the set is turned off. However, feelings of passivity and lowered alertness remain. Survey participants report television has somehow "absorbed or sucked their energy, leaving them depleted."[14] Relaxation occurs quickly when the set is turned on because viewers associate viewing with lack of tension. Brain changes reinforce this association. But stress and lowered mood state occur once the screen goes blank again, reinforcing the urge to leave the set on. And the longer people watch television, the less satisfaction they derive from it.[15] To those who are addicted, the absence of television can cause depression, a sense of loss, anxiety, and cravings for more of television's stimulating effects.

Television and the Adult Brain

Adult brains can create new neurons.[16] [17] But regarding that, Jeff Victoroff, neuropsychiatrist and author of *Saving Your Brain*, notes: "A wealth of new scientific evidence shows us the

difference between the effects of passive and active experience on the brain. Active responses to cognitive challenges are unquestionably what turn on our adult neurons. And here's where we come to the crucial point about mental stimulation and the brain: passive experience does little for the adult brain. To keep the brain learning and growing, we need to generate *active responses to cognitive challenges.*"[18]

Many people watch television thinking that it is educational. But what type of learning takes place while the brain is in a passive state? How much of even "educational" programming is transferable to the brain's higher cognitive centers?

Many people think that once they are adults and their brains are fully developed their choices don't affect brain health. But the adult brain is continually responding to internal and external cues and remodeling accordingly. "[Brain] nerves are constantly making new connections that will serve us better in the things we do frequently. The brain can be shaped by experiences, just as particular muscles respond to particular exercises."[19]

It's true that gross anatomy doesn't change, but "through everyday life, certain neuronal groups are selected to thrive while others die owing to lack of use. If a person is inactive mentally, that individual loses brain cells."[20] On the other hand, "activities that challenge your brain actually expand the number and strength of neural connections devoted to the skill."[21] Examples would include learning a musical instrument, reading mentally challenging material, or learning a new craft or skill.

Adults as well as children can use their brains in an active way and reap the resulting benefits of neural growth, expansion, and resilience. But adults can whittle down a once-sharp intellect through lack of use, causing unused brain circuits to diminish or even die. Without interfacing with others and meeting mental challenges, the mind becomes less able to focus on a task, making the individual less productive and less able to achieve goals in life.

Television and the Developing Brain

The growing brain of a child is especially responsive to environmental and lifestyle factors, and especially prone to television's ability to alter the way the brain thinks and functions. Psychologist Jane Healy is a reading and learning specialist as well as a published researcher in the area of television's effects on the learning brain. She writes: "Scientists are acutely aware that large doses of any type of experience have shaping power over the growing brain."[22] And many children are getting larger doses of television than any other single activity besides sleeping.

Television cannot compete with books, interaction, and real-life experience when it comes to learning. Merely watching letters and numbers fly across the screen does not transfer as well to the areas of the brain involved in mental processing, focused attention, writing skills, critical thinking, and active problem-solving.[23] Also, spending too much time in front of the television can actually diminish these important skills in adults as well as children.

Through excessive television watching, children may actually fail to develop needed circuitry to master critical-thinking skills, while becoming "over-wired" in the parts of the brain that crave novelty and reward but don't demand much thought. With so much of our leisure time spent in front of the television, this fact alone has profound implications for the moral, social, and intellectual advancement of our society.

A recent study in *Pediatrics* discussing television's brain effects reported that "repeated exposure to any stimulus in a child's environment may forcibly impact mental and emotional growth by either set-ting up particular circuitry ('habits of mind') or depriving the brain of other experiences.

Television cannot compete with books, interaction, and real-life experience when it comes to learning.

This shaping process, which affects brain structure and function, seems to influence both cellular development and neurotransmitter regulation."[24]

Television is a two-edged challenge for the developing child. There is the challenge of the brain-altering effects of so much media exposure; but there is also the disadvantage caused by the displacement of many beneficial activities because of time spent watching television. Simply put, there is a lot that *isn't done* because of television.

Dimitri Christakis, a researcher at Children's Hospital and Regional Medical Center in Seattle, Washington, found that for every hour preschoolers watch television, there is a 10 percent increased risk of developing attention problems later.[25] Problems included difficulty concentrating, restlessness, impulsivity, and being easily confused. Noting that television may over-stimulate and permanently rewire the developing brain, Dr. Christakis wrote: "There are lots of reasons for children not to watch television. Other studies have shown it to be associated with obesity and aggressiveness."[26]

Higher learning takes place as a result of active mental exertion, which television generally does not stimulate—it is largely a passive experience.

137

Should we discard television watching altogether then? No. Television can be a source of education, information, entertainment, and even relaxation. Good programs are produced on science, history, nature, religion, art, and human interest. These types of programs can provide a nice diversion and stimulate interest in a new area of study. But higher learning takes place as a result of active mental exertion, which television generally does not stimulate—it is largely a passive experience.

Higher learning could be described as an active process that requires voluntary rather than forced attention, utilizing active reasoning, mental skill, and perseverance. In contrast, passive learning relies on rapid, high-intensity visual and/or auditory stimulation. Passive learning produces a response in the novelty and fear centers of the brain but elicits little mental effort and leaves little time for moral evaluation.

Television and the Neutral Brain

Dr. Antonio Domasio, head of the Department of Neurology at the University of Iowa College of Medicine, may have some further insights on how frequent exposure to violent television and video games numbs the emotions. According to Dr. Domasio, the risk of emotional neutrality increases as the brain is barraged with too much input. This is because the information center of the brain receives and processes data at a much faster pace than the emotional center.

Domasio says: "We really have two systems that are totally integrated and work perfectly well with each other but are very different in their time constants. One is the emotional system, which is the basic regulatory system that works very slowly, with timescales of a second or more. Then you have the cognitive (information) system, which is much faster because of the way it's wired and also because a lot of the fiber systems are totally myelinated, which means they work much faster."[27]

Those nerve circuits critical for forming attitudes, empathy, emotions, and values (the emotional system) lack this fatty myelin coat and process information more slowly than the information system. High-speed visual input may stimulate novelty and fear centers to grab and keep attention—but there is no time for more intricate emotional memory pathways to solidify the experience and assign it a moral value.

High-speed visual input may stimulate novelty and fear centers to grab and keep attention—but there is no time for more intricate emotional memory pathways to solidify the experience and assign it a value.

"Events register faster and faster and more and more remotely," Domasio says, "and you're not even given time to let them sink in. Your feelings for your wife—my feelings for my wife—those feelings that develop slowly are still very different; they're an island of safety. But on the news, things are shown one after another. No matter how terrifying, images are shown so briefly that we have no time to sense emotionally the horror of a particular event."[28] It is not uncommon for news programs to air horrific scenes while displaying basketball scores and stock market figures simultaneously at the bottom of the screen. The end effect is that the horrific scenes no longer evoke moral distress; they are simply more information along with "the rest of the news"!

Television news, now called "infotainment" by some critics, uses two methods in packaging the news to arouse its viewers. First, "arousal can be influenced by story topic or content: violence, disaster, and sex have been shown to elicit arousal in most viewers."[29] Second, lavish and sensational production techniques arouse emotion in the viewer. They include the use of sound effects, music, flash frames, slow motion, and the obtrusiveness of the reporter's tone.[30]

This sensory overload affects both the body and the emotions. In one study, viewing 14 minutes of negative television news bulletins increased stress-hormone production in viewers, as well as personal catastrophizing, worrisome thought, anxiety, and sad mood.[31]

"The image of an event or a person can appear in a flash," Domasio says, "but it takes seconds to make an emotional marking which means that you could potentially become ethically less grounded. You'd be in an emotionally neutral world."[32]

The danger of high-speed input, according to Domasio, is that "there will be more and more people who will have to rely on the cognitive system entirely, without using their emotional memory, in order to decide what's good and what's evil. They can be told about good and evil, but good and evil might not stick."[33]

Forced Attention

In her book *Endangered Minds: Why Children Can't Learn and What You Can Do About It*, Dr. Jane Healy notes several potential effects of television on the brain, including forced attention, neural passivity, and addictiveness. [34]

The ability to pay attention and focus on a task is developed internally. But television artificially manipulates the brain into paying attention by violating certain of its natural defenses with flashing images, sudden close-ups, and invasive sounds (called saliency). Frequent loud noises, camera zooms, and flashing distorted images alert the novelty, reward, and fear centers of the brain of impending danger. This keeps you watching—whether you want to or not. This may contribute to hyperactivity, frustration, and irritability.[35]

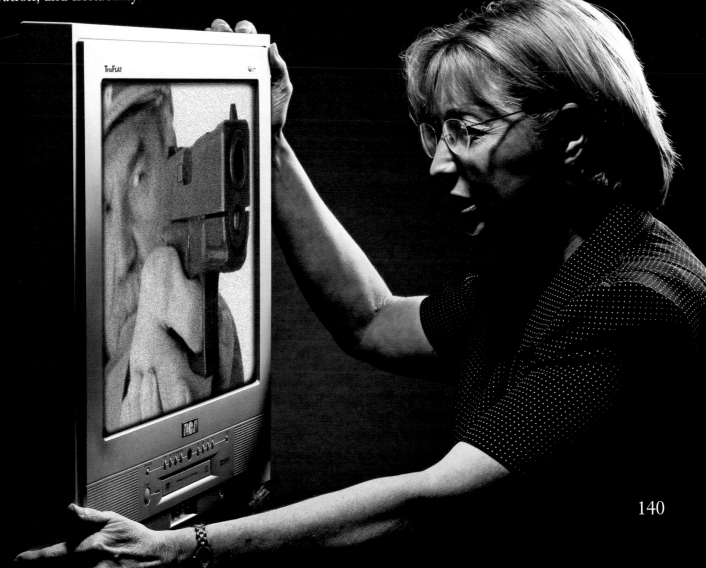

140

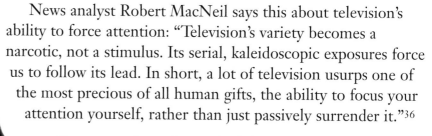

News analyst Robert MacNeil says this about television's ability to force attention: "Television's variety becomes a narcotic, not a stimulus. Its serial, kaleidoscopic exposures force us to follow its lead. In short, a lot of television usurps one of the most precious of all human gifts, the ability to focus your attention yourself, rather than just passively surrender it."[36]

One researcher who studied the effects of television commented on his own embarrassing struggle to pay attention during an interview when the television set was on, even when the conversation was interesting![37] Yale law professor Charles L. Black wrote: "forced feeding on trivial fare is not itself a trivial matter."[38]

Neural Passivity

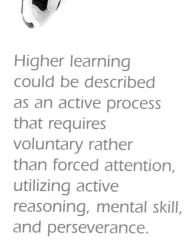

Higher learning could be described as an active process that requires voluntary rather than forced attention, utilizing active reasoning, mental skill, and perseverance.

According to Dr. Healy, television may induce "neural passivity" and reduce "stick-to-it-iveness." Dr. Jennings Bryant of the University of Alabama, found that watching lots of fast-paced programming "reduces vigilance" and diminishes reading and puzzle-solving abilities after viewing. According to Bryant, young viewers "are not as willing to stay with the task." Dr. Bryant, who was on the research and planning committee for The Electric Company, concluded that such programming "may have created a child who was so reinforced to go after the excitement, the blazing stars, etc., that the learning was almost secondary."[39]

Indeed, the weight of evidence suggests that television viewing actually stimulates daydreaming and reduces creative imagination.[40] This is because television largely gains attention through arousal mechanisms rather than stimulation of the intellect.[41]

In addition, television's rapid visual and auditory stimulus can quickly become a narcotic,[42] quickly tuning out the higher learning, concentration, and motivation centers of the brain.[43] [44]

141

The mesmerizing, numbing effect of television is well described by Robert MacNeil: "The trouble with television is that it discourages concentration. Almost anything interesting and rewarding in life requires some constructive, consistently applied effort. But television encourages us to apply no effort. It sells us instant gratification. It diverts us only to divert, to make the time pass without pain."[45]

In early experiments measuring brain wave activity during television exposure, researchers found that switching from reading to television "instantly produced a preponderance of slow alpha waves," which are typically associated with lack of mental activity.[46] Two out of three studies confirmed higher levels of more passive alpha waves while watching television, but higher levels of fast-wave beta activity during reading.[47] [48] Later research discovered shown that simple, uninteresting, or confusing reading had the same effect as television on alpha wave levels.[49]

Entertained to Death

In his book, *Still Bored in a Culture of Entertainment*, psychiatrist Richard Winter makes the point that in days gone by much of community entertainment consisted of getting together with neighbors, popping popcorn, and telling one another stories about themselves and others that kept important memories alive. Technology has changed all that. Philosopher Roger Scruton warns: "Television has confined each young person from childhood onwards before a box of intriguing platitudes. Without speaking, acting or making himself interesting to others, he nevertheless receives a full quota of distractions."[50]

And distractions we get—to the point of being overwhelmed. It is important to remember that the object of an exciting program is ratings; ratings attract advertisers, and advertisers bring revenue. It's about advertising, not information—entertainment is simply the means to the all-important ends: profits.

Television's rapid visual and auditory stimulus can quickly become a narcotic, quickly tuning out the higher learning, concentration, and motivation centers of the brain.

Harvard economist Juliet Schor has presented research to show that the more a person watches television, the more he or she spends. She found that each additional hour of television watched per week led to an additional $208 of annual spending. Those surveyed watched 11.5 hours of television per week, enough to cost them more than $2,300 in unplanned, unnecessary spending.[51] That's why major corporations will spend as much as $1.7 million for 30 seconds of commercial time.[52]

By the age of 20, many young adults have seen more than 1 million television commercials.

By the age of 20, many young adults have seen more than 1 million television commercials. What do children learn from these commercials? "Children learn that they are the most important person in the universe, that impulses should not be denied, that pain should not be tolerated and that the cure for any kind of pain is a product. They learn a weird mix of dissatisfaction and entitlement. With the message of ads, we are socializing our children to be self-centered, impulsive, and addicted."[53]

Commercials could have a more substantial impact on personality development than actual TV programs in that they teach self-indulgence as opposed to contentment, instant satisfaction as opposed to delayed gratification, and consumerism as opposed to thriftiness. Why? Author Henry Lebalme says it could be from "an unrealistic upscaling of desire and a distorted sense of the significance of relatively minor problems."[54] Does my bathroom *really* have to look like a curiosity shop? Is thinning hair *really* going to cause me to lose my friends? An overload of stimulation, information, advertising, and entertainment has produced an unexpected result: boredom.

Dr. Winter explains: "When stimulation comes at us from every side, we reach a point where we cannot respond with much depth to anything. Bombarded with so much that is exciting and demands our attention, we tend to become unable to discriminate and choose from among the many options. The result is that we shut down our attention to everything."[55]

Os Guinness describes it this way: "The flipside of consumerism is complacency. The most compulsive of shoppers and channel-surfers move from feeling good to feeling nothing."[56]

143

That is the very condition that overexposure to entertainment, ads, and nonstop stimulation creates. Fortunately, the body, mind, and brain can be reconditioned to enjoy less stressful overload and more balance between getting and waiting; alternatives to hyper-stimulating entertainment and sensory overload are reviewed in *Designer Activities for an Enriched Life*.

Video Games

Playing video games is not just an isolated passion of children and teenagers. Electronic gaming, whether on consoles, handheld devices, or PCs has become a worldwide pastime of all age groups and both sexes. Global sales of video games in 2002 were $17.5 billion, with Americans tipping the scale at $11 billion in purchases.[57] Of the 60 percent of Americans who play video games, 61 percent are adults, nearly half are women, and the average age is 28.[58] But more of the younger set are logging longer hours in front of computer games.

Video and computer games are a mixed blessing. They can be entertaining and provide an occasional diversion. In contrast to television viewing, interactive computer games require players to participate and develop strategic skills. Some are creative, but an alarming number are violent and pornographic. Psychiatrist Richard Winter points out that "technology seems to act as a giant amplifier of both aspects of the world—all that is wonderful and good and all that is terrible and evil."[59]

And there are increasing problems with addiction and isolation caused by video games. Ten-year-old boys spend almost 10 hours a week playing video games.[60] More than 60 percent of children report that they play video games longer than they intended to,[61] perhaps because the very interactive features that attract players may actually promote addiction in frequent users.

Video games often use a mixture of novelty, reward, violence, and sex to rivet the attention of their players. The games are designed with built-in reward systems that lure players to spend hours achieving artificial goals. Jane Healy describes the "secret weapons" these games employ to attract and hold the minds of players:

More than 60 percent of children report that they play video games longer than they intended to.

144

- feelings of mastery and control by the players;
- exact calibration of the level of difficulty to the player;
- immediate and continual reinforcement;
- escape from the unpredictability of human events and social relationships;
- demanding, colorful, fast-paced visual formats.[62]

These features combine to increase a risk for addictive behavior in frequent players that is similar to drug dependence.[63] Studies show that video game activity is associated with brain changes in dopamine.[64] Repeated overstimulation of dopamine-producing reward centers can lead to addiction, whether it is drugs or highly stimulating activities. The harsh music and sound effects that provide the backdrop of many games act to magnify their addictive potential.

Furthermore, the isolated micro world of highly rewarding game playing does not transfer well to classroom learning. Real-life learning offers less power, excitement, immediate reward, and attention-grabbing tricks, but demands more critical thinking, problem solving, and integration of multiple skills to achieve results. Just because a child masters a game, does not mean that the strategies he or she has developed transfer to real-life skills.

Repeated overstimulation of dopamine-producing reward centers can lead to addiction, whether it is drugs or highly stimulating activities.

In reality, intensive gaming and television viewing may have three critical effects on the learning brain: (1) They may affect the development of language, reading, and analytical-thinking skills; (2) They may affect information transfer between the two hemispheres of the brain. (3) They may discourage attention, organization, and motivational capacities.[65] But despite these facts, what one anonymous author wrote is all too true: "People will come to love their oppression, to adore the technologies that undo their capacities to think."[66]

Addicted to Violence?

Violent video games have recently been linked to less activity in the brain areas that control emotions, impulses, and attention. It has not been shown whether the changes are permanent.[67] In time, it is possible to develop not only an addiction to watching or simulating violence but also to actual violent behavior itself.

People will come to love their oppression, to adore the technologies that undo their capacities to think.

146

Neuropsychiatrist and addiction specialist John Ratey confirms that addiction to anger is a real problem for some people. "Aggressive people often have under-active frontal lobes, the areas of the brain that restrain impulsive action and that supply wisdom, and if these are not working correctly or actively enough, feelings of rage will not be inhibited. Breaking the cycle of low inhibition and overstimulation, however, is made more difficult when a person learns that acting on aggressive impulses will bring a kind of relief. Addiction to aggression as a way to solve problems and relieve frustration can make it very difficult for the angry person to change."[68] Media violence can feed such an anger addiction.

David Grossman is a military psychologist who has spent years studying the methods and psychological effects of training army recruits to circumvent their natural inhibitions to killing. He served as an expert witness in the aftermath of several school massacres, and has studied the effects of violent media on adolescent violence. "More than any other aspect of these new video games," Grossman writes, "it's the accuracy of the stimulation—the carnage, the blood, the guts—that is so advanced. Realism is the Holy Grail of the video game industry. And the latest technology leaves little to the imagination—the stimulation seems less fake, and therefore more effective."[69]

"The interactive quality, the intensity of the violence, the physiological reactions, all serve to connect the player's feelings of exhilaration and accomplishment directly to the violent images. And 'good' feelings keep the player wanting to play."[70]

He adds: "We don't think we have to tell you how deadly the combination can be of viewing ultraviolent images with the amusement park fun of shooting at things until they drop."[71] Add to that the fact that gaming *does* improve eye-hand coordination, and we are faced with the grim probability that these games not only reward players for participating in gruesomely realistic scenes of violence and killing but also teach

We don't think we have to tell you how deadly the combination can be of viewing ultraviolent images with the amusement park fun of shooting at things until they drop.

them a deadly accuracy that increases their ability to maim and kill in real life—and to do it automatically without thinking!

But it is just a game, some say. Dr. Grossman refers to such games as not mere toys but "killing simulators" that teach conditioned-killing responses, much the same way that astronauts use simulators to learn to fly to the moon without ever leaving the earth. His chilling analysis of school massacres in his book *Stop Teaching Our Kids to Kill* is more than convincing.

Television has the same desensitizing effect, conditioning the viewer to enjoy horrific crimes and sexual exploitation, but without the hands-on training. By age 18, an American youth will have viewed 16,000 simulated murders or attempted murders and 200,000 acts of violence. In nearly 75 percent of those violent scenes, the violence is either rewarded or there is no immediate punishment. Violent television programming is linked to higher violence, murder, and attempted murder rates in numerous population studies. Songs with violent lyrics dealing with suicide, sexual assault, murder, and Satanism are also linked with aggressive behavior.[72]

Dr. Grossman explains why we can become immune to violent images and therefore incapable of generating socially acceptable responses: "To make humans continue doing something naturally repulsive, you make it fun for them. This is called classical conditioning. Every day children of all ages and in all stages of brain and ego development watch vivid pictures of human suffering and death for fun and come to associate horror with their favorite soft drink, candy, girlfriend's perfume, birthday party celebrations, or comfort in the hospital bed."[73]

The virtual explosion of "bloodbath" reality television programs and ultraviolent video games that combine violence, trauma, sex, and profanity are creating a culture of dangerously desensitized and addicted children, youth, and adults. Thirty years of research have confirmed our need to reevaluate the addicting and mind-shaping

By age 18, an American youth will have viewed 16,000 simulated murders or attempted murders and 200,000 acts of violence. In nearly 75 percent of those violent scenes, the violence is either rewarded or there is no immediate punishment.

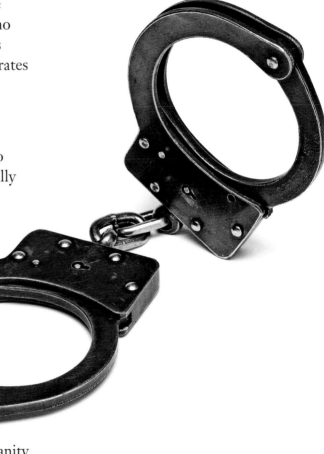

power of the media on the developing and the adult brain. These brain-shaping effects are so stunning that childhood exposure to media violence is a predictor of young adult aggressive behavior, according to a new 15-year study.[74]

Television Health Effects

But television's effects are far from just being mental. Television viewing is linked to obesity among young and old. Numerous studies have concluded that there is a direct relationship between hours of television watched and added pounds.[75] [76] Television viewers are also more likely to have increased heart disease risk factors.[77] There are several reasons for this. Children and adults who spend more time in front of the television are less likely to get needed physical exercise. They are also more likely to respond to the many advertising cues to consume unhealthful snack foods and drinks—with sugary, fatty foods topping the list.

According to Andrew Prentice, professor of international nutrition at the London School of Hygiene and Tropical Medicine, when someone is inactive, controlling appetite is not instinctive; it is something that must be consciously controlled. The less activity one has, the more difficult controlling appetite becomes.[78]

There may be one more intriguing factor. The resting metabolic rate, or the energy your body expends at rest, appears to be lower when watching television than even during rest. This means that excess calories would be turned to fat more readily while watching TV. In this study of 15 obese and 16 normal weight children, "it was concluded that television viewing has a fairly profound lowering effect on metabolic rate and may be a mechanism for the relationship between obesity and amount of television viewing."[79] More studies are needed to confirm these results.

Too much TV-induced stimulation also causes a rush of stress hormones to flood the body, and that is not good for the brain, especially a delicate memory center called the hippocampus. While lack of mental stimulation is linked to increased dementia, it has been hypothesized that stress damage from too much television exposure may also play a role in memory loss.[80]

Thirty years of research have confirmed our need to reevaluate the addicting and mind-shaping power of the media on the developing and the adult brain.

149

Violent television overworks the heart by increasing stress hormone production[81]—the same stress hormones that can damage the memory when throttled too high. That same overstimulation of the stress system has also been linked to increased severity and frequency of asthma[82] and weakened immunities[83] in those who watch violent programming.

Finally, children who viewed television the most frequently were more likely to injure themselves from accidents than infrequent or nonviewers. It is thought that children who watch the depiction of distorted reality on the screen were more likely to imitate dangerous stunts and less able to cope with stressful situations.[84] Conflicts on television are usually settled very quickly or with force, which fail to teach children how to cope with difficult situations.

Television Alternatives

One of the best ways to break television addiction is to resolve that being a bystander to life is more painful and empty than engaging in meaningful activities, even at the risk of disappointment. Television brain lock can be broken; the pleasures of real life can overtake the empty stimulation of living in a fantasy world.

Closely follow the steps outlined in chapters 7-9 of this book, and think about implementing some of the alternatives to television listed in the special section *Designer Activities for an Enriched Life*, and watch your tension—and addiction—melt away!

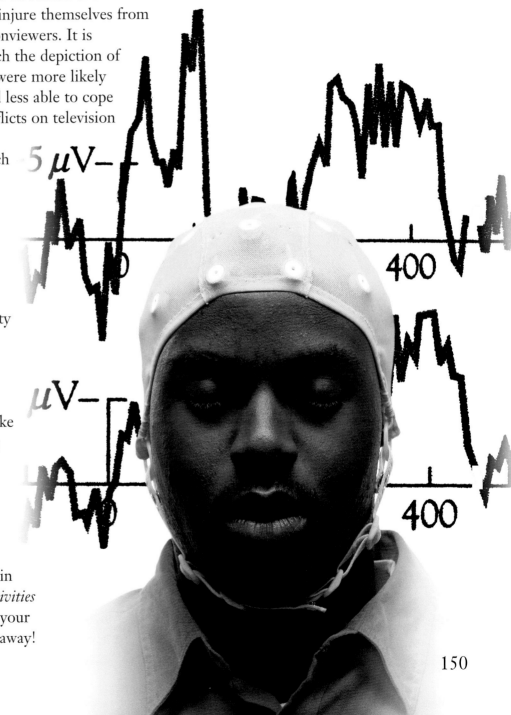

150

There you will find suggested activities that promote fulfillment and can bring you real joy and lasting pleasure. Pleasure comes in many packages, including intellectual growth, positive social relationships, the development of skills and talents, creativity, responsibility, mental and physical health, and the joy of discovery. These activities will enrich rather than impoverish you, and enrich your mind and body as you live in the freedom you were designed to enjoy.

God created us to enjoy life, experience pleasure, form relationships, and develop our mental faculties to a height that surpasses any other creature. Real pleasure, success, happiness, and balance are possible. We can learn to cope with life, enjoy normal daily routines, achieve new successes, and develop meaningful social ties. This is not accomplished via satellite, but by engaging in active learning and relationships. And those are the very things you'll need to keep you on the road to living free!

God created us to enjoy life, experience pleasure, form relationships, and develop our mental faculties to a height that surpasses any other creature.

Designer
Activities
for an Enriched
Life

Connect With Others

◼ **Visiting with family and friends.** Taking time to connect with others—forming close and even casual friendships provides valuable support systems in your life and the lives of those you connect with. Learning the art of visiting is easier than it may seem. Showing an interest in others and giving of yourself to them helps to establish social ties that add savor and happiness to life.

Family sharing time. Families that spend positive time together, such as sharing meals, are on a better footing for growth and happiness. Taking time together each day to share experiences, praying with and for one another, and reading inspirational books and stories can help families grown spiritually, socially, and emotionally. There are hundreds of daily devotional readings that are great for personal use or family sharing. They help equip each member with the necessary tools to meet the challenges each day brings.

158

■ **Attending church,
community programs.**

Community calendars are full of
church and community-sponsored
events that are fun, educational, and
inspiring. Programs that are free or
inexpensive include healthful-living
programs and seminars on money
management, family life, and interior
decorating. There are exercise classes,
Bible study groups, reading rooms,
library programs, and almost endless
musical and instructive events geared
to meet a variety of interests.

Even health food stores and hospitals
often have interesting workshops on
nutrition, skin care, and cooking.
Check with your local library, cham-
ber of congress, or even radio station
to get a calendar of upcoming events.
Local parks, recreation areas, and
zoos offer outdoor education programs for children and adults.
Programs include hiking, horseshoes,
volleyball, canoeing, cross-country
skiing, and nature walks. You will
learn new things, make new friends,
and infuse your life with variety, fun,
and culture.

your children; playing kickball with the neighbors after work some evening; having a water fight with your spouse the next time you wash the car—there are many ways to have fun in a wholesome way that provide a novel change of pace. Some people enjoy throwing a neighborhood party in the backyard. Others prefer popping popcorn and swapping stories with a few friends on the front porch. Whether it's building a bonfire with friends and singing songs or playing hula hoop with your kids—what have you done lately that is just plain fun? Everyone has a fun side that needs to show up every now and then. Remember, real fun is refreshing, not rash; healthful, not harmful. Make a list of fun things you would like to do—and recruit some friends to join you!

162

Enjoying your pets. Pets are great companions. Even your fish can be a friend. Watching fish whirl in a fish tank has a soothing effect on the entire system, relaxing the mind and lowering blood pressure. Interacting with pets can draw out the sweetest sentiments, bring healing to hurting people, and create an atmosphere of mutual care and nurture that aids in human relationships. Whether it's a gerbil or a gelding, the care and management of pets build responsibility, consistency, structure, and social interaction into your life. Pets are also great company. It's not practical or possible for everyone to have a pet, but petting zoos and nature centers provide a great opportunity to enjoy some of God's coziest companions—and have interactive fun.

Learn Something New

■ **Individual study.** Spiritual health is at the center of a freedom-filled life. Taking time for personal reflection, prayer, and Bible study is a powerful agent for change, inspiration, instruction for living, and connection with divine power. There are many valuable Bible study aids and inspirational books that deal with topics of interest to meet individual needs.

Enjoy music. Listen to inspiring music. Music has a powerful effect on mood, memory, and the emotions, all of which ultimately affect behavior.

168

■ **Learn to play a musical instrument.**

Learning to play a musical instrument can be a great way to have fun during downtime. It also connects you with others in a positive social context at musical events. Music can provide entertainment and inspiration during family gatherings, especially if more than one family member plays an instrument.

170

Reading. Taking time to read challenges the intellect, distracts the attention from the mundane, and strengthens brain circuits involved with learning, reasoning, and analysis. Choosing educational, inspirational, and mentally challenging reading material will affect the mental landscape in a positive way. There are biographies and autobiographies of great heroes and missionaries that are thrilling and inspiring reading. There are science and other educational magazines that are interesting, entertaining, and challenging. This type of reading will leave you refreshed, cheerful, and strengthened rather than dull, depressed, and agitated.

Help with homework. Helping your child with homework can open up a world of research and knowledge for you and your child, while building friendship at the same time. It also provides you an opportunity to help your child learn how to tackle frustrating problems that require focus and perseverance. Best of all, when the homework is done, you will have time to play ball or go for a bike ride together to celebrate.

174

Enjoy Leisure Activities

■ **Crafts, hobbies.** Crafts and hobbies are available for every age, and range from short and simple to elaborate and involved. The great thing about these arts is that they can be taken up at any age, whether it's stained glass, pottery, soap carving, or stamp collecting.

Quilting, clock-building, painting, and Lego robotics are just a few of the hundreds of hands-on projects that can fill the hours with fun and the mind with mental stimulation. Another benefit is you will likely connect with other people of like interest and form lasting friendships and social ties. Making something to share with others is a great way to enrich your own life and infuse the lives of others with joy and happiness.

Home projects. Getting involved with home projects can be a great way to save money, learn new skills, and experience the satisfaction of accomplishing a challenging task. Whether it is learning to lay tile on your countertop, making curtains for the den, sponge painting the baby's room, or replacing worn wallpaper, enjoy activities that improve your home and your mind. You will learn to solve problems, gain skills that enable you to help others, learn patience when things go wrong, and have fun working on a project with other family members.

180

Cooking, baking. Learning how to cook simple, healthful food is not only fun but essential for a healthy mind and body. Going one step further, it can be a great source of pleasure to learn how to bake whole grain specialty breads and healthful cookies to enjoy or share. Many people enjoy drying their own fruits or canning fruits and vegetables. Cooking can be an exciting, money-saving, and delicious adventure. Get the family in the kitchen and enjoy cooking together. It will open up a way for you to share good food as well as good company. You can create special occasions to bring joy into your own life and the lives of those around you.

181

Gardening. Even the dullest yard can be transformed with inexpensive, hardy flowers such as mums or marigolds. Planting a vegetable garden, berry bushes, and fruit trees not only provides a source of beauty, but also of good nutrition. Many apartment complexes have patios that will accommodate growing boxes that can produce succulent tomatoes, peppers, and lettuce. Learning how to care for the soil and plants is a mental culture that improves your mood as well as your yard. The exercise helps burn excess calories, regulate hunger, and elevate mood. It is a great feeling to come home from a long day at work and spend a little time releasing the tension of the day by pulling those pesky weeds!

Enjoy the Outdoors

■ **Sightseeing.** There are many free or inexpensive historic sites, museums, and parks that provide scientific, cultural, and educational information. Parks often have trails or self-guided tours that help you identify local trees, plants, flowers, birds, or animals. Such excursions provide refreshment, distraction from the tension of the week, and an affordable "mini-vacation" when that trip to the Bahamas is out of reach.

Exercising. Everyone needs daily exercise, and for most people at least one hour daily is beneficial. Exercise can be indoors or outdoors, mild or grueling. The type of exercise you choose should be the type you like—something you will stick with. Some people love to ride bikes; others prefer golfing, walking, or swimming. There are those who love to meet friends at the gym for racquetball or a full workout under the watchful eye of a trainer. Whatever the form, daily exercise is essential, not optional, for maximum mental and physical health. It reduces depression, tones the mind as well as the muscles, and provides fun, fellowship, and tension release. You can take lessons with some activities such as golf, skiing, or tennis. There are bike clubs, walking clubs, and exercise groups that meet regularly. These are great ways to make new friends, have fun, and feel great, too!

187

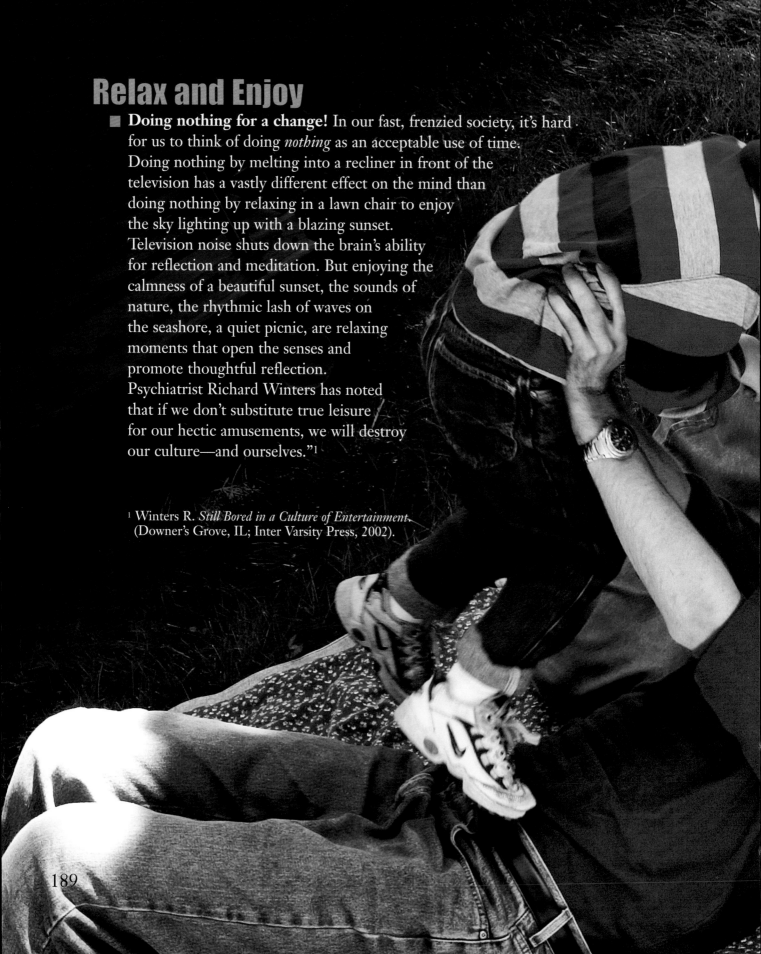

Relax and Enjoy

Doing nothing for a change! In our fast, frenzied society, it's hard for us to think of doing *nothing* as an acceptable use of time. Doing nothing by melting into a recliner in front of the television has a vastly different effect on the mind than doing nothing by relaxing in a lawn chair to enjoy the sky lighting up with a blazing sunset. Television noise shuts down the brain's ability for reflection and meditation. But enjoying the calmness of a beautiful sunset, the sounds of nature, the rhythmic lash of waves on the seashore, a quiet picnic, are relaxing moments that open the senses and promote thoughtful reflection. Psychiatrist Richard Winters has noted that if we don't substitute true leisure for our hectic amusements, we will destroy our culture—and ourselves."[1]

[1] Winters R. *Still Bored in a Culture of Entertainment.* (Downer's Grove, IL; Inter Varsity Press, 2002).

189

190

Getting "off-line" to reflect on our day—our experiences—and our life is a positive way to gather strength and energy for tomorrow's challenges. There is a daily round of demands that are commonplace, confusing, and clamor for our attention. But above that din of noise, in the quiet place of rest, God speaks His messages of love to His children. But He needs our attentive ear—and He needs us to be quiet.

Pat
BODI

193

Delivered

Television Addiction

My children are grown and gone, so I've lived alone for many years. Over time I increasingly used television to fill up empty, lonely hours. Without realizing it, television replaced other activities and became my constant companion. Often I stayed up so late watching television that I would fall asleep in my recliner. The next morning I would wonder why I put myself through such torture. The more I watched, the more isolated, lonely, and helpless I felt. I found myself flipping through the channels just to find something to watch. I was no longer watching a program, but merely experiencing the escape TV provided.

I realized that I would never buy the programs I was watching if they were on video. Yet I actually deprived myself of sleep and watched until a program was over just because it was on TV, even though I had to get up the next day and go to work with a lack-of-sleep hangover. I would get so upset with myself! I knew that television was robbing me of time, social activities, and happiness. I even admitted that I was addicted, yet I seemed powerless to do anything about it.

Then I attended a Lifestyle Matters® seminar entitled The Entertainment Trap. That meeting changed my life! I began telling everyone about it, because I wanted them to know there was a way out for anyone with this addiction.

When I told my mother about what I had learned, she broke her TV addiction, too! She lived in a seniors' apartment and spent endless hours watching movies. But instead of that mindless activity, Mom began to read a lot. I also found lots of additional time to read good books and found myself going to bed much earlier. As my behavior changed, other areas of my life began to change, too. Now, I'm involved in hobbies and social activities that are much more rewarding and pass the time more profitably.

Pat Bodi – Television Addiction

In addition to watching TV, I had begun attending movies. The loose messages of those movies were creeping into my life, even affecting my church life. As a result, I stopped going to movies, too, and am happy to say that I never went to see another one. But I found the TV habit more difficult to break. For the first month I allowed myself one hour of TV a week. But many months later, I found myself again watching a great deal of TV, and experiencing the same old feelings of depression, isolation, and fatigue. I finally removed all but the basic cable I needed to keep my Internet connection for e-mail, which allowed fewer viewing choices. Now, my TV habit is back under control.

I did hit another snag, however: I discovered word games on the Internet. That, too, became an addiction for me. I tried to convince myself it was keeping my brain alive. But I can pick up a crossword book and work a jigsaw puzzle occasionally and accomplish the same thing—without the temptation to waste time on the Internet.

Living free from TV, movie, and Internet-game addiction is possible, even if it has become a way of life. I enjoy healthful cooking, am involved in volunteering, and love to garden. I deal with depression in better ways now, and have more time for walking, reading, and serving God and my neighbors. Try it! You will be a better—and happier—person for it.

Personal Worksheet 5

1. What are the symptoms of a person who struggles with a television or media addiction? Review *Ten Signs of an Addicted Brain* on page 19.* What is the good news for those who struggle with media addictions?** (See pages 150-151.) _____

   _____

   _____

2. What emotional, lifestyle or environmental triggers can set off this type of addictive behavior? How does over-involvement with the media interfere with my job, family, friends, or other interests? What positive steps can be taken to eliminate or reduce exposure to these triggers? What alternatives can replace them?

   _____

   _____

3. What promises can help me when I suffer from restless cravings of heart, mind, and body? Look up 1 Corinthians 10:13 and 2 Corinthians 10:4, 5._____

   _____

   _____

4. What are some strategies and activities that can help me overcome cravings and addictive behavior? What is the value of refocusing attention on other things? What affect will nutrition, exercise, and rest have on this process? Review *Designer Activities for an Enriched Life* on page 153. _____

   _____

   _____

5. What encouragement and power are available to me? Look up 2 Timothy 1:7, 12 and 2 Timothy 4:18. What do I do with guilt? Psalm 86:5._____

   _____

   _____

Answers located on page 342 in the back of book.

* If you are working in a group, review the sections before you meet.
** It is important to rule out other medical conditions. Always work with your physician or healthcare provider. Serious mood disorders or physical symptoms require clinical intervention.

Chapter 6

Behavioral Addictions

"Habits are at first cobwebs, at last, chains."

English Saying

The human brain was created to experience emotion—pain and pleasure, sorrow and happiness. Enjoying a delicious meal, experiencing the intimacy of marriage, basking in the success of a job well done—all release hormones in the brain that convey a feeling of pleasure, which in turn motivate us to continue to engage in those activities.

"Drugs" for the Nondrug User

Excessive excitement and intensity, however, can create changes in the human brain similar to those caused by mind-altering drugs. Some experts have used the term *excitement addiction* to describe dependence disorders that are characterized by impulsive, uncontrolled behavior and a high level of sensation seeking. Labels for addictive, pathological behavior vary, and its classification is uncertain. *Nonsubstance-related behavioral addiction* is another term commonly used to describe

Characteristics of these behavioral dependence disorders include excessive thoughts about the behavior, the inability to resist impulse, the drive to perform harmful acts toward others or oneself, an increasing sense of tension or excitement before acting out, and a sense of relief during or after engaging in the behavior.[2] The most commonly described behavior disorders include pathological gambling, compulsive computer use, kleptomania, compulsive buying, pulling out hair (trichotillomania), and compulsive sexual behavior.[3] In this chapter we will deal with three addictive behaviors that are on the rise: Internet addiction, gambling, and pornography.

E-addicts

According to the Online Computer Library Center, in 2002 there were 8.7 million unique Internet sites, with about 3 million of those sites being open to anyone. This represents a growth of 111 percent since 1998. From 2000 to 2004, worldwide Internet usage jumped from 360 million users to 800 million users—more than a 120 percent increase in just four years.[4]

Although no one knows how many people develop personal problems because of Internet misuse, an ABC News survey conducted in 1999 concluded that as many as 6 percent of Web users could be addicted.[5] Access to the Internet provides users with a phenomenal range of instant information, education, media, shopping, and communication.

The advantages of the Internet are impressive. A wide range of media such as radio, streaming video, slides, and print can provide a data seeker with a gold mine of information. Fast, affordable search engines link students with data, people with people, and shoppers with bargains. To the careful and controlled, it is a blessing. To the unwary and unsuspecting, it can become a burden.

One woman recently decided to find a bargain on silverware on the Internet. She found more than 1 million sites on her search engine, and after hours of mouse clicking she narrowed

it down to 10 online stores. She spent the next two days straining over hundreds of available patterns, subtle price and shipping differences, and varying purchasing options. "I was so exhausted after the ordeal," she confessed, "that I just went down to the local kitchen supply store and bought a set. I lost two days bogged down in a search for a simple product that I could have purchased in one shopping trip. There were just too many choices!"

The Internet is useful in many ways, but it can monopolize more time than we intend. So many choices can be overwhelming. Online, we can go almost anywhere and see almost anything without anyone ever knowing.

The Internet High

The term *Internet Addiction Disorder* was first introduced in 1995 by psychiatrist Ivan Goldberg as more of a spoof than anything else. No one is laughing anymore, however. Whether it's known as Internet Addiction Disorder, Compulsive Internet Disorder, or Pathological Internet Use, addiction to the Internet is emerging as a serious and growing problem.[6]

There is mounting clinical, legal, and anecdotal evidence to suggest that something about being online produces a powerful impact on people. The Internet can and does produce clear alterations in mood, with nearly 30 percent of Internet users admitting to using it to try to alter a negative mood. In other words, they used the Internet like a drug.[7]

This is not really surprising, since all addictions—even behavioral ones—have a chemical component. It's impossible to become addicted to any drug or behavior unless it produces changes in brain chemistry. In an effort to modulate our moods to match our circumstances and experiences, the human brain produces mood-altering chemicals that can be suppressed or released either by drugs taken in or behaviors acted out. One of those chemicals is dopamine. Dopamine release in the brain produces euphoria and is thought to be an important neurochemical event in the development of addiction.

Like other addictions, Internet addiction involves an element of tolerance, where the same amount of usage elicits less of a "high," and increased Internet use becomes necessary to evoke the same amount of pleasure. People who lack self-esteem are more vulnerable to behavioral addictions such as Internet abuse as well as substance abuse.[8]

It is not surprising, then, that Internet addiction has emerged as a new clinical disorder. Interestingly, it seems to snag new users over the more experienced users, although long-term heavy users may be in denial or not recognize signs of addiction.[9]

The Internet can and does produce clear alterations in mood, with nearly 30 percent of Internet users admitting to using it to try to alter a negative mood. In other words, they used the Internet like a drug.

When Internet usage results in academic, social, or occupational impairment, it can be considered problematic. Addicts also report missing sleep and meals, inability to manage their time, spending too much money for online fees and products, using the Internet to relieve a bad mood, preoccupation with the Internet, and withdrawal symptoms such as depression, moodiness, tremors, and anxiety when not online.[10]

On the average, employees with Internet access use nearly 10 percent of a 40-hour workweek on nonwork Internet activities.[11] Secret monitoring of Internal Revenue Service employees found that activities such as personal e-mail, online chats, shopping, and checking personal finances and stocks accounted for 51 percent of employees' time spent online.[12]

Psychologist David Greenfield studied 1,500 companies and found that many employees lose their jobs due to engaging in online pornography and gambling, as well as excessive time spent shopping online.[13] According to Dr. Marlene Maheu, an Internet addiction expert and CEO of Pioneer Development Resources, Inc., 25 to 50 percent of cyber addiction is occurring at the workplace. "That means employees are getting paid to participate in activities that are not work-related,"[14] Maheu wrote.

> Secret monitoring of Internal Revenue Service employees found that activities such as personal e-mail, online chats, shopping, and checking personal finances and stocks accounted for 51 percent of employees' time spent online.

An Internet survey of self-reported problem users found that more than 90 percent thought that without the Internet, the world would be a dull and empty place. Almost 80 percent of respondents said they had daytime fantasies about Internet use, and 80 percent became very nervous if their Internet connection was slow. More than 40 percent felt depressed and guilty after prolonged use of the Web, and 70 percent reported that they became aggressive when others interrupted them while they were using the Internet.[15]

The Internet's Social Fallout

Individuals with substance abuse addictions are more likely than the general population to be addicted to the Internet. One study found that 60 percent of the 20 people in their sample who had Internet Addiction Disorder also had substance abuse addictions.[16] A larger study of 396 subjects found that 52 percent of Internet addicts were also substance abusers.[17]

A study of Internet users in Korea found that individuals who scored high on an Internet addiction scale were also more likely to be involved in dysfunctional social behaviors. Internet addicts were more prone to try escaping reality through the Internet, turning to the Net when they were stressed out by work or depressed. Internet addicts also reported a higher

A number of factors add to the appeal of the Internet. Online content is immediate, constant, uncensored, and unregulated.

degree of loneliness, depressed mood, and compulsivity than casual Internet users.[18] As with other addictions, poor stress-coping skills underlie many of these behaviors.

But regardless of the type of addiction, it dehumanizes or depersonalizes the addict. It takes away an individual's ability to discriminate between acceptable options. Choices are disconnected from consequences and reason from reality. The brain's normal order becomes reversed: Instead of pleasure for survival, it becomes survival for pleasure—pleasure seeking, for pleasure's sake.

Net Appeal

A number of factors add to the appeal of the Internet. Online content is immediate, constant, uncensored, and unregulated. The Internet is interactive and gives users a sense—however false—of being anonymous. As a result, people who wouldn't think of breaking the law "in public" find it much easier to engage in devious or even criminal behavior "in private."

While not harmful in itself, the Net makes everything easy and quick to acquire, and therein lies the potential for abuse. The combination of ease of access, availability, low cost, anonymity, timelessness, lack of inhibition, and dearth of boundaries all contribute to the total Internet experience.

The same factors that make the Internet such a powerful factor for good also make it much easier to engage in well-established forms of compulsive behavior such as gambling, shopping, stock trading, and destructive sexual behavior.

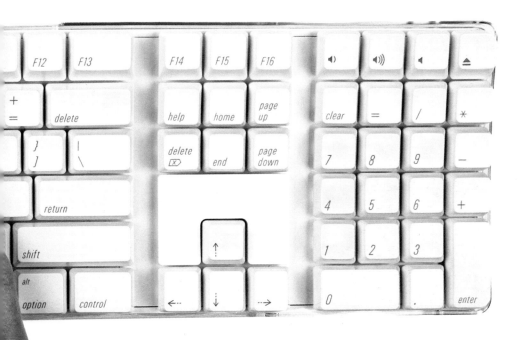

The Internet's superficial sex sites can never replace the emotional and psychological benefits of a face-to-face relationship.

Unfortunately, the same factors that make the Internet such a powerful factor for good also make it much easier to engage in well-established forms of compulsive behavior such as gambling, shopping, stock trading, and destructive sexual behavior.

As people with compulsive tendencies learn all too quickly, traditional methods of engaging in addictive behavior pale in comparison to the speed and efficiency of the Internet. The Internet allows addicts to engage in highly pleasurable activities without human interface, and in so doing, opens the doors for greater abuse. Without the normal human interaction involved in purchasing stocks, gambling, or shopping, there is a far greater likelihood of compulsive behavior or abuse.

This is especially true in the sexual arena. The Internet is a virtual smorgasbord of sexual activity, allowing for accelerated but superficial intimacy unchecked by the usual social inhibitions. Boundaries fall by the wayside as Internet users who likely would never have considered an affair in real life progress from chat rooms to cybersex to emotionally void real sex. Without the buffer of a healthy social context and meaningful emotional and psychological bonding, many are finding that the lure of superficial sex traps them in a world of depression, isolation, and addiction.

Normal activities such as shopping, stock trading, and participating in auctions are also uniquely impacted by the Internet. For instance, in the absence of social cues that exist at the corner drugstore, products somehow seem more stimulating and potent on the Internet. The shopper is not physically browsing and handling the merchandise, clerks or other customers are not available for input, the distraction of seeing or visiting with other shoppers does not exist, and the process of standing in line and waiting to pay does not occur. All these interruptions and distractions provide more time for reflection and avoidance of impulse buying.

Money can also seem less real on the Net, another factor that leads many buyers to purchase against their better judgment. The result is a consumer binge-remorse-purge cycle that we know as buyer's remorse. Goods that shouldn't have been purchased in the first place are returned, resulting in added handling charges and headache to the buyer—not to mention the merchant.

Not the Enemy

Despite the negative outcomes that Internet addicts experience from excessive time spent online, the Internet itself is not the enemy. The "Information Superhighway," as it is sometimes called, provides many important and necessary benefits to society. It is fast, ecologically sound, convenient, and informative. But it also has some potholes and "soft shoulders" many are not aware of. For some, the on-ramps to the superhighway soon become continuous cloverleaves, with no way to exit!

Like drug and alcohol users, Internet addicts are turning to a diversion to help them escape reality and the problems of everyday life. While it's true that the Internet is not inherently bad and that online interaction does fill a social void for some people, there are also significant risks involved. While not all Internet addicts are sexual addicts, the time they spend on the Net definitely puts them at greater risk of being introduced to pornography.

The Internet also enables people to more easily assume new identities. Other Internet users then interact with these "false users" and may incorrectly assume that the online relationship is the same as the real thing. The Internet becomes a real problem when people are so engrossed and enmeshed in online activities that they neglect their health, relationships, jobs, and other responsibilities. As with many of life's pleasures, when it comes to the Internet, moderation is the key. See the special sections entitled *Are You an Internet Addict?* **and** *Seven Steps to Tame Internet Addiction*.

Despite the negative outcomes that Internet addicts experience from excessive time spent online, the Internet itself is not the enemy.

206

Gambling: The Fever to Win

David Johnson,[19] a former state auditor in the Midwest, was the picture of frugality for most of his life. He clipped grocery coupons, paid off his house early, and paid his credit card bills in full monthly to avoid any interest expense. But when the 50-something Johnson began gambling on an Indiana riverboat casino as an occasional diversion, it quickly developed into an obsession. He ran through his life savings like a fire in an August desert, losing $175,000 during a three-year period. Most of that money was poured into the slot machines he found so mesmerizing that he pumped coins into them at a rate of 15 per minute.

During one gambling binge, Johnson lost $21,000 in 48 hours, then $38,000 during a four-day gambling spree. But even after Johnson declared bankruptcy and was banned from the casino, his gambling—and his losses—continued. What led Johnson, a man with a lifelong record of careful money management and a career in the oversight of financial matters, to lose his normally prudent nature—and his nest egg—at the slot machines? Johnson became addicted to gambling, "the addiction without a drug."

In 1996, Americans wagered $586.5 billion in all forms of legal gambling. Overall, between 75 and 90 percent of Americans gamble.

High-Risk Groups

In 1996, Americans wagered $586.5 billion in all forms of legal gambling. Overall, between 75 and 90 percent of Americans gamble. In the year 2000, 66 percent of U. S. youth gambled. The average cost at the state level for each gambling addict is more than $13,000 a year.[20] With the steady growth of the gaming industry, gambling addiction is also on the rise. It is estimated that 3 to 5 percent of the population is engaged in pathologic gambling.[21]

Although anyone can develop an addiction, people who already have a behavioral or substance abuse addiction are the ones most likely to fall into another one. Studies have shown that being born into a family of gamblers, illicit drug users, smokers, or alcoholics can increase the risk that one will become a gambler.[22] [23] Rates of alcohol abuse in pathological gamblers have been reported in the ranges of 45 to 55 percent and 65 to 85 percent for nicotine dependence.[24] According to one analysis, males, minorities, unmarried people, and people with a history of depression and/or substance abuse are all at a higher risk for pathologic gambling.[25]

A National Pastime

No longer isolated to Nevada, gambling is emerging as a major national pastime in the United States. Bingo, the traditional game of chance for senior citizens, has been eclipsed by parlor betting, sports-book wagering, slot machines, riverboat and Native American casinos, state and national lotteries, and off-track betting.

Legalized lotteries have been called *the tax on the poor* because they appeal to low-income groups and seniors on fixed incomes. It's hard for anyone to see the long-term consequences of buying strings of $1 tickets. But according to Dr. Valory Lorenze, executive director of the Compulsive Gambling Center in Baltimore, it is "indisputable" that legalized lotteries increase gambling addiction.[26]

> Studies have shown that being born into a family of gamblers, illicit drug users, smokers, or alcoholics can increase the risk that one will become a gambler.

208

Dr. Ron Perkinson, clinical director at Keystone Treatment Center in Canton, South Dakota, compares video lottery addiction to crack cocaine addiction in susceptible players.[27] "You get mesmerized," says Nathan Sunderland, who is overcoming his gambling addiction. "Your blood pressure rises, and your frame of mind just locks everything else out."[28]

According to Dr. John Kindt of the University of Illinois, up to 90 percent of addicted gamblers begin by gambling in state lotteries.[29] And the National Gambling Impact Study Commission reported that the availability of state-sponsored lottery games increases the prevalence of at-risk gambling by 80 percent.[30]

Internet Gambling

But has the Internet really played that big of a role in the proliferation of gambling? Consider this: The density of Gambler's Anonymous chapters is positively associated with the availability of casinos, card rooms, slot machines, sports betting, jai alai, and off-track betting.[31] So, with the wide variety of online gambling available today, the Internet has certainly contributed to the growing national obsession with gambling.

While the individual stories of behavioral addicts vary, they tend to follow a fairly standard pattern. In the case of gambling, the odds of winning are almost always in favor of the casino. But despite the odds that they will lose, many problem gamblers start out with a winning phase. They have an initial big win, when a small bet beats the odds and results in a big payoff. This success leads to more gambling, and the initial winnings are eventually squandered. But given time, the compulsive gambler suffers a large loss, and will then "chase" that loss, betting more and more money in an effort to "reverse the bad luck" and recover his or her loss.

The behavior usually progresses from occasional betting to habitual gambling. The urge to gamble becomes so great that the tension can be relieved only by more gambling. But, as with any addiction, a tolerance soon builds, and higher stakes and greater risk of personal loss become part of the gambling "high."

As with other addictions, gambling consumes a lot of time and mental energy, as well as a substantial amount of money. This leads to the neglect of other interests such as health, family, and work. As a result, the gambler may experience severe family problems and financial ruin, and exhibit criminal behavior in an attempt to support his or her habit.

Although all forms of gambling have the risk of abuse if overplayed, some are more addictive than others.

The Gambling Brain

We have mentioned that scientists have traditionally confined their definition of *addiction* to describe substance abuse. But new knowledge about the brain's reward system suggests a similarity between substance addictions and other compulsions, such as gambling. As far as the brain is concerned, a reward is a reward. The human brain is designed with a desire to avoid the pain of loss. And the reinforcement system of gambling relies on intermittent wins as a way of rewarding the individual's behavior.

The constant losses involved in gambling feed the compulsion to achieve the "big win" in order to make up for the big losses. Pathological gamblers are aware of the long-term negative consequences of their behavior, but the brain-lock, or compulsion, they have developed causes them to persist in making choices that promise immediate reward.[32]

The craving to gamble can be as strong as that of drug abusers; their "highs" can rival those induced by actual drug use. As with drug addicts, pathological gamblers suffer from withdrawal symptoms and are at risk of sudden relapse, even after many years of abstinence. Medical images of gamblers' brains have shown that when gamblers see others gambling or hear them talking about gambling, they experience changes in the brain's limbic region similar to those of cocaine addicts.[33] Another study of pathological gamblers showed significant changes in cortical arousal when the gamblers were playing cards with money at stake, as opposed to simply playing cards with no money at risk.[34]

The gambler's brain-lock can be broken; but it requires determination, vigilance, prayer, and support.

Obviously, addictive activities such as gambling, with their repetitive, high-emotion, high-frequency experiences, can and do change the circuitry of the brain. This neuroadaptation, as it is called, helps perpetuate compulsive behaviors such as gambling. There is also evidence that several neurotransmitters, including serotonin and dopamine, are involved in the development of pathological gambling.[35] The fact that certain medications targeting serotonin and other neurotransmitters have been effective in treating pathological gambling lends support to the above hypothesis.[36]

Like other addicts, pathological gamblers have been found to have dysfunctional reward pathways in the brain. The structure of the cortex, for instance, which facilitates decision-making processes, is negatively affected, reducing the individual's ability to make informed decisions quickly.

Fortunately, the gambler's brain-lock can be broken; but it requires determination, vigilance, prayer, and support. It is also important to work with specialized healthcare providers to ascertain the presence of other disorders that may coexist with this problem. See *Help for the Gambler*.

Pornography

Like many pornography addicts, Jack's addiction to sexually explicit material started in adolescence and was preceded by sexual abuse. Jack learned to use pornography to ease his pain. Yet somehow, instead of healing his wounds, pornography only led Jack deeper and deeper into addiction.

Although Jack cared deeply for his wife and family, no one knew of Jack's problems with masturbation and sexual fantasy, not even his wife.

In his own words, "Inside I was dying—dying for someone to help me out of this trap; wishing that I could tell someone."

Jack, a respected architect, never dreamed that his addiction would lead him to an attempted rape. As he slid down the slippery slope of sexual seduction, he required more graphically explicit materials to achieve the same high. "I came to that

Twenty-five percent of search engine requests, or 68 million per day, are pornography related. Thirty-five percent of all downloads, about 1.5 billion monthly, are pornographic. Sixty percent of all Web site visits are sexual in nature.

crossroad where porn wasn't enough for me anymore," Jack wrote. "I needed a real person. I would never have believed that I would rape, but over a period of time the viewing of pornography eroded away all the good in my life." Though he has suffered greatly and caused much agony and heartache, Jack found release from the bondage of sexual addiction through prayer and counseling. Like Jack, many men, and an increasing number of women, struggle with pornography and sexual addiction, suffering the resulting isolation, devastation, and self-destruction.

The Prevalence of Porn

The easy availability of pornography is stunning. Its heavy usage is even more surprising. Twelve percent, or 4.2 million, of all Internet sites are pornographic,[37] and only 3 percent of them require adult verification.[38] Twenty-five percent of search engine requests, or 68 million per day, are pornography related. Thirty-five percent of all downloads, about 1.5 billion monthly, are pornographic. Sixty percent of all Web site visits are sexual in nature.[39]

Thirty-seven percent of clergy say they struggle with cyberporn.[40] The cybersex industry generates approximately $1 billion annually, and that number is expected to climb to $5 to $7 billion in the next five years.[41] Estimates of the size of the whole pornography industry range from $4 to $10 billion per year.[42]

The largest consumers of Internet pornography are the 12- to 17-year-old age group. Ninety percent of 8- to 16-year-olds say they have run into at least some pornography online while doing their homework.[43] Being exposed to traumatizing, shocking images can produce disgust and fascination simultaneously. Forty-four percent of adolescents polled have visited X-rated sites or sites with sexual content.[44]

Ten percent of adults admit to an Internet sexual addiction. Forty thousand expired Web sites have been re-routed,[45] which means that Web users who type in the name of an expired Web business are automatically sent to pornography sites.

212

Perhaps as a result of these Internet sites, the pornographic film industry is now bigger than ever, making some 6,000 X-rated movies a year and grossing more than $4 billion.[46] In 1998 the FBI opened 700 cases dealing with online pedophilia, and by 2000 that figure had quadrupled to 2,856 cases.[47] Perhaps even more troubling is how the Internet has become a very useful tool for pedophiles and sexual predators as they distribute child pornography, engage in sexually explicit conversations with children, and seek victims in chat rooms.

Pornography: A Progressive Addiction

Dr. Victor Cline, a clinical psychologist at the University of Utah and a specialist in the area of sexual addictions, has observed four steps of addiction that most of his clients who have been involved in pornography experienced:

Step 1: Addiction. Once consumers of pornography get hooked, they keep coming back for more. The sexually graphic images provide the user with a "high," followed by a sex release, most often through masturbation.

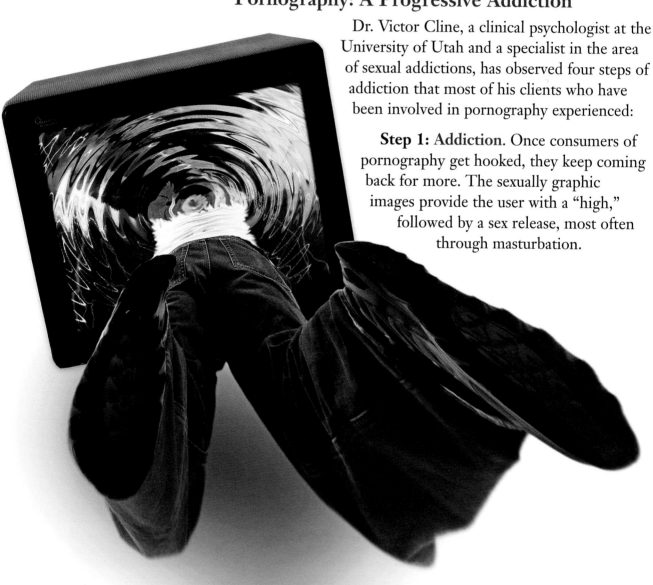

Step 2: Escalation. During this phase, consumers of pornography require more frequent stimulation and graphic exposure to reach their desired "high."

Step 3: Desensitization. Material that was originally perceived as unthinkable, shocking, illegal, repulsive, or immoral is now seen as acceptable, legitimate, and commonplace by the viewer.

Step 4: Acting out sexually. This last step describes an increasing tendency to sexually act out the behaviors viewed in pornography, including promiscuity, voyeurism, exhibitionism, group sex, rape, sadomasochism, or child molestation. Interestingly, sexual dysfunction during normal relations can occur, propelling the addict toward seeking more potent stimulation.

According to one study, early exposure (under 14 years of age) to pornography is related to greater involvement in deviant sexual behavior, particularly rape. Fifty-three percent of child molesters deliberately used pornographic stimuli as they prepared to offend.[48]

In another study, male subjects exposed to six weeks of standard, hard-core pornography developed an increased sexual callousness toward women; began to trivialize rape as a criminal offense or no longer considered it a crime; developed distorted perceptions about sexuality; developed an appetite for more deviant, bizarre, or violent forms of pornography; devalued the importance of monogamy and lacked confidence in marriage as either a viable or lasting institution; and viewed promiscuous relationships as normal and natural behavior.[49]

Child pornography produces especially troubling results, including: those who view it engage in increased incidence of rape and sexual violence; pedophiles use it as a tool to coerce child victims; children who see it have increased sexual addiction profiles; unplanned pregnancies are common as a result; it can incite children to act out against other children; it can have a devastating impact on exposed children's attitudes, values, emotions, and identity. [50]

The more pornography one accesses, the higher the risk that he or she will act out what they see.

214

Obviously, pornography is not an innocent pastime. The more pornography one accesses, the higher the risk that he or she will act out what they see, including sexual assault, rape, and molestation.[51] Sexual addiction results when one becomes compulsively dependent upon sexual thoughts or activity to produce changes in his or her mood. And many times, what may begin as a casual curiosity all too often develops into a compulsive sexual addiction.

Many frequently engage in this casual sexual curiosity to escape an inner void or emotional pain, but the very thoughts or acts engaged in can increase the individual's guilt. Thus the sex addict falls into a vicious cycle, a progressively downward spiral that leads into deeper and more serious addictive behaviors, increased guilt, and greater tolerance to obscene images. Thus, reality and fantasy become blurred for those who are trapped in the whirlpool of pornography.

Sexual power is one of the most potent powers we possess. It enables us to multiply and replenish the earth. Like God, we can "create" children in our own image, and after our likeness, through sexual reproduction. Appropriate sexual expression between a married man and woman has built-in checks and balances. But pornography is a subliminal quest for unlimited sexual power, without concern for the object of one's passion.

Remapping the Addicted Brain

While individuals may view pornography without making a lifelong habit of it, its effects are progressive, addictive, and damaging in all cases. Using pornography nearly always diminishes the viewer's capacity to love and experience appropriate intimacy in a normal relationship. It reduces the opposite sex to body parts instead of whole personhood, and puts a dark and sordid hue on the ultimate expression of the deep love and trust that God designed for a husband and wife to enjoy together.

Pornographic images are so powerful that they neurochemically blitz the brain, overriding normal impulses. Sophisticated medical diagnostic techniques have confirmed that explicit sexual images do, indeed, alter normal brain function. Research

Sexual power is one of the most potent powers we possess.... Appropriate sexual expression between a married man and woman has built-in checks and balances.

has also shown that a pornographic environment "colonizes" a viewer's brain, producing structural changes that are involuntary and long lasting.[52]

Sex addiction changes brain chemistry similar to drug or alcohol addictions, so it becomes difficult for such individuals to experience sexual satisfaction apart from pornographic images. And there are often the same feelings of agitation, depression, aggression, anxiety, and withdrawal to contend with when one is no longer engaging in the activity.

As with other addictions, it is important to work with a healthcare provider for mental and physical evaluation and treatment. Fortunately, recovery is possible, including the restoration of normal sexual thoughts, feelings, and function. In the same way that negative choices can map the brain to produce

216

harmful habits, positive choices can remap, or rewire, the brain to break the deadlock of behavioral addictions and achieve a freedom-filled life.

As mentioned in chapter 1, the incredible process of remapping the brain is described this way: "Networks that succeed in processing new experiences or behaviors end up as strong, permanent members of the neuronal neighborhood, while unused networks, cut off from the ebb and flow of information, wither away and die. In effect, the brain's structure *becomes* the information that it receives, and so how it perceives that information determines its future state. Changing your pattern of thinking also changes the brain's structure."[53]

During abnormal behavior such as compulsive gambling or obsessive sexual activity, "the neurons get stuck in a rut of abnormal patterns of activity, becoming underactive or overactive or just nonperforming, it being either too easy or too hard for them to fire. A person who forcibly changes his behavior can break the deadlock by requiring neurons to change connections to enact the new behavior. Changing the brain's firing patterns through repeated thought and action is also what is responsible for the initiation of self-choice, freedom, will, and discipline. We always have the ability to remodel our brains."[54]

Neuropsychiatrist Jeffrey Schwartz puts it this way: "The time has come for science to confront the serious implications of the fact that directed, willed mental activity can clearly and systematically alter brain function."[55] In other words: God designed your brain so you can think and will your way to a new you! Individual choices cause "one brain state to be activated rather than another."[56] That is, mental action can alter brain chemistry. Schwartz concludes: "With the ability to shape our brains comes the power to shape our destiny."[57] And with God's help, we can do just that.

The Spiritual Side of the Battle

It seems to be basic human nature to reassure ourselves that most areas of our lives are under control, while hiding or denying problems in other areas. Thus, the pathological gambler may

> The time has come for science to confront the serious implications of the fact that directed, willed mental activity can clearly and systematically alter brain function.

reason that he or she is fine because "at least I'm not engaged in pornography"; the Internet addict may be a Christian who is morally averse to gambling; and sex addicts may comfort themselves that they are not substance abusers.

The truth is, however, that any behavioral addiction can burn out the good in a person's life, gutting it with a firestorm of destruction and despair. And no one is completely immune from developing an addiction.

The Bible teaches that Christ came to "deliver *all* those who through fear of death were subject to *lifelong bondage*."[58] He understands the problem! Furthermore, He has promised that through connection with Him we need not be "conformed to this world," but can be "transformed" by the "renewing" of our mind.[59] God will help our desires and thoughts to change, and give us the power to live a new life—free from bondage.

But we need to be vigilant and careful to shun harmful thoughts and choices and cultivate new ones: "Do you not know that to whom you present yourselves slaves to obey, you are that one's slaves whom you obey, whether of sin leading to death, or of obedience leading to righteousness"?[60]

This text shows us that the power of choice can have an amazing effect on us for good or for destruction. When we yield ourselves to God He can strengthen our impoverished will and give us the power to follow through with new decisions. And those new decisions actually begin to rewire our brains, making each step of recovery easier and long-term victory more sure.

Victory over behavioral addictions has two dimensions; the mind and the body. The mind must be renewed, and the body must be weaned off the grooved, habituated chemical surges associated with the harmful habit. Chapters 7-9 can be of great benefit to those who are afflicted with addiction to drugs or destructive behaviors and give them the keys to living free! See also *Designer Activities for an Enriched Life* on page 193 for great alternatives to old habits.

Victory over behavioral addictions has two dimensions; the mind and the body. The mind must be renewed, and the body must be weaned off the grooved, habituated chemical surges associated with the harmful habit.

Are YOU a Gambling Addict?

220

Problem Gamblers Frequently:

- Have a desire to increase the amount of their bets.

- Are restless or irritable while trying to cut back.

- Gamble with increasing frequency and amounts of money.

- Spend an excessive amount of time gambling at the expense of job or family time.

- Become preoccupied with gambling or with obtaining money for gambling.

- Feel an aroused sense of "being in action" while gambling.

- Use gambling as an escape mechanism.

- Continue to gamble despite negative consequences, such as large losses and work or family problems.

- Borrow money to gamble, taking out secret loans or maximizing credit cards.

- Brag about wins but forget to tell about losses.

- Have frequent mood swings—higher when winning, lower when losing.

- Gamble for longer periods of time or for more money than originally planned.

- Engage in secretive behavior such as hiding betting slips or receipts, and having mail or bills sent to another address.[1]

[1] Compulsive gambling. *Psychology Today* 2002 Oct 10.

DISCONNECT NOTICE

...unt has a Previou... ...ance due. We have scheduled your...
...on or after 10/2... ...RIC POWER requests payment be made in the
...nection. AMERIC... ...t that service is disconnected, a reconnection
...RE 10/25/01... ...required.
...and a den... ...

...made,... ...anks and disregard this notice.
...ce for... ...stor rights and other information.
...will no... ...e requirements stated on this notice.

Account Balance		Amount Du...
$	64.24	
	1.21	
$	65.45	
$		
...ge $		...$ 114.39

...nt Due. . . . .
..., Add $0.92 After This Date

may refer to our Customer
Handbook for information regarding
your rights and responsibilities.

Indiana Michigan Power is
authorized to transact business in
Michigan as American Electric Power

Ques...
or Se...
1-800-2...

222

Help for the Gambler

Help for the Gambler

As with other addictions, the first step toward help for the pathological gambler is recognizing that there is a problem. The following are some steps that you—or someone you know—can take to address the challenge of compulsive gambling. Also follow the guidelines in chapters 7-9 of this book.

- Identify the "triggers" that make you want to gamble. Practice new, constructive thinking patterns or activities that help you avoid those triggers.

- Join a gamblers' support group.

- Realize that total abstinence is the only cure for the gambling addict.

- Ask your doctor about any medical intervention that may be appropriate.

- When you are tempted to gamble, remember that the impulse will pass.

- Avoid being around others who gamble.

- Spend time with people who will encourage you in positive pursuits.

- Find someone to talk to about your desire to quit gambling, or consider counseling.

- Ask God to help you overcome the habit and engage in new, rewarding activities. See *Designer Activities for an Enriched Life* on page 153.

- Remember that changing your actions helps to change the way your brain works—it will get easier. Even the most tenacious addictions can be overcome.

The best way to avoid developing a problem with gambling is not to gamble at all. The Bible teaches very plainly that the mind-set of easy gain that gambling encourages is contrary to sound principles of life and mental health. While there

225 [1] Proverbs 23:5, [2] Proverbs 15:27, [3] Proverbs 8:18, [4] Galatians 5:22-23, [5] 1 Timothy 1:7, [6] Ecclesiastes 2:26, [7] John 8:36, [8] John 14:2

is honor in making an honest living and even increasing wealth, we are warned of the folly of trusting in riches for true happiness and security: "Wilt you set your eyes upon that which is not? For riches certainly make themselves wings; they fly away as an eagle toward heaven."[1] We are warned that feeding an obsession for gain is a potent source of misery: "He whose desires are fixed on profit is a cause of trouble to his family; but he who has no desire for offerings will have life."[2]

In place of empty cravings and unsatisfying temporary wins, God promises us the "durable riches"[3] of self-control;[4] a balanced life;[5] wisdom, knowledge, and joy;[6] salvation from the bondage of bad habits;[7] and, at last, a beautiful tax-free mansion in heaven.[8]

Are **You** an **Internet** Addict?

How do you know if you are an Internet Abuser?

If you answer yes to at least five of the following questions, you may have a problem with Internet addiction:

- **Preoccupation**—Do you feel preoccupied with the Internet (you think about your previous online activity or anticipate your next session)?

- **Increasing desire**—Do you feel the need to spend more and more time on the Internet in order to receive satisfaction?

- **Irresponsibility**—Do you forgo important social, occupational, or recreational activities in order to make time for Internet use?

- **Out of Control**—Have you repeatedly made unsuccessful efforts to control, cut back, or stop Internet use?

- **Withdrawal**—Do you become grumpy, jittery, or experience other classic signs of withdrawal when trying to reduce time spent on the Net?

- **Overdoing**—Do you stay online longer than originally intended?

- **Social risk**—Have you jeopardized, or risked, the loss of a significant relationship, job, or educational or career opportunity because of the Internet?

- **Denial**—Have you lied to family members, therapists, or others to conceal the extent of involvement with the Internet?[1]

[1] Internet addiction disorders: causes, symptoms and consequences. Ferris JR. Virginia Tech, Psychology.

7 Steps to Tame Internet Addiction

7 Steps to Tame
Internet Addiction

If you have seen yourself all too clearly as you've read this section on Internet addiction, don't despair. Recognizing that there is a problem is the first step toward curing an addiction. Here are some steps you can take to overcome Internet addiction. See chapters 7-9 for vital keys to lasting victory.

- **Limitation**
  Take a vacation from the Net. Give yourself a day, a week, or even a month off. During this time period, try to use the computer only occasionally or for necessary tasks. When Internet use is necessary, establish time limits and stick to them.

- **Diversion**
  Spend time developing other hobbies or interests.

- **Distraction**
  Whenever you are tempted to log on to the Internet, take a brisk walk or engage in some other type of exercise.

- **Monitoring**
  Talk to a friend or family member about what is happening in your life. Tell him or her your concerns about Internet use, and set aside quality time to build your social relationships.

- **Support**
  Talk with a counselor or join a support group.

- **Socialization**
  Spend time developing new relationships and friendships.

- **Self Control**
  Shorten your Internet sessions as much as possible. Avoid unnecessary surfing. Use a timer or get software that shuts off the computer after a certain period of time. Plan activities that will limit your time and access with the computer, such as lunch dates with friends. If all else fails, discontinue your Internet access.

Because of the nature of this addiction, this person has chosen to share his story but to remain anonymous.

235

Delivered

Pornography

Pornography became my addiction when I was going through puberty. In my brother's room one day I found pornography magazines. I began masturbating every day. When I realized that my masturbation was an addiction that seemed impossible to overcome, the habit had already done its damage. I realized that this addiction began to consume much of my precious time. My grades in school went from A's to D's within one year. I noticed my ability to remember began to diminish. I started experiencing muscle pains near my private areas, and my nerve endings began to ache. I began to hate my addiction to pornography and masturbation, but no matter how hard I tried, I could not overcome this horrific habit.

Then one day I picked up a little book someone had given me called *Happiness Digest*. I figured it couldn't hurt, so I began reading the chapter called "Give Your Guilt Away." It was then that I first realized that I needed God's help if I was going to overcome. I remember crying out, "God, help me!" I knew that if I were to be set free from this addiction I had to have the strength and forgiveness of God. As soon as I asked Him to forgive me of this horrible sin and to give me the strength to overcome, I felt a peace that I cannot explain. I knew at that moment that God was going to teach me how to overcome.

Daily, I spent time reading about the wonderful life of Jesus. Even so, my addiction didn't just vanish. I had to learn to stay away from places I had associated with this addiction. No longer could I spend lots of time alone, so I began to make an effort to be around other people. Whenever I experienced a craving to look at pornography, I would, with great effort, redirect my mind to think of the wondrous love and power of Jesus. As I thought of Jesus I could feel His power and presence in my life. It was a power that gave me faith that I could be healed from my addiction. Little by little I noticed that I practiced this abusive habit less and less, until I knew that Jesus had given me complete victory.

Delivered
Pornography

Reading stories in the Bible such as how Jesus healed the lepers, how He raised Lazarus from the dead, and how He forgave the woman caught in adultery when others just wanted to stone her, is how I get strength to stay free. But most important, sharing what I have learned with others helps keep me on the right path.

God has blessed me with a beautiful wife and a wonderful child. My life's work is selling uplifting, educational books. I am thankful that God has given me this victory, and I know He can do the same for others caught in this trap.

I have learned that nothing but the love of God can give true victory over any addiction. Matthew 11:28 says: "Come unto me, all ye that labour and are heavy laden, and I will give you rest." Romans 12:21 says: "Be not overcome of evil, but overcome evil with good." And, Revelation 12:11 says: "And they overcame him by the blood of the lamb, and by the word of their testimony; and they loved not their lives unto the death." I am thankful for my life of victory every day.

Personal Worksheet 6

Behavioral Addictions

1. How would you describe the basic symptoms of a person who has a behavioral addiction? Review *Ten Signs of an Addicted Brain* on page 19.* What is the good news for those who struggle with behavioral addictions?** _____

_____

_____

2. What emotional, lifestyle or environmental triggers set off this type of addictive behavior? What positive steps can be taken to eliminate or reduce exposure to these triggers? What alternatives can replace them?

_____

_____

3. What promises can help me when I suffer from restless cravings of heart, mind, and body? Look up 2 Peter 1:4 and 2 Samuel 22:17, 18, 33-37. _____

_____

_____

4. What are some strategies and activities that can help me overcome cravings and addictive behavior? What is the value of refocusing attention on other things? What affect will nutrition, exercise, and rest have on this process? Review *Designer Activities for an Enriched Life* on page 153. _____

_____

_____

_____

5. What encouragement and power are available to me? Look up Psalm 40:1-3 and Psalm 121. What do I do with guilt? Ezekiel 36:25-27. _____

_____

_____

Answers located on page 343 in the back of book.

* If you are working in a group, review the sections before you meet.
** It is important to rule out other medical conditions. Always work with your physician or healthcare provider. Serious mood disorders or physical symptoms require clinical intervention.

Chapter 7

Healing The Broken Brain

Keys to Life: Connection and Community

"Begin to weave and God will give you the thread"

German Saying

Strategies for Success

How do you change bad habits for good? Stephen Covey in his book *Seven Habits of Highly Effective People* reminds us that there are three things to consider when developing habits. You need to know what to do, you need to know how to do it, and you need to be motivated to do it. And there is one more vital element: You need the power to do it.

What's the piece that's missing for you? Do you know what you need to do to break free from your bad habit or addiction? Perhaps you know what you need to do but you don't know how to do it. You try and try but nothing seems to be working. Or perhaps you know what to do and how to do it, but you just don't have the passion or motivation to stick with it. You may have great intentions—"Monday I'll quit; I'll start over." But the staying power seems to be lacking in your life.

As it has been explained, the brain is very responsive and changeable throughout life. You can change even when habits have been long entrenched in your lifestyle. Repetition is the creator of habits. The more times a thought or action is repeated, the more cemented it is in the brain. The keys in these chapters will help you learn to be consistent in making positive choices. You will also discover the source for motivation and power that is essential for forming new habits.

Keys To Life

Not only are these keys powerful tools for overcoming bad habits and addictions, they are also the keys to successful, happy living. These keys will help you realize your full potential. Simple yet powerful! Free and yet extremely valuable! They are for everyone—whether you are struggling with a bad habit or not.

Keys signify ownership, status, and worth. The keys to an abundant life are varied: Some are spiritual, some are emotional and social, and some are lifestyle. But they all unlock treasures that help develop their owner's true status and worth, and that owner is you. A key is an especially valuable thing if it opens a treasure box. It is even more valuable if that treasure box is yours. But you must use the key to unlock each treasure for yourself. No one can do that for you. These chapters place the keys of life in your hands.

Each key is closely linked to other keys; none stands alone. For instance, when you strengthen one area of your life, such as having a positive mental attitude, it affects your physical health. When you live a healthful lifestyle and enjoy good physical health, it affects your mental health. When you have a strong spiritual life, your mental and physical health are enhanced. Working from all three angles will give you the tools for living free. You can start from any angle; each supports the other.

The more times a thought or action is repeated, the more cemented it is in the brain.

Key #1: Create a Connection
Embrace God

One of the hardest struggles of the human heart is to realize the need of a power outside of oneself. It is natural to be independent, to try to solve all of life's perplexities without help. But God, who created us, knows we need His help, power, and guidance in order to successfully manage ourselves and our life situation. We need to let God have control in our lives.

Science is confirming that "spiritual well-being is at the center of a healthy lifestyle."[1] Individuals who personalize their religion, cultivate faith in God, and internalize spiritual values generally have better coping skills and less depression under stressful life events.[2] The cultivation of a deeply personal religion is "strongly associated with life satisfaction."[3] One review stated it this way: "A large proportion of published empirical data suggests that religious commitment may play a beneficial role in preventing mental and physical illness, improving how people cope with mental and physical illness, and facilitating recovery from illness."[4]

242

Often the single biggest issue for someone struggling to break free from an addiction is trust. It is hard to relinquish the excessive need to control people or circumstances in an attempt to factor out potential pain. But if the need to control is not replaced with trust, a person will eventually replace one addiction with another.

The Bible teaches us that when we turn our lives over to God's control, He will equip us to face life's challenges, give us a new way of looking at life, give us reason to hope and trust, guide us in the right way, and at last grant us eternal life. The counsel is inviting: "Trust in the Lord with all your heart, and do not rely on your own insight. In all your ways acknowledge Him, and He will make straight your paths."[5]

Connect With God Through Prayer

Prayer is a two-way conversation with God. There is no being in the universe more personally interested in you than God. Prayer opens your heart to hear His voice and receive His love, power, and guidance.

If the need to control is not replaced with trust, a person will eventually replace one addiction with another.

243

Modern science is beginning to recognize that "prayer is an integral component of the spiritual life of mankind. Clients in crisis may need prayer for encouragement, comfort, and support."[6] In addition, "prayer allows people to express themselves during crisis and emotional turmoil. It can serve as an important source of personal strength and as a foundation for self-resilience during times of adversity."[7] A study involving nearly 3,000 adults ages 19 to 97, found that recent alcohol disorders were less common among those who frequently read the Bible or prayed privately.[8]

Another study showed that persons who considered themselves to have a personal connection with God or a higher power were much more likely to experience better health.[9] Among teenagers, "personal religiosity is positively correlated with rejection of substance abuse, even after controlling for individual differences in personality."[10]

But in reality, prayer is a phenomenon whose results defy statistics, scientific measurement, and even our limited human reasoning. Prayer is the key to a limitless treasure, because when we pray we are connecting with the Infinite God and our Creator, who asks us to come to Him with our needs. "Trust in Him at all times; O people, pour out your heart before Him: God is a refuge for us."[11] God stands behind His promises. "Prayer is the opening of the heart to God as to a friend. Not that it is necessary in order to make known to God what we are, but in order to enable us to receive Him. Prayer does not bring God down to us, but brings us up to Him."[12]

Through prayer God can cleanse us from destructive habits. "And I will make you free from all your unclean ways."[13] He also promises us the power to stop doing the things we know are destroying us: "And I will put my spirit in you, causing you to be guided by my rules, and you will keep my orders and do them."[14] "Likewise the Spirit helps us in our weakness; for we do not know how to pray as we ought, but the Spirit himself intercedes for us with sighs too deep for words."[15]

Modern science is beginning to recognize that prayer is an integral component of the spiritual life of mankind.

244

As God changes our attitude about our destructive habits, He promises to fill us with peace as He helps us negotiate life's challenges and trials: "Have no anxiety about anything, but in everything by prayer and supplication with thanksgiving let your requests be made known to God. And the peace of God, which passes all understanding, shall keep your hearts and minds through Christ Jesus."[16] Prayer is the key in the hand of faith that unlocks heaven's treasure-house of power.

It starts with a simple prayer: "God, teach me how to pray. Show me your way. Help me to love what you love and dislike what you dislike."

Connect with God through Study

Have you ever been hopelessly lost on a trip, with no map and no one around who seemed to know your destination? You drive around and around and get nothing but frustration and an empty tank of gas. In a similar way, people try to fix their problems, find happiness, and forge a future without seeking God or reading His Word. It doesn't take long to wind up empty and frustrated.

God's Word, the Bible, provides instruction for living. It gives insight and understanding for the big picture in life as well as the details. "The entrance of Your words gives light; It gives understanding to the simple."[17] The Bible inspires hope, faith, and courage in the heart of the reader. It revives the sorrowful and depressed. "Your word [is] to me the joy and rejoicing of my heart, for I am called by Your name, O LORD God of hosts."[18] It also brings conviction of sin and offers forgiveness and cleansing through the Savior, Jesus Christ. "If we confess our sins, He is faithful and just to forgive us our sins and to cleanse us from all unrighteousness."[19]

In the same way that we can't survive physically by having an occasional meal, we can't survive spiritually by listening to an occasional sermon or having an occasional Bible study. Transformation, growth, and maturity in our thinking and lifestyle are a process, not an event. When you have

Transformation, growth, and maturity in our thinking and lifestyle are a process, not an event.

surrendered your life to God, don't expect to wake up one morning and have everything figured out and be able to perform perfectly in every area of your life. You need daily time in God's Word. And daily, little by little, the time and effort you invest will transform your life and character.

God's grace will cover your mistakes and give you the perseverance you need to continue your journey. Your thinking, attitude, and lifestyle will daily come more into harmony with His will. Over time, positive choices that were once difficult and took a great deal of prayer and struggle will become a part of the new character God is creating in you. "Therefore, if anyone is in Christ, he is a new creation; old things have passed away; behold, all things have become new."[20] God will speak to you personally in His Word. He is there for you.

Key #2: Create a Community

God created us with a need for one another. It is important, so far as possible, to create a community of support. Surround yourself with people who will encourage and support you in your positive choices. Sever the relationships that you know are pulling you in the wrong direction.

Any building that stands the test of time and weather must not only have a good foundation; it also must have a solid support system built into that structure. Having an internal foundation of trust in God, hope, and prayer is vital. But social support is like the walls of that structure. It is important for developing the ability to cope with life's challenges, developing social skills, empathy, sound judgment, and wisdom. It is not uncommon for people to retreat into a world of isolation and addiction because they lack these basic functional tools necessary for emotional and social survival.

Support is not relying wholly on others or circumstances for self-esteem, security, and self-definition. People and circumstances change; but God's estimation of your value does not change. He declares that you are His treasure, and that you are greatly loved.[21] Having a good support system is healthy and beneficial, but frail human beings are subject to err, and our basic sense of worth cannot be based on the opinions of others. Even best friends can disappoint us at times.

The only One who loves us perfectly is God, because He *is* love.[22] He loved us before we loved Him, and He loves us even though we are flawed. When we accept His perfect love and His estimation of our value, then we are free to love others in spite of their flaws. Others cannot pay back years of emotional debt that is owed. Our need for support and love from others must be balanced by an understanding of our basic worth; in this way our expectations of others will not be unreasonable and exaggerated. We will also experience less pain when people disappoint us.

Our need for support and love from others must be balanced by an understanding of our basic worth; in this way our expectations of others will not be unreasonable and exaggerated.

Building a network of social support to aid recovery from addiction often requires severing unhealthy relationships that are destructive and feed on failure. Jane struggled with cocaine and alcohol for years, and found herself back in jail after she rationalized that she could help fellow addicts who were still using drugs. The desire for maintaining old ties was stronger than the conviction that she must change her associations. The internal strength and personality tools for helping her friends were not developed.

Predictably, she soon joined them in their destructive activities. She spent four months in jail for that decision. Now she is out of jail and, realizing her mistake, has surrounded herself with positive people who do not use drugs or alcohol. Jane attends a support group, and has established church ties and social relationships at work with people who do not live in the world of drugs and alcohol. She has completed high school, and has set her sights on college.

Someone once said: "Always be reading a book that is a little too hard for you, and surround yourself with people who are a little wiser than you." When we associate ourselves with people who have positive attitudes, good problem-solving abilities, and healthy relationships, we can learn from their example.

Healthy social ties are worth developing. Numerous studies have linked a positive social life with improved mental health, less sickness and depression, higher levels of optimism, and longer life.[23] [24] [25] Find ways to connect with people who provide a positive influence on your life. People join church groups, bicycle clubs, cooking classes, exercise classes, hobby groups, community projects, and volunteer associations. These are all great ways to connect with positive people and have fun at the same time.

It takes time to develop strong bonds of friendship and community with others. Take time to strengthen your friendships. Get closer to supportive family members. Be actively involved in your church family and community organizations. Time invested in cultivating positive friendships and activities is time well spent, and will expand, enrich, and energize your world. You will find unexpected opportunities to give support as well as receive it, and thus create some of life's richest experiences.

Find ways to connect with people who provide a positive influence on your life.

Experience Forgiveness

Sometimes the greatest hindrance to forming lasting relationships is unrealistic expectations of others, and holding on to hard feelings when others make mistakes. Holding on to past hurts can hinder present relationships because of unresolved bitterness, anger, and lack of forgiveness. Angry, bitter people have a hard time making or keeping relationships for this reason. It is often difficult for them to keep problems in their proper perspective. They will catastrophize and picture the worst scenario in every situation, which usually *does* make it worse—and that's not a workable formula for building lasting friendships.

Is there someone whom you need to forgive? There is an old saying that "when you forgive, you set a prisoner free—and that prisoner is you." The dictionary defines *forgiveness* as "giving up resentment, granting relief from payment, or ceasing to feel resentment against an offender."[26] Forgiving an injury is an active virtue that requires a conscious decision to part with angry, hostile, bitter feelings associated with the wrongs committed against you. It is a process of emotional release that can be difficult but is nonetheless essential to spiritual, mental, and physical well-being. "Forgiveness is not a quick fix," cautions Robert D. Enright, Ph.D. It is a "matter of willed change of heart, the successful result of an active endeavor."[27]

Anger, hostility, resentment, and bitterness are associated with numerous physical and psychological ailments, and even a shortened lifespan. Often unforgiving people not only hurt themselves but others, either psychologically or physically. Hurting people hurt other people. Unforgiving people often have a hard time forgiving themselves of the wrongs they have committed, and are "worm-eaten" with denial, guilt, and shame.

Motivational speaker Zig Zigler has said that it is a dangerous thing to drive a car by looking in the rearview mirror, and people who journey through life dwelling on past wrongs and injuries miss present opportunities and the hope of a better

> When you forgive, you set a prisoner free—and that prisoner is you.

250

future. Just the act of remembering a past slight is associated with increased blood pressure, heart rate, and muscle tension.[28] One study of college students showed that those who were less forgiving in general had higher blood pressure levels, even when relaxed.[29]

Growing evidence shows that people who are inclined to forgive others enjoy better mental and physical health than those who hold grudges, unless they are repeatedly excusing someone who is abusive.[30] Refusal to forgive is most common among people with high anger and fear levels and low self-esteem, but easier for people who manifest humility.[31] Humility is the opposite of pride. It is the absence of a spirit of revenge. It is the ability to reflect objectively and give consideration to the needs and perspective of others. But humility is not accepting responsibility for or condoning the bad actions of others. Humility is not shame, guilt, or self-blame. As a matter of fact, people who blame themselves for bad events and believe that things will never change are more likely to suffer from physical and emotional problems.[32]

It is a dangerous thing to drive a car by looking in the rearview mirror, and people who journey through life dwelling on past wrongs and injuries miss present opportunities and the hope of a better future.

Is it possible to break the chains of anger, blame, guilt, self-hatred, revenge, and lack of forgiveness? Is it possible to experience the freedom of forgiveness when sexual, physical, or emotional abuse has occurred? Can peace fill the soul when you have experienced trauma, violence, treachery, or abandonment? Can you forgive yourself when your life has been riddled with drug or alcohol abuse, or compulsions and character traits that have hurt yourself or others?

Everett Worthington, the director of the Templeton Forgiveness Research Campaign, an organization that monitors and measures the physiological effects of forgiveness, was forced to transfer the principles of forgiveness from paper to practice. One day after mailing his manuscript outlining a step-by-step process of forgiveness, he learned that his mother had been murdered. After an initial reaction of disbelief and anger, in time he was able to work through those feelings and forgive the perpetrator of the crime, releasing himself from continual pain.[33]

It has been said that "to forgive is divine," and indeed it is. The Bible tells us to "forgive, and you will be forgiven." (Luke 6:37.) We all fall short of perfect love, so God calls us to forgive others the wrongs done to us. He tells us never to avenge ourselves, but leave our situation to the judgement of God: "Vengeance is mine, I will repay, says the Lord" (RSV). We have no promise that this life or the people in it will be fair. Sin wouldn't be sin if it didn't hurt the innocent. God has promised that He will balance the accounts of all, for He is a God of justice as well as love. In the meantime, He wants us to be free from the pain of harboring hatred toward ourselves or others.

As a child Joyce Meyer was sexually abused for many years by her father. She wrote in her compelling book, *Beauty for Ashes*, "Receiving forgiveness for past mistakes and sins, and forgiving others for their mistakes and sins, are two of the most important factors in emotional healing. Forgiveness is a gift given for those who do not deserve it."[34] Forgiveness is a divine attribute, a gift from God that we receive when we ask for it by faith.

Receiving forgiveness for past mistakes and sins, and forgiving others for their mistakes and sins, are two of the most important factors in emotional healing.

252

The Bible says God puts our sins as far away from us as the East is from the West. He will cleanse us from the unrighteousness that caused the problems in the first place, and fill the vacuum with His own loving attributes. (See 1 John 1:9; Psalm 103:12; Hebrews 10:12.) We are also admonished to make restitution, as far as possible, for wrongs that we have committed. (See Matthew 5:24.) This means righting the wrongs done to others by specific confessions and paying back damage done, as far as possible. This cleansing activity helps us to reason more deeply from cause to effect, and associate wrong actions with consequences. It also helps us to face our wrongs, build new behavior, and experience the freedom of making things right.

But God knows that we can never fully pay back the debt owed for certain wrongs committed. He also knows that those who have hurt us cannot pay back the debt owed to us. Joyce Meyer concludes: "There are many Scriptures that tell us that God vindicates. (Isaiah 54:17.) God is the One who recompenses us. He is our reward. (Isaiah 35:4.) He is a God of justice, which only He can bring. He alone can repay you for the hurt done to you, and He alone is qualified to deal with your human enemies."[35]

She adds a personal note: "Many years ago I had a choice. I could choose to remain bitter, full of hatred and self-pity, resenting the people who had hurt me as well as all those who were able to enjoy nice, normal lives, those who had never been hurt as I was. Or, I could choose to follow God's path, allowing Him to make me a better person because of what I had been through. I thank Him that He gave me grace to choose His way rather than Satan's way."[36] It is a choice that every human being can make, no matter how plagued with anger and resentment he or she is.

Finally, the steps to experiencing forgiveness are straightforward. **First**, face your anger. Recognize the feelings that are altering your attitude and behavior. **Second**, ask God to give you the gift of forgiveness for the wrongs you have committed, and determine to make things right as far as possible. **Third**, decide to forgive those who have hurt you. Ask God for the grace to leave others in His hands, and claim the promise that He will compensate you, or make up the difference, for any hurt done to you. (Isaiah 61:7.) **Fourth**, actively forgive. Acknowledge your pain, but allow the experience to deepen your own wisdom, compassion, and empathy for others. Act on your new decision by the way you speak and behave. **Fifth**, discover release from the emotional prison of unforgiveness. Realize that you are not alone, and that those who hurt are usually hurting people themselves. Use the experience of forgiveness to help others, and use the negative experience to grow in wisdom and develop a new purpose in your life.

This chapter has focused on two vital keys: connectedness with God and with one another. These two keys form the foundation for a lifestyle rooted in victory, growth, and security. In the next chapter we will build on this foundation by exploring practical keys to creating a positive lifestyle and environment.

Use the experience of forgiveness to help others, and use the negative experience to grow in wisdom and develop a new purpose in your life.

When **Someone** You love is addicted

Ask yourself: "Am I codependent?"

Those who are codependent let another person's behavior affect them to the point where they become consumed with controlling that person's behavior in trying to make it stop, or use the other person's behavior to avoid dealing with their own problems or addiction.

Codependency can include:

1. Enabling the addicted person to continue in their addiction by shielding them from the consequences of their addiction.

2. Taking the blame for the addiction of another, and trying to be "good enough" in the hope that their addiction might stop.

3. Losing control through a personal addiction, non-fulfillment of life responsibilities in school, work, church, or volunteerism, or illegal activities.

4. Escaping through isolation to get away from the anxious and tense atmosphere, or trying to stay as quiet as possible to avoid additional problems.

5. Providing contrast entertainment or diversion to ease the anxiety and tension at home.

The above roles are the result of either not dealing with or inappropriately dealing with feelings of anger, hurt, low self-esteem, abandonment, self-hate, and more.

255

The 7 **R**'s for living free from codependency:

1. **R**ealize that you need help yourself. Seek guidance of professionals who work with the significant others of persons with an addiction. Make connections with church or community support groups (see index).

2. **R**esist the urge to rescue. Understand the importance of 'Tough Love' and 'Setting Boundaries' - tough love refers to a discontinuance of enabling as described above, and setting boundaries refers to making decisions and choices that lead to positive, spiritually enhancing changes in your life.

3. **R**ecognize that you are not responsible for the choices your loved ones make.

4. **R**elease your loved one to God. 'Let go and let God' - this means give your loved one and his or her addiction over to God through prayer.

5. **R**emove yourself from harm's way. If you are in a dangerous situation, leave and seek help at once.

6. **R**ecapture the importance of taking care of yourself mentally, physically, and spiritually. The keys to Life (chapters 7-9) can help you in this endeavor.

7. **R**est in the assurance of God's love and plan for you.

Personal Worksheet 7

Healing the Broken Brain
Keys to Life: Connection and Community

1. Create a Connection.* What is often the single biggest issue for someone struggling to break free from an addiction?** (See page 243.) _____
   _____
   _____

2. Pray for Guidance. What are the benefits of prayer? How can I develop a positive, consistent prayer life?
   _____
   _____
   _____

3. Connect Through Study. What are the benefits of Bible study? How can I develop a positive, consistent study life? _____
   _____
   _____

4. Create a Community. What are the benefits of positive social support? What supports are available to me?
   _____
   _____
   _____

5. Freedom in Forgiveness. What are the results of failure to forgive? How can a person experience freedom in forgiveness? _____
   _____
   _____

Answers located on page 343 in the back of book.

* If you are working in a group, review the sections before you meet.
** It is important to rule out other medical conditions. Always work with your physician or healthcare provider. Serious mood disorders or physical symptoms require clinical intervention.

Chapter 8

Healing The Broken Brain

Keys to Life: Lifestyle and Environment

"This one makes a net,
This one stands and wishes,
Would you like to make a bet
Which one gets the fishes?"

Chinese Rhyme

Key #3: Create a Positive Lifestyle

You can create a lifestyle that will protect your mind, spirit, and body. Small choices make a big difference. A positive, healthful lifestyle builds security, nurture, consistency, and stability into your life. Simple strategies such as eating a healthful breakfast, drinking plenty of water, going for walks, reading inspirational materials, and positive thinking and speaking can make a big difference. Some people fail to overcome addictions due to a terrible neglect of their personal lifestyle. For example, if a person gives up an alcohol addiction but consumes only junk food, caffeine, and sugar, it makes it much harder to overcome cravings and stay off alcohol. Lifestyle choices affect body, mind, and spirit.

Feed Your Mind

Reading inspirational and character-building material just 20 minutes a day amounts to about 20 books a year. Reading 20 positive books a year on achieving excellence, building a solid character, building relationships, and learning about those who succeeded in life despite obstacles, can have a telling effect on the mind, character, and brain. As neuropsychiatrist John Ratey puts it: "Experiences, thoughts, actions, and emotions actually change the structure of our brains."[1]

Zig Zigler talks about taking advantage of "automobile university." He encourages people to use their driving time in their cars to listen to inspiring and educational material. Your mind cannot occupy a positive thought and a negative thought at the same time. The Bible states it this way: "As the thoughts of his heart are, so is he."[2] No one is built up by looking at, contemplating, or reading trashy materials that devalue human life, discourage noble traits, and destroy godly values. When you fill your mind with that which is noble and good, it will have a powerful shaping effect on your mind, body, and spirit.

Choose Healthful Foods

The proper care of the body will also have an influence on your mind and spirit. Enjoy wholesome foods that provide energy, vitality, and strength. Eating a diet rich in junk food, refined sweets, and processed food does not provide the nutrition needed for mental processing, nervous system health, and mood regulation.

Nutritionist Elizabeth Somers describes the effects of such a diet: "Repeated poor food choices can set fundamental patterns in the production of the brain chemicals that regulate appetite and mood so that you become a victim of mood swings, food cravings, poor sleep habits, and other emotional problems because of poor eating habits."[3]

Janice Keller Phelps, a physician who ran a drug detoxification clinic in Seattle for 20 years, worked with more than 20,000 addicts. A recovered alcoholic herself, she believes that most addicts have a basic sugar addiction with an underlying depression. She writes: "Sugar addiction is the world's most widespread addiction, and probably one of the hardest to kick. Because it is shared by so many addictive patients, I believe it is the 'basic addiction' that precedes all others. Most of my addicted patients tell me that at one time they craved sugar almost daily. Furthermore, few people recognize their sugar addiction."[4]

To lessen a sugar craving, eat whole foods with complex carbohydrates that provide healthful energy to your body and brain. Choose fresh fruits and vegetables, whole grain breads and cereals, beans, nuts and seeds. These tasty, satisfying foods strengthen your physical and mental health. If you are not getting the nutrients that you need, cravings will soon take over. When you eat well your mind will be sharper to discern temptation and stronger in judgment to solve problems. You will have more brain energy to deal with stress, challenges, and new situations. See *"Understanding Carbs"* (page 73) and *"Easy Ways to Reduce Your Sugar Intake"* (page 77).

To lessen a sugar craving, eat whole foods with complex carbohydrates that provide healthful energy to your body and brain.

262

Dietary fat influences the health of the brain as well as other organs of the body. The type of fat you eat affects how permeable, fluid, and responsive your cells are to chemical messengers. Plant fats encourage flexible, responsive cell function. Flexible cells mean healthier heart, vessel, and brain action. Some great plant sources of healthful fats include olives, avocados, nuts, flax and other seeds, olive oil, and canola oil. See *Fat: Essential for Life* on page 81.

Saturated animal fats such as red meat and butter, and trans fats that are commonly found in chips, fries, and pastries, are vessel hardening and not the best for optimal brain function. But omega-3 fats are good for the head and heart. In particular, they have been shown to help reduce aggression and depression in some people.[5] Good plant sources include ground flax seed, walnuts, soy beans, and canola oil.

Regular Meals

Breakfast is vital to start your day right. Eating breakfast gives a satisfying feeling so you are less likely to reach for caffeine or sugar to raise your mood or energy levels. Eating plenty of whole grains and fresh fruits gives you slow-release energy that will fuel your mind and body for the day's tasks.

If you don't eat breakfast your body will run on nervous energy. When that happens, a stress hormone, cortisol, is produced which raises the blood sugar level. High stress hormone levels combined with poor nutrition will make you more edgy and more susceptible to depression and mood swings.

So, be proactive instead of reactive. Eat a hardy high fiber breakfast. This will help you deal with stress better so you will be less likely to run to the vending machine when problems arise. A good breakfast will also lessen your cravings for sugar, caffeine, and snacks.

Don't deprive yourself the pleasure of a healthful, well-planned lunch. Enjoy your meals at regular times. Going too long without eating can make your blood sugar and your mood take a dive. If you have supper, lighten it up. One of the big

Small choices make a big difference. A positive, healthful lifestyle builds security, nurture, consistency, and stability into your life.

263

reasons that people skip breakfast is because they load up on heavy foods at night. Then they don't sleep well, wake up feeling groggy and unrefreshed, and have no appetite. So train your appetite to enjoy foods at the time your body needs them most: in the early and middle parts of the day.

Including plenty of fresh fruit varieties, leafy green and other vegetables, whole grains, beans, nuts, and seeds is going to provide a rich array of vital nutrients. These nutrients work together to improve mood, reduce cravings, provide energy, and improve mental function. With lots of high-fiber plant foods at mealtime, there will be less of an urge to snack.

Try to avoid the hunger trap or the constant eating trap that can trigger a bad mood. See the special sections on *Building a Better Menu* on page 289 and *Health in a Hurry* on page 285 for practical suggestions. For more in-depth discussion on the benefits of plant nutrition on hunger and cravings, see The Satiety Factor on page 64 and Brain Healthy Fats on page 69.

Cut the Caffeine

Need to overcome a caffeine habit? Caffeine has been dubbed "the bad habit glue," because it reinforces other habits such as alcohol, sugar consumption, and smoking. It is also highly addictive in its own right. (See pages 112-118.) When overcoming caffeine, make sure you get plenty of rest. Getting up tired in the morning makes caffeine very tempting. Go to bed earlier, especially during the first week of kicking the caffeine habit. When you get up, drink a few glasses of water. Following the guidelines for healthful eating, exercise, and rest in this section are vital to overcoming the caffeine habit.

As you implement these lifestyle tools, you will begin to experience real strength of mind and body instead of nervous stimulation. It takes time to recover lost strength and heal an overworked nervous system, but good nutrition and lifestyle immediately begin to repair the body and mind. The benefits of perseverance are inestimable, as strength, vigor, and natural vitality are restored in your life.

Healthful nutrients work together to improve mood, reduce cravings, provide energy, and improve mental function.

Turn on the Fountain

Drink plenty of refreshing water all through the day. Water vitalizes your body because it eliminates toxins, improves circulation, speeds nutrients to the cells, and perks up a dull brain. Water intake prevents mild dehydration, which can trigger irritability and false hunger signals. The average adult needs about eight glasses a day. Getting plenty of water is essential for vitality and a proper functioning metabolism.

Other healthful alternatives to stimulating, dehydrating beverages include 100 percent fruit juice (in moderation), herbal teas, and grain beverages such as Roma or Postum. Keeping your body fresh and clean inside and out with plenty of water is an important key to a healthful lifestyle. A relaxing bath cleanses, acts as a tonic, soothes the nerves, and is a pleasant diversion. So, get into the water habit!

Exercise for Excellence

Getting plenty of physical exercise has a powerful effect on the mind as well as the body. When you *feel* better, you *think* better. Exercise has been shown to improve mood;[6] lower stress, depression, and anxiety levels;[7] and increase brain power![8] It also helps to increase energy levels and improve the quality of sleep for most people.[9]

The following true story took place in the 1930s. A discouraged, despondent man came to see Dr. Harry Link, a famous doctor in New York City. The despondent man had lost his job. He felt like nobody loved him anymore. He wanted to commit suicide to end his troubles.

Dr. Link explained that he had been too sedentary, having exercised only his mind while neglecting his body. "I will give you a program of manual work," he said, "and soon you will be feeling better." "I don't like manual work," said the man. "I don't want to work. I want to commit suicide." Dr. Link did his best to persuade the man to accept a program of work, but it

Water vitalizes your body because it eliminates toxins, improves circulation, speeds nutrients to the cells, and perks up a dull brain.

265

was no use, and at last in exasperation he said, "All right then, commit suicide. But if you do, why not do something out of the ordinary, something heroic, and get into the headlines when you die."

The man liked the idea. "What do you suggest, Doctor?" he asked. The doctor said, "I have never heard of a man running himself to death. If you want to get into the headlines, run around the block until you drop dead, and every newspaper will have it on the front page." "That's what I'm going to do," said the man, and off he went to make the news.

He went home, wrote his letter of farewell, then started running. He ran and he ran, but he couldn't drop dead. He got so tired, he said, "I'll have to finish it tomorrow night." He went back home and slept better than he had for a long time. The next night he ran again, around and around; but he couldn't drop dead, and—you've guessed it—he didn't drop dead at all! He literally ran himself back to health and strength![10]

Exercise promotes physical health by reducing the risk and progression of heart disease, stroke, diabetes, and cancer. It also improves mood and mental function.

What is the best form of exercise? The one you are willing to do! Brisk walking, hiking, bicycling, swimming, golfing, skiing, canoeing, chores such as splitting wood, gardening, jumping on a trampoline, stair climbing, stationary exercise machines—all provide good exercise and help reduce stress. Remember: Motion balances emotion. So when you feel down, get up and get moving, both mentally and physically. Beat a bad mood—just get on the move!

Exercise has been shown to improve mood; lower stress, depression, and anxiety levels; and increase brain power!

266

Get Your Rest

It is difficult for some people to see that rest for their mind and body are important enough to plan for. We can be so filled with busy planning, problem-solving, and stimulating media that our minds never have "down time" for reflection, meditation, and relaxation. There is too much "brain stuff" going on, so real learning, wisdom, and growth cannot take place! The brain is too busy filtering useless "noise" and has no time for reflection.

Spending time in nature is one of the most soothing, refreshing, and yet invigorating activities for an overworked mind and body. Learning to distinguish between stimulating entertainment and refreshing recreation can help you use your leisure time to your best advantage. Walking in the woods, working in the garden, or watching a beautiful sunset are great ways to enjoy nature and absorb its calming influence.

Spending time in nature is one of the most soothing, refreshing, and yet invigorating activities for an overworked mind and body.

267

Another vital component of a healthful lifestyle is plenty of refreshing sleep, which should optimally occur during nighttime hours, including two or three hours before midnight. Research suggests that deep, uninterrupted sleep is when the majority of memory storage takes place in the brain. In a study published in *Science*, researchers reported that deep sleep is critically important to the learning process, and that people tend to absorb knowledge about new skills while sleeping.[11] A good night's sleep can also help to keep stress hormone levels down the next day![12] Other positive effects include better blood sugar control[13] and a stronger immune system.[14] It's easy to overload the day with so many busy activities that there is no time for sleep! Sleep time is not wasted time—it is vital to health, good judgment, and balanced mood.

The Bible teaches the importance of rest for body, mind, and spirit. Jesus noticed His weary disciples and encouraged them to come apart and "rest awhile."[15] At Creation, God set aside the seventh day as a special day of rest, worship, and fellowship.[16] And He invites us to enter into His rest.[17]

Create an Environment

Plan for success. Create a mental environment that will help you live a healthful, successful lifestyle. Get rid of as many reminders of your past habits or addictions as possible. As the saying goes, *Out of sight, out of mind.* Focusing on new thoughts and behaviors will naturally crowd out old harmful patterns. You can't think positively and negatively at the same time, so choose positive thoughts. Don't wait for your feelings to guide you into positive thinking. Use positive thinking to guide your feelings.

Create a physical environment geared toward success. It would not be wise for an ex-smoker to leave ashtrays and cigarettes all over his or her apartment. For someone who has been involved with pornography, the calendars, magazines, videos, and Web sites must be eliminated. For the junk food addict, the food items that trigger binging must be removed from the house.

Research suggests that deep, uninterrupted sleep is when the majority of memory storage takes place in the brain.

268

One woman who compulsively read romance novels decided to quit and burned 300 of them in her backyard. She learned from experience the truth and power of the Bible counsel: "And you may not take a disgusting thing into your house, and so become cursed with its curse: but keep yourselves from it, turning from it with fear and hate, for it is a cursed thing."[18] Decisive action makes decided changes in the brain.

Often there are other habits or associations, called triggers, surrounding addictions that also need to be changed in order to avoid "turning on" the addictive behavior. For instance, if in the past you have not been able to drive by a certain donut shop because the sight of it triggers an irresistible desire to indulge, find a new route and avoid the shop altogether. Focus on some aspect of the new route, and think about your great meal or evening that you will enjoy when you get home. Remind yourself that the craving will pass.

If you are used to having a morning cup of coffee and a cigarette while you watch the news, develop the habit of a morning walk instead. Enjoy a refreshing glass of water, juice, or herbal tea instead of coffee. Avoid the TV in the morning and listen to the news on the radio on the way to work. In this way you are dealing with the *triggers* as well as the *tokens* of addiction, and changing your routine helps engrave new associations in your brain.

Neuroscientist John Ratey puts it this way: "Each and every new experience causes the neuronal firing across some synapses to strengthen and others to weaken. The pattern of change represents an initial memory. As neurons in the chain strengthen their bonds with one another, they then begin to recruit neighboring neurons to join the effort. Each time the activity is repeated, the bonds become a little stronger, and more neurons become involved, so that eventually an entire network develops that remembers the skill, the work, the episode, or the color. At this stage, the subject becomes encoded as memory."[19] Forming new habits to override old ones is as important as quitting the old habits themselves!

Often there are other habits or associations, called triggers, surrounding addictions that also need to be changed in order to avoid "turning on" the addictive behavior.

If you are living in an environment where you do not have complete control over all the triggers, you can change how you *relate* to the things that are beyond your control, what you *do* during times of temptation, and how you *compensate* for the elimination of the old behavior. If your spouse is drinking coffee, smoking, and watching the news in the morning, you can still make positive choices. Go for a walk in the morning and then enjoy a healthful breakfast together. In this way you are embossing new memories and associations in the brain, and helping old ones to die away.

Remember: Temptation usually passes in a few moments. Act quickly and divert your attention. Use the key of prayer to gain strength to resist. "God is our refuge and strength, a very present help in trouble."[20] Go for a 10 minute walk. Call a friend. Take a bath or shower. Take a 10 to 15 minute power nap.

Placing yourself in a positive environment can be a powerful tool in building a better brain. It can be rewarding to volunteer at a school, church, or hospital. Another way to keep active and learning is by taking a class. You can keep your brain productive and growing by surrounding yourself with supportive people and a supportive environment.

270

Past weaknesses will still have to be guarded, but in time, those old triggers will weaken. You are developing new habits, new associations, and new ways of relating to your environment. You are building a new *you*! You are gaining control of your life.

Manage Stress

It is important to find escape valves for stress before it builds up and becomes unmanageable. Manage your stress before it manages you. Watch for the telltale signs of stress, and diffuse it before it detonates you! Be aware of stress traps that you set for yourself. Managing stress involves making choices, forming priorities, adopting attitudes, and taking actions that enable you to maximize your potential without overloading your abilities. Pare down or wear down!

People who are chronically stressed often feel that their lives are out of control. Balancing your life puts you back in control and helps you avoid unnecessary stress. Here are several stress-taming tips you may find useful:

Identify your most important goals and prioritize your time accordingly.

Set a realistic schedule.

Monitor your schedule, including the amount and intensity of your activities. Limit the number of decisions you make in a day.

Avoid clutter.

Regulate the rate of change taking place in your life at one time, including jobs, moving, travel, and even holidays.

Eliminate personal debt, especially credit card debt, and don't buy on impulse.

Take time to help others—it's a good way to put your own life in perspective.

Giving yourself the gift of a daily schedule that includes stimulating and inspiring reading, healthful food choices, exercise, and plenty of rest is vital to mental, emotional, physical, and spiritual well-being. It is balance in these areas of life that opens a treasure chest of blessings and benefits, creates a hedge

271

of protection against stress, depression, defeat, and addiction, and opens a doorway to a new life and a new you. It is God's plan to move you from survival to maintenance, from maintenance to success, and from success to significance. As you use God's keys to recovery, accept His love and healing power. Success and meaning will become yours!

Get Rid of That Worrywart

Worrying creates stress. When you embrace God and learn to trust Him, there's no need to worry. Worry is automatic for some people; it is the opposite of trust. One author wrote that "worry is interest paid on trouble before it falls due."[21] One woman was such a habitual worrier that when her husband went on business trips, she would leave messages on his cell phone that said: "Please tell me what is going on, so I will know what to be worried about!" British writer Arnold Bennett had a unique description of the ravages of worry: "Worry is evidence of an ill-controlled brain; it is merely a stupid waste of time in unpleasantness."

It is God's plan to move you from survival to maintenance, from maintenance to success, and from success to significance.

272

Developing trust also helps to "cool down" overactive areas of the brain.

People who suffer from anxiety tend to be *ruminators*; that is, like cows that chew their cud all day, ruminators tend to rehearse real or imagined difficulties over and over again until they are almost unable to think of anything else—unless it is another worry. And worry *does* alter brain chemistry and function, elevating the stress hormone norepinephrine and lowering the calming hormone serotonin.[22] Worry gives even small problems big shadows, and disables the brain for engaging in true problem solving during real challenges. Like anything else, worry can become a habit; but thankfully, like other habits, it can be broken. Jesus said: "But which of you by being anxious can prolong his life a single moment?"[23] As a matter of fact, the Bible is not only emphatic about the futility of worry, it also proposes a solution: "Do not be anxious about anything; but under all circumstances, by prayer and entreaty joined with thanksgiving, make your needs known to God. Then the peace of God, which is beyond all human understanding, will stand guard over your hearts and thoughts, through your union with Christ Jesus."[24]

The decision to stop engaging in useless worrying is just that—a decision. The Bible tells us to replace the anxious feelings with thoughts of thankfulness and expressions of trust and gratitude. We are told to leave our needs in the hands of God. When we do this, God Himself has promised to teach us how to trust—and not to worry.

He says, "Come to me, all you who are troubled and weighted down with care, and I will give you rest."[25] The God who created you invites you to come to Him with all your brokenness, concerns, and problems. He has a plan, and He will strengthen you and give you peace, even in the midst of trouble! Developing trust also helps to "cool down" overactive areas of the brain involved in anxiety, worry, negative thinking, and fear. (These areas are the deep limbic system, the cingulate gyrus, and the basal ganglia.)

273

It is easy to think that if we have enough external benefits such as money, looks, friends, talent, or power, we will be happy, in control, and free from worry. Do you think that is true? People can have every earthly advantage and yet still worry. But you *can* break the worry habit—and learn to trust in God.

No More Pity Parties

Pity *parties* recycle your life through reliving failure over and over again. Feeding on failure, either yours or others, fosters more of the same.

Elizabeth Elliot, who was left a young widow when her missionary husband was murdered by the natives he ministered to, has said that "self-pity is a death that has no resurrection, a sinkhole from which no rescuing hand can save you because you have chosen to be there." Self-pity has been defined as "a self-indulgent dwelling on one's own sorrows or misfortunes."[26] It is one of the most tempting of human traits, while at the same time one of the most self-disintegrating activities a person can engage in. There is no hope in self-pity, no plan, no purpose, and no promise. It fogs our vision and is a self-indulgent counterfeit of genuine sadness or grief, which can produce valuable fruit.

Self-pity is a death that has no resurrection, a sinkhole from which no rescuing hand can save you because you have chosen to be there.

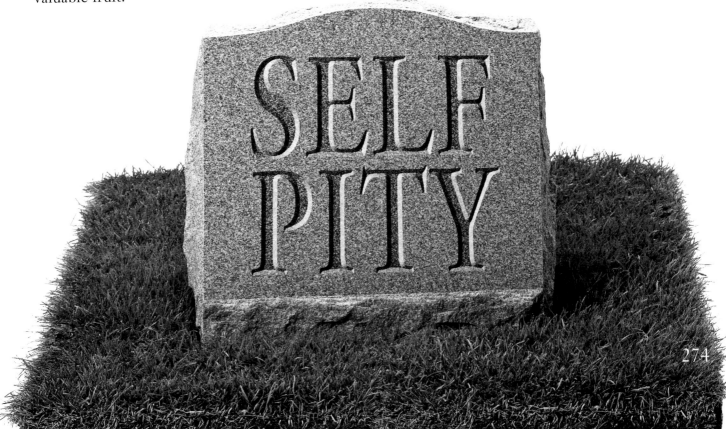

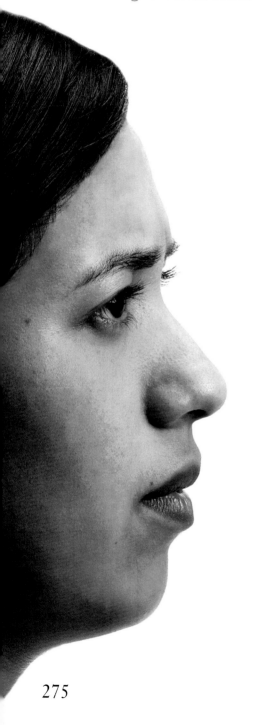

It would be foolish to think that every day our path will be strewn with rose petals but no thorns; that there will never be times of grief or sadness. It is like a sign on an executive's desk that read: "You are smiling because you don't understand the situation." Neuropsychiatrist John Ratey discusses how to harness the emotion of sadness to produce positive change: "Sadness takes us off-line so that we can regroup and reevalutate. It may even cause us enough 'pain' that we are motivated to change."[27]

Sadness may result in a feeling of numbness, which "may be adaptive, granting relief in the case of a terrible loss or giving a person some 'down time' to prepare for the next stage in life or to incorporate a major change."[28] But prolonged sadness can cause sustained overactivity in a fear center of the brain and in the right frontal lobe. This can result in depression, anxiety, and an inability to adapt to new information and engage in constructive problem solving. According to Ratey, "Depression is less genetically based than any other mental illness, and is the one most dependent on environmental factors."[29]

How can we put a fence around sadness so it can do its work without opening a dangerous door to depression? First, learn to detect and reject self-pity. Self-pity can be our worst enemy, if we yield to it. But when sad and overcome with grief, remember that relating to life's challenges in a positive way can turn the worst situation into a strengthening, learning experience. Second, when confronted with trouble, or if you make a mistake, don't give up; get up—and get going! Elbert Hubbard said, "The cure for grief is motion." Walking, gardening, or engaging in some physical activity or project helps mental processing and helps "throttle down" an overactive right frontal lobe, which is associated with anxiety.[30]

Overactive right frontal lobe activity is associated with sadness, but left frontal lobe activity is associated with positive mood. "Happiness and sadness are separate functions, and they represent opposite patterns of activity in the hemispheres of the brain."[31] The Bible counsels us to dwell on subjects that are true, honest, just, pure, pleasant, positive, virtuous, and worthwhile (Philippians 4:8). In this way we can help to heal the broken brain and help to balance unequal activity in the two hemispheres.

275

Research suggests that simply changing the expression on your face from a frown to a smile can significantly impact a depressed or stressed mood state and alter brain chemistry.[32] Even the practice of quieting the mind through deep, continued thought can help reverse some of the ill effects of stress.[33] The Bible states it this way: "I considered my ways, and turned my steps to Your statutes."[34] In another place it says: "Keep a watch on your behavior; let all your ways be rightly ordered."[35] Learn to monitor your moods, and keep a conscious check on negative thinking.

As much as possible, avoid places, people, and activities that are depressing. Planting yourself in front of the television and getting lost in a violent movie will only increase overall feelings of helplessness and stress. It is not good for the mind or morals to watch or read materials for entertainment that are traumatic, violent, depressing, immoral, or worthless. But turning your energy to the needs of others helps to ward off depression and increase feelings of self-esteem. Focus on activities that are refreshing, relaxing, healthful, moral, and mentally stimulating. See *Designer Activities for and Enriched Life* on page 153.

We can actively cultivate the mental traits of gratitude, optimism, diligence, and perseverance under stress; they are all linked to better mental and physical health.[36] We are individually responsible for the choices we make, including how we relate to people, situations, and challenges. Blaming others for our own poor choices and responses never accomplishes growth or change. Taking personal responsibility is liberating—it frees you to *act* instead of *react*.

Celebrate Life

There is so much to celebrate in life—you have strengths to build on and resources at your disposal that you may never have been aware of until reading these chapters. Everyone is different, and it is important not to compare what you have or don't have in relation to someone else. You are special, and God has a special plan for your life. Begin building with what you have and the resources you can identify and use, and watch new growth happen in your life.

Simply changing your expression from a frown to a smile can significantly impact a depressed mood state and alter brain chemistry.

It is important to focus on short- as well as long-term goals. For instance, an obese person may set a goal: "I am going to walk 10 miles a day and lose 200 pounds." This is an unrealistic way to approach an admirable long-term goal. It is more realistic to say: "I have 30 minutes a day I can devote to walking, and I am going to focus on losing 10 pounds." Looking at the big picture can be discouraging and overwhelming. As the saying goes: "It is a trial by the mile and hard by the yard. But it's a cinch by the inch."

Making a plan and rehearsing it in your mind can help you practice making positive choices. Before you start your day, talk to God. Visualize your day and how you will make positive choices. Trust that God will be with you throughout the whole day helping you prioritize your schedule, make right choices, and be productive with the talents He has given you.

If you should fall down, know that you can get up again. Forgive yourself and decide right then to get back on your victory path. Learn from your mistake and grow.

The next chapter is the story of one woman's journey to living free, and how implementing these keys brought her lasting change.

Sadness takes us off-line so that we can regroup and reevaluate. It may even cause us enough 'pain' that we are motivated to change.

Exercise
it Goes to your Head

We hear a lot about the benefits of regular exercise on physical health. But what about mental health? Your best exercise machine may be your dog. Just taking the dog for a daily walk can yield some surprising benefits—for you as well as Bowser!

Reduces Stress

■ Even a single bout of exercise can be a valuable short-term therapy for reducing tension, depression, anger, and confusion.[1] [2]

■ A ten-minute brisk walk will yield one hour of increased energy and reduced tension, whereas a sugary snack will ultimately result in fatigue and tension.[3]

■ Moderate-intensity exercise is even more beneficial than high-intensity exercise for anxiety reduction.[4]

■ Regular exercise increases the ability to handle stress by causing fewer stress hormones to be released when stress does occur.[5]

Improves Mood

■ Students who exercise regularly show lower levels of anxiety, shyness, loneliness, and hopelessness than their less active peers.[6]

■ Moderate, regular exercise has a positive impact on mood, vigor, psychological well-being, creativity, and self-esteem in all age groups.[7] [8] [9] [10]

■ Animal studies show that regular exercise can reduce symptoms of depression, and may alleviate some major depression.[11] [12]

Boosts Brain Power

- Exercise increases cerebral blood flow, increases neurotransmitter availability and efficiency, and affects brain structure.[13]

- Small increases in aerobic fitness improve mental fitness, particularly executive control functions of the brain, which have to do with planning, coordinating, and filtering out distracting information.[14]

- Animal and human studies show that repeated physical activity triggers chemical changes in the brain that enhance learning and memory.[15] [16]

- Children learn better when the brain is stimulated by exercise.[17]

- People over age 60 who walk rapidly for 45 minutes three times a week can significantly improve mental processing abilities that would normally decline with age.[18]

Helps You Sleep

- Exercise can help alleviate sleep problems in older adults.[19]

- Exercise can be effective in improving sleep quality, depression, strength, and quality of life.[20]

- Treating chronic fatigue with appropriate exercise can improve sleep and mood.[21]

- Exercising in the evening does not disturb sleep.[22]

Building
a Better
Brain

Choose Healthful Brain Foods

1. Enjoy complex carbohydrates. They include whole grain breads and cereals, nuts, beans, and plenty of colorful vegetables and fruits. Complex carbohydrates keep the feel-good hormone, serotonin, balanced. Plant foods help the brain work more efficiently and have been shown to improve overall mental and physical functions.

2. Eat a variety of colorful fruits and vegetables. For instance, purple, red, and blue fruits and vegetables are rich in phytochemicals called anthocyanins, which help scavenge free-radical damage in the body and brain. Orange, yellow, and green vegetables are rich in stress-lowering carotenoids. Enjoy a rainbow of garden colors every day!

3. Eat at least an ounce (1/4 cup) of nuts or seeds each day. Nuts, especially walnuts, pecans, Brazil nuts, and almonds, are a good source of healthful fats. Walnuts and ground flax seed are especially rich in omega-3 fats, which are beneficial in the structure of the nerve cells in the brain. Nuts also contain brain-healthy monounsaturated fats.

4. Eat at regular mealtimes for optimal brain function. Begin the day with a healthful breakfast. Take time for lunch. Have an early supper. Regular meals keep the blood sugar, hormones, and appetite balanced. Regular meals can help you deal with stress better.

5. Drink plenty of water. Water helps you stay alert, keeps nutrients flowing, and cleans out your system. Replace high-sugar and caffeinated drinks with water. Drink water between meals for the best digestion of food at mealtime.

Stimulate your brain with mental challenges

Keep learning new things. Get involved in community-based classes at your local college, art center, or library. Develop a new hobby. Plant a garden. Read books on subjects that are unfamiliar to you, such as gardening, government, history, or science. When taking your daily walk, find new paths. Work a puzzle. Learn a musical instrument. Learn a new language. Learn to build a better mousetrap! Keep your mind actively learning.

Exercise

Daily walking is an excellent exercise for brain health. Accumulate 10,000 steps or five miles a day. You may want to use a pedometer to monitor your progress. Walk for at least 30 to 60 minutes each day. Ten-minute walks are refreshing and energizing and can boost your mood for an hour. Walking can reduce tension and anxiety, relieve depression, help control blood sugar, boost the immune system, and control weight gain.

Rest

Adequate sleep tonight will help you retain the information that you learned today. Sleep helps what you learn take root in your long-term memory. If you are able, go to bed early enough, about 9:30 or 10:00 pm, to get pre-midnight sleep. That way you can wake up refreshed in the morning. It may take some practice to readjust your body clock, but getting enough sleep helps you deal with stress and helps balance blood sugar and stress hormone levels. Take time for a rest during the day. If you are sitting for long periods of time, take a 5 to 10 minute break each hour for optimal brain function. Get up and walk around, drink a glass of water, or just reflect on the things you are thankful for.

Look on the sunny side

Look on the positive side of life. A discouraged mind-set cannot find solutions. Write down 10 things you are thankful for each day. Sing songs while you travel in the car. Express appreciation for others. Notice the beauty around you, and appreciate the qualities of those around you without dwelling on their flaws. Look for opportunities to express optimism and thankfulness.

Manage stress

Turn off the radio and TV, and use downtime for real reflection. Pace yourself each day. Do your best and leave the rest. Allot an amount of time for a task and stay within your budgeted time. Often the perception of a situation and the way we handle it create more stress than the situation itself. Realize and accept your limitations. Nobody is perfect, not even you. Start the day with a simple prayer, "God, help me use my time and talents in the best possible way today—and give me joy in the process."

Connect with others

We need one another. Take time for friends and family. Surround yourself with people who love you, encourage you, and want the best for you. Do something nice for someone else as often as you can, even if it's just a friendly call or card.

Connect with God

Take time to connect with God. Enjoy walking in nature; talk to God in prayer; read the Bible; enjoy other inspirational books; join others in worship. Time with God strengthens you physically, mentally, and spiritually, and replaces restlessness with peace.

Health
in a Hurry – Eating Out
Successfully

Fast Food Can be Healthy Food!

Fast food fare doesn't have to be unhealthful. Here are some delicious fast-food options you can enjoy that are healthful replacements for a miserable meal when you're out and about—and in a hurry!

Grocery Store, Health Food Store, or Deli Options:

Sandwich items: hummus; soy cream cheese spreads; bean dip; frozen garden patties; veggie sandwiches; baked tofu slices; veggie cheese slices; soy mayonnaise; bean burritos (without lard); guacamole or fresh avocado with sprouts, tomato, and cucumber slices; nut butter and applesauce.

Salads: tabouli; pre-made mixed greens or spinach salad; fruit salad; veggie slices and dip plate; pasta; vegetable or shredded cabbage salad made with olive oil.

Breads: whole wheat wraps or pita bread; whole grain bread, rolls, or crackers; baked chips.

Soups and entrées: vegetarian vegetable or bean soup; pasta with marinara sauce; baked potatoes or roasted veggies; tofu dishes.

285

286

Other: mixed dry roasted nuts or sunflower seeds; dried or fresh fruit; soy yogurt; fruit smoothie; air-popped popcorn.

Subway or Other Deli Sandwiches: Choose whole grain bread; add lots of veggies and ask for a garden burger instead of meat.

Wendy's: Baked potato with broccoli; salad bar.

Steak House: Baked potato; vegetable and salad bar.

Restaurants: Vegetable plate; vegetable or bean soups; mixed-greens or spinach salad; whole grain breads; baked veggie wraps or vegetarian patties, if available.

Ethnic Restaurants: Greek; Lebanese; Chinese; Indian; Mexican; Italian—choose their vegetarian options.

Taco Bell: Bean burrito without cheese—add side orders of lettuce, rice, and guacamole to your burrito.

Vegetarian Restaurants: Visit www.happycow.net and www.vegdining.com to see if there are any good ones in your area.

Eating Out With Success

Before you go to an event or out to eat:

1. Tame your appetite:

If you become famished, it will be hard to make healthful choices when you order in a restaurant. Practice prevention, don't become famished.

- Eat high-fiber foods with every meal.

- Stay on a reasonable eating schedule. Space meals every 4 to 6 hours.

- Choose water or herb tea if you need a beverage.

2. Talk to yourself. Rehearse your choices.

- Remind yourself why you are eating out or going to the event.

- Imagine yourself making healthful choices at the event.

- Bring healthful choices, if appropriate.

- If possible, decide what you will eat before you go.

3. Transform your meal.

- Ask your server what he or she would recommend as a healthful selection.

- Look at the menu as a directory of foods available at that restaurant and then build your own meal.

- Choose vegetable or bean soup.

- Create your own plate. Order a' la carte instead of a specified dinner selection.

- Ask for salad dressing on the side.

- Choose pasta or a non-meat entree.

- Ask for a vegetarian plate.

- Share a dessert with someone or choose fresh fruit.

Eat with an attitude: Eat slowly. Enjoy the food and the company. After you have eaten, put your napkin on your plate and push it away, or push yourself away from the table. Sip an herbal tea if you must remain. Relax!

Building
a Better
Menu

A Better Menu Can Help Build a Better Brain.

Building a better menu will build a better brain, a better body, and a better you! Plant-based nutrition gives you more of what you need to help your mental engine purr instead of ping.

Get more fiber and complex carbohydrates: Choose whole grain breads and cereals, beans, fruits, vegetables, nuts, and seeds. They give you more of the good things you need to get through each day.

Plant foods give you more:

- **Nutrition:** more vitamins, minerals, antioxidants, and phytochemicals.

- **Quantity:** more food to eat with fewer calories.

- **Fiber and Satiety:** a fuller and more satisfied feeling.

- **Color:** beauty and phytochemicals.

- **Flavor:** tantalizing tastes from fresh, succulent fruits and crunchy veggies.

- **Variety:** abundance of variety in the produce department.

- **Balance:** a balance of nutrients that are naturally low in calories.

- **Energy:** complex carbohydrates for optimal energy.

- **Productivity:** a brain that works more efficiently.

- **Beauty:** clear skin, bright eyes, and a slowdown of the aging process.

- **Confidence:** to know you are doing the right thing.

Choose healthful fats: Eat nuts, seeds, olives, olive oil, and avocados for the best fats. Omega-3 fats are especially beneficial. They are found in flax seed, walnuts, and soy. Use non-hydrogenated spreads instead of butter or trans-fat-filled margarines.

Drink water: Water is the best thirst quencher and brain energizer compared to other drinks. Choose water instead of high-sugar, caffeinated beverages or alcohol.

Building a Better Breakfast

A good breakfast is one of the most important strategies for a successful day. It will power up your brain, body, and mood and give you energy to meet the challenges of the day.

A high-fiber breakfast will keep you satisfied so you will be less likely to crave unhealthful snacks and stimulating drinks. You will have more nutrition and less unwanted weight gain. You will have calmer nerves, better blood sugar control, and better ability to cope with stress when you power up your day with a good breakfast.

Easy breakfasts

You can enjoy a healthful breakfast in three easy steps:

1. **Get your grains:** You can enjoy a bowl of high-fiber cereal. Make sure each serving is at least three or more grams of fiber. Or heat up some oatmeal or other whole grain cereal. Enjoy cereals with B_{12}-fortified soy or rice milk. Treat yourself to some whole grain toast or a bagel with a natural peanut butter or non-hydrogenated spread. Make sure each slice of bread has two or more grams of fiber.

2. **Grab that fruit:** Add two or three choices of fresh fruit. Enjoy a variety of fruits. Treat yourself to fresh kiwi, pineapple, cantaloupe, plums, berries, apricots, peaches, or pears as well as the more familiar favorites such as apples and bananas.

3. **Go for the nuts:** Enjoy brain-boosting fats in the form of walnuts, pecans, Brazil nuts, and almonds. You may eat them raw or lightly roast them at 200 degrees for about 30 minutes to bring out their tantalizing taste. You can grind flax seed in a blender or coffee grinder and enjoy it on your cereal. For the freshest taste, store nuts and seeds in the freezer.

Building a Better Lunch

Taking time for a healthful lunch keeps your mental engine purring, your blood sugar balanced, and your energy levels high. It helps keep your mood elevated, and it reduces tension and fatigue.

Taking time for lunch punctuates your day with pleasure and can connect you with friends, coworkers, and family. It also gives your body the nutrient and energy boost it needs to keep you balanced and your spirits buoyed the rest of the day.

A good midday meal will help you deal with stress better and keep you from craving those unhealthful drinks and foods that make you bounce off the walls and increase tension and fatigue.

Easy lunches

You can enjoy a healthful lunch in three easy steps:

1. **Enjoy your raw foods:** Begin your midday meal with a nice helping of fresh mixed-greens salad, raw veggie sticks, or fresh fruit.

2. **Energize with fiber-rich fare:** Tickle your taste buds with bean or vegetable soups, whole grain breads, brown rice and tofu dishes, wholesome pastas, vegetarian patties on whole grain buns, baked or steamed potatoes with creative toppings such as tofu sour cream or olive oil and dill.

3. **Be veggie smart:** Color up your cuisine by including plenty of freshly steamed greens. Enjoy a variety of greens such as collards, kale, and spinach. Experiment with lightly steamed broccoli, cauliflower, squash, purple cabbage, and the scores of other delicious veggies that provide essential stress-lowering nutrients.

296

Building a Better Supper

If you have enjoyed a fiber-rich breakfast and lunch, you can eat an early supper and keep it light. This will help you sleep better and avoid indigestion.

Easy suppers

You can enjoy a healthful supper in three easy steps:

1. **Keep it simple:** Supper can be simple but elegant, nutritious, easy, and attractive. If supper is the only time your family eats together, use the suggestions for lunch for your evening meal. Otherwise, these simple supper ideas will give you plenty of what you need.

2. **Keep it colorful:** Here are some easy options:

   - Enjoy a light mixed-greens salad with split pea or vegetable soup. Spread some hummus (a garbanzo spread*) on whole grain crackers.

   - Warm up some leftovers.

   - Enjoy a fruit plate with soy yogurt and popcorn.

   - Enjoy a few baked nuts with some fresh fruit or a bowl of granola and soy milk.

   - Make yourself a sandwich with some steamed or raw veggies on the side.

   - Have a fruit smoothie and popcorn.

   - Whip up a burrito with refried beans, salad greens, and salsa.

3. **Keep it light:** If you are sedentary in your job and eat an appropriate amount of nutrient-rich food for breakfast and lunch, you will feel better with a light supper, or you may decide you do not need supper at all. In that case, enjoy a tasty herb tea or a little V-8 juice to fill that "spot" as you relax and enjoy the evening.

    * To make your own hummus. Blend one can drained garbanzos, 1 T lemon juice, 2 cloves garlic, 1 tsp salt, and 1 T sesame tahini until smooth. Add a little water to blend, if needed. May add chopped parsley.

Recipes

▶ Easy Oatmeal

1 - 2 C Water (may add part juice or soymilk)
Pinch of salt (optional)
1/2 C Frozen fruit or 2 T Dried fruit—raisins, dried cherries,
dried peaches, or pears
1 C Old-fashioned oatmeal

Bring 1-2 C water to boil. Add salt and fruit, if desired. Add 1 C oatmeal. Bring back to a rolling boil. Cover with lid. Take off the burner. Let sit for 10 to 15 minutes. Top with fresh fruit, nuts, applesauce, and/or soymilk.

▶ Bake-While-You-Sleep Steel Cut Oats or Irish Oatmeal

1 C Steel cut oats or Irish Oatmeal
4 C Water
1/2 tsp salt
1/2 C Dried fruit
2 T coconut
Sweetener, as desired.

Place in a deep casserole dish. Cover. Bake for 1 hour at 350°.
(Place a baking sheet under the cooking dish just in case it boils over.)
Set oven on time-bake to start one hour baking one hour before you get up in the morning. Wake up to a delicious breakfast!

▶ Beans Deluxe

1 Onion, diced
1 Carrot, diced
1 15 oz. can Beans
1/4 tsp Onion powder
1/4 tsp Garlic powder
1/4 tsp Cumin or basil

In a nonstick pan, braise onion and carrot in a little water. Add beans and seasonings. Continue to stir and slightly mash beans as they cook for 10 to 15 minutes.

Serving Suggestions: Serve over brown rice, stuff in pita bread or roll in whole wheat tortilla shell. Add tomatoes, green peppers, lettuce.

▶ Grrreat Greens

1 bunch Greens—collards, turnip greens, and/or kale
(7 C fresh greens = 2 C cooked greens)
1/2 Onion, diced
2 T Olive oil
1 T Sesame seeds, toasted
Salt, to taste
Lemon juice, to taste

Choose one or more types of greens: collards, turnip, or kale. Wash and slice. Sauté onion. Add sliced greens. Add water as needed to keep from scorching. Cook about 10 minutes until tender and bright green. Season with salt, olive or sesame oil, sesame seeds, and lemon juice.

▶ Vegetable Bean Soup

Sauté   1 C Chopped celery
          1 C Chopped carrots
          1/2 C Chopped green pepper
          1/4 C Chopped onion
          1 clove Garlic, minced

Add: 2 16-oz cans Whole tomatoes, with liquid
          1 15-oz can Red kidney beans, drained
          1/2 tsp Basil
          1/2 tsp Oregano
          1/2 tsp Cumin
          1 Bay leaf
          1 tsp or less Salt

Cook 15 to 20 minutes. Yields about four 8-oz servings.

▶ Picnic Baked Beans

Preheat oven to 350°.

Mix: 4 C Cooked beans (navy or pinto)
          3/4 C Water
          1/2 C Ketchup or tomato sauce with 1/8 tsp garlic and onion powder

Add: 2 T Dried onion or 1/2 grated onion
          1 Carrot, grated
          1 Apple, grated
          1 Red pepper, diced

Preheat oven to 350°. Bake covered for 45 minutes to 1 hour.

▶ Alfredo Tofu Pasta Sauce

1 10.5-oz. package Soft tofu
1 1/2 C Unsweetened soy milk
1-2 Garlic cloves (depends on how much you like garlic)
1 T Olive oil
3 T non-dairy Parmesan cheese or nutritional yeast flakes
1-2 tsp Salt (or salt to taste)
1 tsp Onion powder
1 tsp Dried Basil
1 T Dried parsley

Blend tofu, milk, garlic, olive oil, Parmesan cheese salt and onion powder. Mix in basil and parsley. Cook and drain 1 16 oz.. package of the pasta of your choice. Pour over drained, hot pasta.

▶ Garlic, Basil, or Parsley Pesto

Chop the following ingredients finely in a food processor:

5-6 Garlic cloves
3-4 T Olive oil
1/4 C Pine nuts or walnuts
1-2 C Fresh basil or parsley
1/4 C Non-dairy Parmesan cheese
1/2 tsp Salt

Mix all ingredients in a food processor. Cook and drain 1 16 oz.. package of your favorite pasta. Gently mix pesto with the pasta and serve hot.

▶ Zesty Green Salad

Arrange all or some of the following on your plate, in a bowl, or in a veggie wrap to your taste. Enjoy with your favorite healthful dressing or topping.

Spring-mix salad greens (available at any grocery store)
Fresh baby spinach
Avocado, sliced
Olives, black
Walnuts, sprinkled
Red and/or green pepper, slice
Carrots, shredded or sliced
Cucumber, sliced
Cranberry, dried, sprinkled
Tomato, cherry
Onion, green, sliced

▶ Lemon Olive Oil Dressing

1/4 C Olive oil
1/2 C Lemon juice
1 clove Garlic, minced or garlic powder
Add salt or seasoned salt to taste.

Mix. Pour over salad.

▶ Black Bean Salad

Mix together:

3 15-oz cans Black beans, drained and rinsed
2 C Frozen corn, thawed
2 Large tomatoes, diced
1 Large green bell pepper, diced
1 Large red and/or yellow pepper, diced
1/2 C Chopped red onion
3/4 C Chopped cilantro (optional) or parsley

Seasoning:

3/4 C Fresh lemon juice
2 cloves Garlic, minced
2 tsp Cumin
1 tsp Coriander
1/2 tsp Salt

Mix together beans, corn, tomatoes, bell pepper, onion and cilantro. Mix seasoning. Pour over bean/vegetable salad and lightly toss.

▶ Three-Bean Salad Deluxe

1 16 oz. can Garbanzo beans, drained
1 16 oz. can Kidney beans, drained
1 16 oz. can S & W dill green beans (with liquid), or a similar brand
1 C Artichoke hearts (water-packed), drained and diced
1/2 16 oz. can Black olives, sliced
1 Red pepper, diced
1/2 C Onion, green or purple, diced
2 C Shredded Savoy cabbage (or other cabbage)
1 tsp Dill weed
1/2 - 1 tsp Salt
1 tsp Onion powder
1/2 C Fresh lemon juice
3 T Olive oil
1/2 C Fresh parsley, chopped

Mix. Serve as a salad, wrap in whole wheat tortilla shell or stuff in whole wheat pita bread.

▶ Fruit Shake

1 C Soy or other milk; or juice of your choice
1 C Frozen fruit: Strawberries, raspberries, blueberries, peaches, and/or pineapple
1 Banana (extra good if the banana has been frozen)
Dates or honey to sweeten to taste
1 tsp Vanilla, if desired

Blend juice (or milk) with frozen fruit and banana. Add more liquid to desired thickness. Sweeten if desired.

▶ Easy Pizza

Whole wheat pizza shell or whole wheat pita bread.
Cover lightly with prepared spaghetti sauce.
Top with veggies: green and yellow peppers, mushrooms, zucchini, onion, and olives.
Sprinkle with veggie cheese or nutritional yeast flakes if desired.

Bake in 450° oven for about 15 minutes.

▶ Carob Peanut Butter Fudge

2 C Carob chips
1 C Peanut butter
1 12 oz. box Silken tofu, firm style

Blend well in a food processor. Stir in pecans or walnuts if desired. Pour into 9-inch x 13-inch pan. Freeze overnight. Thaw for about 10 minutes. Cut into squares. Serve while cold. (Becomes very soft when it reaches room temperature.)

▶ Creamy Wake-up Drink

2–2 1/2 C Milk (soy or rice) or 3/4 C dry soy milk with 2 C water
1 C Raw oatmeal
2 T Nuts, pecans or walnuts
1 tsp Flax seed (optional)
1/2 tsp Vanilla (optional)
4 Dates or 1 T Sweetener

Whiz all ingredients in blender. May add ice. May add fresh or frozen fruit. For a high-protein drink add more powdered soy milk.

▶ LuAnn's Tofu Walnut Meatballs or Burgers

Makes about 40 balls (10 servings).

    1 16-oz. pkg Firm tofu (water-packed, produce style)
    1/2 C Water
    2 T Light soy sauce (or Bragg's Liquid Aminos)
    1-2 tsp McKay's Beef-style seasoning or vegetable boullion
    1/2 tsp Ground sage
    1/2 tsp Dried basil
    1/2 tsp Onion powder
    1/4 tsp Garlic powder
    2 C Soft bread crumbs
    1/2 C Uncooked quick-cooking oats
    3/4 C Finely chopped walnuts
    2 T Dried minced onion

1. Using a blender or food processor, blend or process the tofu, water, soy sauce or Bragg's Liquid Aminos, beef-style seasoning, sage, basil, and onion and garlic powders until smooth; set aside.

2. In a mixing bowl, stir together the bread crumbs, oats, walnuts, and dried onions. Pour the tofu mixture over the dry ingredients and stir until well mixed. Allow mixture to stand for about 5 minutes before shaping into balls.

3. Preheat the oven to 350°. Lightly spray a large baking sheet with no-stick cooking spray or brush with olive oil; set aside.

4. Using wet hands or a small ice-cream scoop, form the mixture into about 40 balls, arranging on the prepared baking sheet.

5. Bake in the preheated 350° oven for about 30 minutes or until lightly browned. May be used immediately or frozen for use, as needed.

Serving ideas: Prepared balls may be arranged in a shallow baking dish, topped with a favorite sweet-sour/barbecue sauce or brown/mushroom gravy, served with brown rice or whole grain noodles. They may also be added to spaghetti sauce and served over whole grain spaghetti.

Source: Adapted by LuAnn Bermeo from Best Gourmet Recipes From the Chefs of Five Loaves Deli & Bakery, by Neva Brackett.

▸ Purple Cabbage

1/2 head Purple cabbage, sliced
1 Onion, diced
1 Apple, grated
2 T Lemon juice

Sauté onion and purple cabbage until soft. Add apple and cook another 5 minutes. Add lemon juice. Mix lightly and serve.

▸ Popcorn

Air pop popcorn or prepare 1 C popcorn with 1-3 T olive oil..

3 ways to season:

1. Sprinkle with olive oil and salt
2. Nutritional yeast flakes and Liquid aminos
3. Tahini—add 3 T slowly, while mixing the popcorn with a spoon; then

Add salt
And/or nutritional yeast flakes
And/or cumin, paprika, onion and garlic powder

▸ Walnut Maple Cookies

Makes 12 cookies

2 1/2 C Walnuts, ground
2/3 C Whole wheat pastry flour
1 tsp Salt
1/3 C Ground flax seed
1/3 C Carob chips
1/2 C Maple syrup
2 tsp Vanilla

Mix well. Drop cookies on prepared baking sheet. Flatten with fork. Bake 10-15 minutes in 350° oven. Let cool before removing from baking sheet.

From *Depression, the Way Out*, Neil Nedley, MD

▶ Oatmeal Cherry Cookies

1/2 C Honey
1 T Molasses
1/2 C Oil
1 T Vanilla
1 tsp Salt
1/2 C Soy milk
3/4 C Walnuts
3/4 C Dried cherries*, soaked in hot water, drain water
2 1/2 C Quick oats
1/4 C Whole wheat flour
1/4 C Unbleached white flour

Beat first seven ingredients together. Mix remaining dry ingredients in another bowl. Combine liquid and dry ingredients, stir well. Let sit for10 minutes to firm up. Drop by 2 T portions onto prepared baking sheet.

Flatten slightly and shape. Bake at 350° for 25 minutes.

313

Personal Worksheet 8

1. Take Care of Your Mind.* What positive choices can I make in the following areas to improve life skills, mental culture, and reduce addiction risk?** See *Building a Better Brain* on page 281. Set realistic goals in each area.

   Attitude: _____

   Speech and conversation: _____

   Reading material: _____

   Television: _____

   Internet: _____

2. Take Care of Your Body. What positive choices can I make in these lifestyle areas to improve health and vitality, energy and mood, and reduce addiction risk? See *Building a Better Menu* on page 289. Set realistic goals in each area.

   Eating habits: _____

   Water intake: _____

   Exercise: _____

   Sleep habits: _____

3. Celebrate Life. What is the difference between sadness and depression? (See pages 275-276.) What are the dangers of self-pity? What choices can I make in the following areas to cultivate resiliency, self-control, and hope when I face challenges?

   Mental: _____

   Physical: _____

   Spiritual: _____

Answers located on page 343 in the back of book.

* If you are working in a group, review the sections before you meet.
** It is important to rule out other medical conditions. Always work with your physician or healthcare provider. Serious mood disorders or physical symptoms require clinical intervention.

Chapter 9

The Attitude Factor

Spiritual and Emotional Healing

"Everything can be taken from a man but one thing: To choose one's attitude in any given set of circumstances."

Viktor Frankl

How to Trick an Elephant

Failure is learned. Consider this illustration: Baby elephants are cute, but adult elephants are dangerous if not under the control of their trainer. In order for a 160-pound man to have complete control of an elephant that can weigh up to 6,000 pounds, the elephant must be conditioned early in life. The baby elephant is tethered to a heavy chain that is staked deep into the earth. He can pull with all his might, but he is no match for the deeply anchored stake and strong chain that hold him captive. He becomes conditioned to accept his slavery, and as he grows in size and strength he is unaware that the strong bonds that have held him captive are powerless to control him now. Little does he realize that one determined pull will break his bonds forever. His brain tells him he is enslaved; he accepts it, and therefore he *is* enslaved.

In a similar way many are conditioned to accept addiction and failure as a way of life. They are tethered to the past, unable to break free from negative experiences that have molded them, and equally unable to realize present opportunities for freedom that meet them. They may have experienced trauma or had few role models very early in life. Now they are the victims of destructive habits and self-defeating personality traits that only deepen the gulf between them and other people, destroy opportunities for positive life experiences, and prevent unmet needs from being fulfilled.

Vicki Griffin Shares her Story

At a very young age I was in the middle of frequent violent physical and emotional abuse. I learned very early that my environment was not safe or predictable, and I did not see an example of rational problem solving or conflict resolution.

The helplessness I felt and the fear of going home began a pattern of running away from home, beginning at age five. I didn't get far, because there was nowhere to go—but without realizing it, escape and relief from depression became a central focus in my life. I ran away from home often, and by age 11 I had developed a serious case of bulimia, which lasted for 20 miserable years. I had gradually developed the idea that if I looked and performed perfectly I would be happy and successful in life. Media messages about the superiority of super-thinness reinforced my unrealistic mindset.

I used food to escape my painful life and as a substitute for unmet needs. Crash dieting and severe calorie restriction created enormous food cravings that were coupled with a fear of gaining weight. I was constantly hungry and unreasonably depriving myself of food, which drove the binging behavior. I started using drugs to drive myself to accomplish more and stave off hunger. When I did eat it was coffee, candy, and junk food. I was fueling my body with foods that made me run on nervous energy instead of real nutrition. People do have their own crazy reasoning for doing things, and I was no exception. I developed an angry personality, which drove me to run with a fast crowd and live recklessly and superficially. My diet and lifestyle contributed to the depression and fatigue I felt all the time.

Decision Time

People who live in a world of anger, abuse, and depression are at increased risk for addictions. They often do not have the internal skills to recover from even minor disappointments. Their life of addiction is often a futile effort to avoid the inevitable pain and uncertainty of life, which they are ill-equipped to handle, either psychologically, emotionally, or spiritually. Their brains have been programmed to fail, and they *do* fail, because they believe the negative messages they learned early in life. The brain cooperates with their decisions, thoughts, and expectations, and deeply engrafts these patterns into the psyche, so that unreasonable thoughts, unrealistic expectations, and irrational behavior govern the life. The Bible calls it bondage.

My family and I were victims of ignorance and dysfunction. What we did not know is that there was a way out. We did not know that God was able to break this very type of bondage in our lives, set us free from the prison house of sin, and give us power to overcome these terrible patterns of living. The prophecy about the Messiah states: "The Spirit of the Lord is upon Me, because He hath sent me to preach good tidings to the meek; he hath sent me to bind up the brokenhearted, to proclaim liberty to the captives, and the opening of the prison to them that are bound."[1] Help was available—we just didn't know it!

My parents were in bondage, and so was I. My environment was definitely against me in terms of addiction risk. So were my genetics, as I was the offspring of a seriously depressed mother. God knows about these factors; they are not too big for Him to deal with. He is able to provide help in the physical, emotional, social, and spiritual realm. He can set our thinking and our lives straight if we will allow Him to work in our lives. "He raises the poor out of the dust, and lifts the needy out of the ash heap."[2]

That doesn't mean that treatment for depression or medical intervention for these disorders is never in order. Work closely with a trusted doctor or healthcare provider.

Vicki Griffin

318

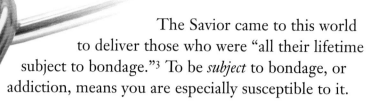

The Savior came to this world to deliver those who were "all their lifetime subject to bondage."[3] To be *subject* to bondage, or addiction, means you are especially susceptible to it.

People entangled in the net of bad habits need more than recovery from addictive behavior: They need a renewal of their mental, emotional, and physical faculties and spiritual restoration. Overcoming an addiction is a big step, but staying free takes patience, perseverance, and staying power. God provides the staying power needed as well as a plan for living. But it takes focus, commitment, and patience.

Not too long ago a lovely young teenage girl sat in my office with her frantic mother. She was bulimic, and because her mother knew it and did not want her to throw up her meals, she would not let her close the bathroom door. This poor girl had developed a ritual of throwing up in Ziploc bags and hiding them in her room. The stench filled her room. She was in prison.

My heart went out to this young woman, and as we talked together I poured out my sympathy, soul, and counsel trying to reach her. At times her grey eyes would soften, only to harden right up again. Finally, I stopped our session and asked her point blank: "Do you want to stop doing this?" "Part of me does, and part of me doesn't," she said flatly. My heart sank. Help was available, but she didn't want it—at least not very badly. That was the end of our meeting, but hopefully not of her story.

Change can be painful, even when it is good. When Jesus came to the man who had been languishing for 38 years, paralyzed from the neck down, He asked him a seemingly ridiculous question: *"Would you like to be made whole?"*[4] But it is actually a very important question; perhaps the most important question to address when considering the cost of leaving a life of paralyzing dysfunction, addiction, and failure. The cost is actually quite high. Habits are at least predictable, even if they are bad ones. They are also insulating in the sense that you are not participating in a new life with all the risk of new failures and more rejection.

To be subject to bondage, or addiction, means you are especially susceptible to it.

319

As I got older, I stopped running with a fast crowd, but the bulimia was still the center of my experience. I attended a university, and there met and married my husband Dane. He was kind, considerate, and a real friend. What more could a girl ask for? When we were first married I was fiercely independent. I had not surrendered my own will and way to God, and so I did not have His power or perspective in my life. Up to this time I didn't realize that I didn't trust anyone and was unable to resolve conflicts. I also didn't realize how selfish and self-centered I was. I found out very quickly.

I could not see who Dane really was because I was tethered to my past. In fact, if he happened to hurt my feelings my defense would be to threaten to leave or retreat into a world of self-pity. My bulimia actually worsened. I simply could not endure this new and different experience called marriage. My own thinking and expectations were warped. I expected perfect love, the type of love that only God can give. I demanded perfection of myself as well, and couldn't forgive myself if I made a mistake. I wanted a painless life, but I could be negative, self-centered, and demanding. Without realizing it I was expecting Dane to create a perfect cocoon of safety for me and make perfect decisions. The problem was, he was human and had flaws just like I did. I seemed to be on a fatal course to ruin my life, even though I was well-educated, had a wonderful spouse, two beautiful children, and a nice home.

The pain of growth is pain with a purpose, pain with the promise of healing.

Early in our marriage we heard a powerful message about how Christ came to die on the cross and create a reservoir of righteousness and power to those who were trapped in sin and rebellion. The speaker told us that God loves us, not for who we are, but because of who He is, and that He died to reclaim us as His own children and make us new. Our part is to stop resisting His dominion in our lives, and with His help put away our rebellious attitude. I heard the call loud and clear.

Pain Is Inevitable—Misery Is a Choice

I knew it was time to turn my life over to God. I had experienced a lot of evil, and so I knew there was a devil. But now I knew there was a God who was even more powerful than the devil, and that God was asking me to give Him control in my life.

I asked God to change my desires and thinking. Daily I asked Him to help me recover the lost ground that had been stolen from me. I made a choice to learn a better way and leave my past behind.

Up to this point my bulimia was so severe that I would throw up as many as a dozen times a day—I simply could not allow myself the pleasure of a meal. I was underweight and exhausted, even spitting up blood—a dangerous sign.

The moment I made the decision to turn my life over to God, the bulimia was over. It was almost unbelievable, but I had no more desire to throw up. I felt that I could eat and be satisfied. That emptiness in my life had been filled. I began to spend time daily in Bible study and prayer. Now I wanted to change my lifestyle and live differently. I came to understand that this included the way I dressed, ate, entertained myself, thought, and lived. My style of living had reinforced my addiction, and it all had to change. I stopped worrying about my weight. I knew that if I followed a healthful lifestyle my weight would be fine. At times old thoughts would try to creep in and take over, but my focus was set, and I felt that now I knew what to do, how to do it, and Who to go to for help.

I learned that a diet rich in nutrients and fiber would give me satisfaction, fullness, and nutrition without having to worry about my weight. I learned to enjoy a wholesome breakfast, a hearty but healthful lunch, and a light supper. Eating healthfully took away my cravings for junk food or snacks. I could enjoy sweets occasionally without losing control. I was satisfied—and the good food that I ate helped me think better, improved my mood, and gave me more energy.

When I was delivered from the bulimia, I also turned my back on tobacco and caffeine—cold turkey. I was averaging about 10 cups of coffee a day. I prayed that the headache wouldn't split my brain in two, and it didn't. I was through with letting caffeine and nicotine control me.

God loves us, not for who we are but because of who He is.

321

I began to exercise every day, and found that it helped control anxiety and improve my mood. It was fun, too, and I experienced more energy and slept more soundly. I threw away the magazines that featured rail-thin models in tight clothing and stopped setting unrealistic goals. I realized that femininity and sensuality are two different things. I now wanted to be feminine and modest, not sensual and seductive. I had discovered a sense of true inner worth.

I no longer accepted the superficial suggestions of the media that physical beauty is the major determinant of worth. It is the inner character that is of true worth, not outward beauty which can fade.[5] That doesn't mean that our physical appearance isn't important. It is a good thing to be well groomed and in shape physically.

This was not the beginning of a mistake-free journey. But I had a goal and a Helper. I learned to forgive myself and others, and just start over again. I learned from my poor choices and learned what to do to keep from getting into situations or thinking that would lead me in the wrong direction.

Dane needed help too, and his life was also changed by God. Together we determined to grow day by day, learning and practicing right principles of living.

Vicki and her husband Dane have been married for 28 years.

Defeat to Deliverance

I have been free from bulimia for 20 years now. On this journey, I discovered that while it is easy to get distracted, staying focused on seven major lifestyle goals helps to keep me on the right course.

1. Nutrition. Nourishing food strengthens not only the body, but the brain. Plant foods are rich in compounds and nutrients that lower stress and improve mental function and mood. Avoid junk food, saturated animal fat and trans fats, caffeine, and large amounts of refined sugar. When you eat better, you will feel better and have the energy to make better choices.

You can give your brain a workout by reading a challenging book, working a crossword puzzle, or learning a new skill.

2. **Exercise.** Exercise improves head as well as heart health: it is critical to mental as well as physical health. It has been said that motion balances emotion. Exercise lowers stress, depression and anxiety; it improves mood, well-being and mental processing; and increases learning power.

3. **Rest.** Our bodies are designed for rest as well as for action. It is important to plan times of recreation and relaxation to minimize the depression that is linked to constant mental and physical strain. Also, regular, early-to-bed sleep patterns rejuvenate the brain; help control stress hormone and blood sugar levels; reduce irritability, fatigue, and stress; and increase energy!

4. **Work.** Real work satisfaction does not come from a better job, but doing a job better. When you approach your job with that philosophy, a better job may come. But you will have work satisfaction along the way. The point is, no job is unimportant or insignificant. If it is the job you have been given to do, it is the most important job in the world. It can become an achievement instead of an activity. Attitude is everything.

5. **Relationships.** Cultivating healthy relationships is a lot like cultivating a garden. The more focused attention and care a garden gets, the more fruit it produces. In the same way, taking time to cultivate and maintain positive friendships and social relationships bears the fruit of joy, empathy, and unselfishness. Taking time for healthy relationships creates opportunities for giving as well as receiving.

6. **Mental fitness.** Physical fitness requires determination, perseverance, and practice. Mental fitness does too. You can give your brain a workout by engaging in challenging mental activities such as reading a challenging book, working a crossword puzzle, playing a musical instrument, or learning a new skill. Such activities increase the brain's

neuronal neighborhoods, creating new connections and increasing mental agility. This improves the speed and accuracy with which the brain can solve problems and meet challenges. Challenge your brain and change your world.

7. Spiritual health. Spiritual health is at the center of a healthy lifestyle. It is making peace with God and allowing His plan, purpose, and power to guide your life. Through Bible study, prayer, and practicing the principles of life taught by the Word of God, we may achieve steady growth and improvement in our lives.

Staying the Course

I also discovered seven helpful principles for maintaining a path of growth and freedom from addiction, as well as reducing the risk of relapse:

1. Stay focused. It is easy to get bogged down in the demands and details of the day and lose sight of your larger goals. Appreciating and focusing on your larger goals turns ordinary activities into achievements and every effort into an adventure and learning experience. By embracing the fundamental principles of successful living you will learn to eliminate hindrances to achieving your most important goals.

2. Set realistic expectations. The key to staying motivated is setting realistic expectations. Evaluate your previous experience and current situation. What is a realistic, reachable goal for you in the area you are considering? Achieving a small goal is more valuable than brooding over impossible expectations. Dreams can become realities or nightmares depending on the size of the steps! Remember; it's a cinch by the inch, but it's hard by the yard and a trial by the mile! Little steps lead to big victories.

3. Expect challenges. We can turn our mistakes into victories if we learn from them, become more vigilant, adopt new strategies for success, and thereby grow in wisdom. Successful people are not mistake-free; they just don't give up when things go wrong. Mistakes can be the greatest stepping stones to achieving your goals if you refuse to be defeated by them.

What you make up your mind to be, you will be. Our attitude is probably the most powerful indicator of success or failure in the pursuit of change.

4. Maintain a positive attitude. Check those negative thoughts! To a large extent, we have the ability to choose how we will think and feel about a situation. Make the choice to focus on solutions rather than problems. Look at difficulties as opportunities for gaining strength to meet challenges. Find a valuable lesson in every challenge. Cultivate thankfulness, optimism, and trust in God in the situations you can't change.

5. Seek support and accept responsibility. Spending time and forming relationships with people who have positive life skills is one of the best ways to learn new habits and ways of thinking. We become what we surround ourselves with. Social ties create mutual accountability and give us the opportunity to demonstrate and build responsibility and consistency into our lives. The principles of support, accountability, and responsibility enable us to develop deep, meaningful relationships with others.

6. Practice new choices. Extreme makeovers may work on TV home remodeling programs, but remodeling a life is a process that takes place over time. Fast is fragile, but slow is steady, stable, and comes to maturity over time. It is the very slow, steady process of repeatedly making positive choices that builds mind, body, and spirit. Never underestimate the power of little, daily positive choices in overcoming big, bad habits. Repetition and patience are the keys to crafting a healthy lifestyle.

7. Connect. Circumstances alone cannot change the heart. The best of intentions can plunge without the preserving power of prayer. God is personally interested in your healing, growth, and progress and He will guide, sustain, and empower all who come to Him in prayer.

Make up Your Mind

What you make up your mind to be, you *will* be. Our attitude is probably the most powerful indicator of success or failure in the pursuit of change. Neuroscientist John Ratey from Harvard University states it this way: "It has become obvious that we can actually change our brains. By altering the external environment or the internal environment of our bodies, we can take better advantage of our strengths and amend our

The possibilities for change are bounded only by our imagination, our willingness to assess our brains accurately through self-reflection, and our commitment to do some hard work.

weaknesses. The possibilities for change are bounded only by our imagination, our willingness to assess our brains accurately through self-reflection, and our commitment to do some hard work. One necessary precursor to change, though, is often a change in attitude."[6]

Adopting healthful lifestyle habits requires planning and prioritizing each day. But positive choices have a powerful sculpting effect on the brain and promote long-term recovery from addictions.

Reading wholesome material gives the brain and emotions better fuel for facing and fixing problems. Choosing supportive friends who encourage positive choices, helps make the path easier. Determining to look at life's challenges as learning and growth experiences rather than caving in to self-pity develops perseverance, courage, and optimism. Saying *no* to negative thoughts and habits frees up mental energy for positive choices.

> Determining to look at life's challenges as learning and growth experiences rather than caving in to self-pity develops perseverance, courage, and optimism.

326

Saying *yes* to healthful food, exercise, uplifting reading and media, wholesome friends, and positive attitude will help reshape your mind to create a new and better you!

Wisdom Works

Counseling can be a useful tool, even from wise and stable friends. When confronted with negative experiences, I have learned to identify certain types of thinking and responses that are unrealistic and ineffective. If I indulge in those thoughts, I am more likely to become depressed, anxious, and respond inappropriately. I have gone to those who react appropriately in similar situations and asked them how they would reason and relate to the challenge. They explain to me how they would approach the situation and why they think the way they do. This can be a great way to learn successful strategies. Addicts have distorted thinking and coping skills and can learn from others how to think and reason in a healthful way. Talking with others who have overcome addictions can help you come up with strategies to deal successfully with life.

"When the student is ready, the teacher appears." As you seek, you will find. Other people can help you in this journey. Proverbs 11:14 says: "When there is no helping suggestion the people will have a fall, but with a number of wise guides they will be safe." Choose wise guides to help you shape your new lifestyle.

For example, I often ask those I trust how they think and reason through a situation. Their practical wisdom has kept me from making unwise decisions or needlessly offending people. I'm learning better logic and how to deal with tricky situations through their example.

Emotions also need taming. That doesn't mean you will never show your emotions, but wisdom and reason need to be in control, keeping emotions in check. Wisdom waits and trusts. Emotions act out of impulse. It takes practice to be patient and wait. Try to avoid the extreme highs and lows in your emotions—there is always a rebound, and it is usually fatigue and depression.

Learning to reject patterns of thinking and behavior that don't work and accepting new and positive ones actually rewires the brain.

327

The way you speak will help you balance your emotions. If we speak recklessly and carelessly it can get our emotions all stirred up, making the situation worse.[7] A lifestyle that protects against fatigue, hunger, inactivity, overactivity, and stress is also helpful in managing your emotions.

Learning to reject patterns of thinking and behavior that don't work and accepting new and positive ones actually rewires the brain. Notice this powerful statement from neuroscientist Jeffrey Schwartz: "The time has come for science to confront the serious implications of the fact that directed, willed mental activity can clearly and systematically alter brain function; that the exercise of willful effort generates a physical force that has the power to change how the brain works and even its physical structure. The result is directed neuroplasticity. The cause is what I call directed mental force."[8]

He adds: "It is the activity—taking possession of new knowledge, manipulating it and finding new connections, and, more than any other brain activity, generating new ideas and teaching them—that seems most likely to rev up synaptic synthesis [new brain connections]."[9]

Confident and Connected

Applying the Keys to Life will help you physically, mentally, emotionally, and spiritually. Building on these foundational keys, your personal confidence will grow over time. You will learn to act from wisdom instead of impulse. You will no longer need to compare yourself to others, because you will realize your true worth as a child of God. Your lifestyle will build your body, mind, and spirit. And your mouth, emotions, and actions will be under the guidance of God. Old habits may assert themselves at times; your path may be littered with mistakes. But with these keys there is progress, growth, and increasing strength. These are the keys to life—eternal life—a life of Living Free!

Your Will Empowered!

Many are inquiring, "How am I to make the surrender of myself to God?" You desire to give yourself to Him, but you are weak in moral power, in slavery to doubt, and controlled by the habits of your life of sin. Your promises and resolutions are like ropes of sand. You cannot control your thoughts, your impulses, your affections. The knowledge of your broken promises and forfeited pledges weakens your confidence in your own sincerity, and causes you to feel that God cannot accept you; but you need not despair. What you need to understand is the true force of the will. This is the governing power in the nature of humanity, the power of decision, or of choice. Everything depends on the right action of the will. God has given to men and women the power of choice; it is theirs to exercise. You cannot change your heart, you cannot of yourself give to God its affections; but you can choose to serve Him. You can give Him your will; He will then work in you to will and to do according to His good pleasure. Thus your whole nature will be brought under the control of the Spirit of Christ; your affections will be centered upon Him, your thoughts will be in harmony with Him. Desires for goodness and holiness are right as far as they go; but if you stop here, they will avail nothing. Many will be lost while hoping and desiring to be Christians. They do not come to the point of yielding the will to God. They do not now choose to be Christians. Through the right exercise of the will, an entire change may be made in your life. By yielding up your will to Christ, you ally yourself with the power that is above all principalities and powers. You will have strength from above to hold you steadfast, and thus through constant surrender to God you will be enabled to live the new life, even the life of faith.

White EG. *Steps to Christ* (Review and Herald: Hagerstown, MD) pp. 47, 48.

329

Personal Worksheet 9

1. Success in life has more to do with attitude than aptitude. What positive attitudes would I like to strengthen? Which negative attitudes do I need to modify in order to move forward in my personal growth?* _____

   _____

   _____

2. What characteristics can be developed as a result of a close connection with God? Look up Galatians 5:16-24 and 1 Corinthians 13. _____

   _____

3. What are seven lifestyle priorities noted in this chapter, and why is each one important?** _____

   _____

4. What mind-set does God challenge me to adopt? Look up Galatians 6:7-9; Proverbs 4:26, and Haggai 1:5-7.

   _____

   _____

5. What are the seven strategies for reaching and maintaining my most important goals? How can each one aid in achieving sustained growth? _____

   _____

   _____

Answers located on page 343 in the back of book.

* It is important to rule out other medical conditions. Always work with your physician or health-care provider. Serious clinical disorders such as anorexia nervosa require clinical intervention.
** If you are working in a group, review the sections before you meet.

Substance Addiction
Withdrawal
Symptoms

Common Symptoms of Withdrawal

For the most part, withdrawal symptoms are opposite in nature to the direct effects of the substance that caused the dependence. Not all addictions lead to withdrawal, but for the ones that do, it is important to know what to expect by being aware of the symptoms that occur when use is discontinued. The following information comes from the *Diagnostic and Statistical Manual of Mental Disorders*.

Amphetamine Withdrawal
(Includes Cocaine)

The following symptoms develop within a few hours to several days after last heavy or prolonged use:

1. fatigue

2. vivid & unpleasant dreams

3. can't sleep or sleeping too much

4. increased appetite

5. psychomotor retardation or agitation

6. down, or depressed, mood

333

Sedative, Hypnotic, or Anxiolytic Withdrawal
(Prescription or Over-the-Counter Drugs)

The following symptoms develop within several hours to a few days after last use:

1. autonomic nervous system hyperactivity (sweating, pulse rate greater than 100, palpitations, etc.)

2. increased hand tremors

3. can't sleep

4. nausea or vomiting

5. transient seeing, touching, or hearing hallucinations or illusions

6. psychomotor agitation

7. anxiety

8. grand mal seizures

(NOTE: If withdrawing from or ceasing use of this type of substance, seek medical attention immediately; it is one of the most life-threatening withdrawals.)

Opioid Withdrawal
(Heroin, Methadone, Prescription, or Over-the-Counter Drugs, such as Vicodin, Oxycodone, etc.)

■ Opioid withdrawal can occur within minutes to several days after heavy or prolonged use or after taking an opioid antagonist after discontinuing use.

■ It varies in intensity from no detectable symptoms to extreme discomfort graded as follows:

Grade 0—craving, anxiety, drug-seeking behavior

Grade 1—yawning, sweating, excess tearing, runny nose

Grade 2—prolonged and abnormal dilation of the pupil, gooseflesh, muscle twitching, loss of appetite

Grade 3—can't sleep; increased pulse, respirations, and blood pressure; abdominal cramps; vomiting; diarrhea; weakness

Alcohol Withdrawal

■ Cessation of (or reduction in) alcohol use that has been heavy and prolonged; two or more of the following develop within several hours to a few days after discontinuing use:

1. autonomic nervous system hyperactivity (sweating, pulse rate greater than 100, palpitations, increased blood pressure and temperature)

2. increased hand tremors

3. can't sleep

4. nausea or vomiting

5. transient seeing, touching, or hearing hallucinations or illusions

6. psychomotor agitation

7. anxiety

8. sense of agitation

9. delirium tremens

10. grand mal seizures

Nicotine Withdrawal

■ Abrupt cessation of daily nicotine use for several weeks or more; within 24 hours the presence of four or more of the following signs will occur:

1. depressed, or down, mood

2. can't sleep

3. irritability, frustration, or anger

4. anxiety

5. difficulty concentrating

6. restlessness

7. decreased heart rate

8. increased appetite or weight gain

Caffeine Withdrawal

■ Headache is the primary cue of withdrawal from caffeine; it typically occurs 12 to 24 hours after the last ingestion of caffeine.

■ Feeling sleepy and tired are also major symptoms of caffeine withdrawal—especially during the second and third day.

Marijuana Withdrawal

■ Cues of withdrawal from marijuana are not experienced until at least one week after the last dose of marijuana has been taken, and they include:

1. diarrhea

2. teeth chattering

3. wet dog-like shakes

4. salivation

5. drooping of the upper eyelid

6. yawning and restlessness, piloerection (body hairs stand on end).

These symptoms often mirror those experienced with a mild case of flu and are not frequently acknowledged to be due to an addiction.

The path that a person takes in withdrawal is impacted by other factors, such as age, gender, concurrent illnesses, race, ethnicity, use history, and pregnancy. It is highly recommended that if you are experiencing withdrawal, seek professional help from your health-care provider for safe detoxification. Do not try to handle it on your own.

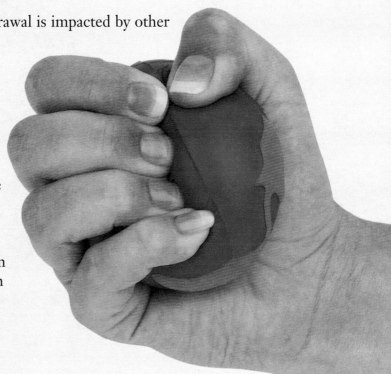

Untreated withdrawal is a major cause of relapse and inability to heal from addictions. Long-term or post-acute withdrawal persists for years for some people. To address this, one must focus on preventing relapse and living free through the keys outlined in chapters 7 and 8.

Substance Addiction Recovery Resources

Alcoholics Anonymous (AA) World Services, Inc.

Box 459
Grand Central Station
New York NY 10163
212-870-3400
www.AA.org

Al-Anon Family Group Headquarters, Inc. Alateen

1600 Corporate Lending Parkway
Virginia Beach VA 23454-5617
757-563-1600 (8:00 am - 6:00 pm, EST)
www.al-anon.org

American Society of Addiction Medicine

4601 North Park Avenue, Arcade Suite 101
Chevy Chase, MD 20815
Phone: 301-656-3920
Fax: 301-656-3815
www.asam.org
email@asam.org

Codependents of Sex Addicts (COSA)

National Service Office
PO Box 14537
Minneapolis, MN 55414
www.cosa-recovery.org
info@cosa-recovery.org
For those affected by someone else's
sexual behavior.

S-Anon Family Groups

Word Service Office
PO Box 111242
Nashville, TN 37222-1242
615-833-3152
www.sanon.org
sanon@sanon.org

Sexaholics Anonymous International Central Office

PO Box 111910
Nashville, TN 37222
615-331-6230
www.sa.org

Narcotics Anonymous

World Service Office in Los Angeles
PO Box 9999
Van Nuys, CA 91409
Phone: 818-773-9999
Fax: 818-700-0700
www.narcoticsanonymous.org

Loma Linda Behavioral Medicine Center

1710 Barton Road
Redlands CA 92373
800-752-5999
24-hour help line. Inpatient and outpatient chemical dependency recovery services for adults, adolescents, and children.

Ministry Care Line

3535 Southern Boulevard
Kettering OH 45429
800-324-8618
www.kmcnetwork.org/kccc
For clergy and their families.

SDAXA (Seventh-day Adventists for the Extinction of Addictions)

Regeneration Ministries
Hal Gates, Director
20015 Bothell Everett Highway
Bothell WA 98012-7198
800-732-7587
425-481-7171
www.regenerationministires.com
www.plusline.org (Resource information help desk.)

Betty Ford Center

39000 Bob Hope Drive
Rancho Mirage CA 92270
800-854-9211
admissions@bettyfordcenter.org
For persons addicted to alcohol and/or other drugs.

Hazelden Educational Materials

Pleasant Valley Road
PO Box 176
Center City MN 55012-0176
800-328-9000
www.hazelden.org

Kelly Foundation

2801 West Roosevelt Road
Little Rock AK 72204
800-245-6428
www.kellyfdn.com

National Association for Christian Recovery

PO Box 215
Brea CA 92822-0215
714-529-6227
www.christianrecovery.com
Provides a quarterly magazine *STEPS* as well as regional and national conferences.

The Substance Abuse and Mental Health Services Administration

National Clearinghouse for Alcohol and Drug Information
P.O. Box 2345
Rockville MD 20852-2345
800-729-6686
www.health.org
Ask for the name of the RADAR coordinator in your state. They have free loan items and pamphlets available.

Resources for Alcohol and Drug Abuse Treatment

1. Alcoholics Anonymous: www.alcoholicsanonymous.org or yellow pages under AA Central Office. AA meetings occur every day in the morning, noon, and evening. Some are nonsmoking; some are for men or for women only. Some are small, and some are large. It helps to ask someone to be your sponsor, He or she can then guide you through the process of growth. That person can be a temporary sponsor until you find someone with whom you are very comfortable. There is much literature available at the meetings to help your understand yourself better.

2. Al-Anon: www.al-anon.org or yellow pages under Al-Anon. The same applies as mentioned above, but for family members.

3. Narcotics Anonymous: www.narcoticsanonymous.org and www.naranon.com or yellow pages under Narcotics Anonymous for those who use illicit drugs and their family members, respectively. Many people go to both types of meetings.

4. American Society of Addiction Medicine: 301-656-3920 or www.asam.org. These are physicians who are specifically educated about the unique problems associated with alcohol and drug use. Ask about other treatment resources, doing an intervention if the alcoholic or addict is resistant to help, or referrals to experienced counselors.

Personal Worksheet Answers

Personal Worksheet #1

1. Your answer. (Note: All habits are learned by practice and repetition.)

2. True. See review sheets.

3. All human beings are in need of divine help and strength; all are bent toward self-destruction without God's intervention.

4. Your answer.

5. Jesus died for us in order to give us the divine help and strength we need to overcome destructive thinking and habits.

Personal Worksheet #2

1. Your answer.

2. Your answer.

3. It is never too late to learn new and better ways. God Himself will teach us what we need to do.

4. Your answer.

5. God has promised to set us free from life-long addictions by filling our lives with His power and principles of living.

Personal Worksheet #3

1. Your answer.

2. Your answer.

3. God has promised to satisfy my unfulfilled longings, fill me with His goodness, and guide me through the "dry" times of bad circumstances.

4. Your answer.

5. God is never too tired to hear from us, and never too far away to help us. He will be right there for me when I need Him.

Personal Worksheet #4

1. Your answer.

2. Your answer.

3. The Lord has promised to relieve my distress, lead me in a better way, and replace my anxious longings with His presence and comfort.

4. Your answer.

5. God invites me to call on Him in my need; He will be my protection and give me the victory over cravings and wrong actions. He will forgive me and help me to look forward in life, and not dwell on past failures.

Personal Worksheet #5

1. Your answer.

2. Your answer.

3. God has promised to deliver me from falling under temptation. He will give me new impulses, thoughts, and ideas. He will give me the power to obey those right impulses.

4. Your answer.

5. God will help me develop balanced thinking and help me keep the victories I have gained as I grow in strength. God forgives me of my wrongs and helps me learn new ways, not hanging on to guilt.

Personal Worksheet Answers

Personal Worksheet #6

1. Your answer.

2. Your answer.

3. God will deliver me from lustful impulses. He will make me stronger than my addiction and set me on solid ground in my life.

4. Your answer.

5. He will pull me out of the quicksand of bad habits and establish His plan in my life. He will watch over me and protect me as I learn and grow. He will forgive me of my wrongs and cleanse me from wrong desires.

Personal Worksheet #7

1. Your answer.

2. Your answer.

3. Your answer.

4. Your answer.

5. Your answer.

Personal Worksheet #8

1. Your answer.

2. Your answer.

3. Your answer.

Personal Worksheet #9

1. Your answer.

2. The fruit of a character cultivated by God is positive, unselfish, wholesome, and balanced. Angry, negative thinking and lack of forgiveness produce unhappiness and depression; forgiveness, positive thinking, and mercy cultivate peace and happiness.

3. Your answer.

4. God calls me to reason from cause to effect, and realize the powerful shaping influence of positive as well as negative choices.

5. Your answer.

343

Footnotes

Chapter 1 – The Addicted Brain

1 A review of 50 years of research on naturally occurring family routines and rituals: cause for celebration? Fiese BH, et al. *Journal of Family Psychology* 2002 Dec:16(4)381.

2 LeDoux J. *Synaptic Self* (New York, NY: Penguin Publishing, 2002) p. 134.

3 Pinel J. *Biopsychology* (Needham Heights, MA: Pearson Allyn & Bacon, 2000) pp. 368-9.

4 The most important unresolved issue in the addictions: conceptual chaos. Shaffer HJ. *Substance Use Misuse* 1997:32(11)1573.

5 Behavioral addictions: do they exist? Holden C. *Science for People* 2001 Nov:294(5544)981.

6 Ibid.

7 Ibid.

8 Katherine A. *Anatomy of a Food Addiction* (Carlsbad, CA: Gurze Books, 1996) p. iii.

9 Reward deficiency syndrome: a biogenetic model for the diagnosis and treatment of impulsive, addictive, and compulsive behaviors. Blum K, et al. *Journal of Psychoactive Drugs* 2000 Nov:32(Suppl: i-iv)1-112.

10 Beating abuse: glutamate may hold a key to drug addiction. Powledge T. *Scientific American 2002* Jan: 20.

11 Glutamate transmission and addiction to cocaine. Kalivas P, et al. *Ann NY Acad Sci* 2003:1003:169-75.

12 Ibid.

13 Reward deficiency syndrome: a biogenetic model for the diagnosis and treatment of impulsive, addictive, and compulsive behaviors. Blum K, et al. *Journal of Psychoactive Drugs* 2000 Nov:32(Suppl: i-iv)1-112.

14 Juvenile violence and addiction: tangled roots in childhood trauma. Van Dalen A. *Journal of Social Work Practice in the Addictions* 2001:1(1)25-40.

15 Childhood family problems and current psychiatric problems among young violent and property offenders. Haapasalo J, Hamalainen T. *Journal of American Academic Child Adolescent Psychiatry* 1996:35(10)1394-401.

16 Posttraumatic stress disorder in incarcerated juvenile delinquents. Steiner H, et al. *Journal of American Academy Child Adolescent Psychiatry* 1996:36(3)357-65

17 Juvenile violence and addiction: tangled roots in childhood trauma. Van Dalen A. *Journal of Social Work Practice in the Addictions* 2001:1(1)25-40.

18 Ibid., p. 30.

19 Ibid.

20 Environmental regulation of the development of mesolimbic dopamine systems: a neurobiological mechanism for vulnerability to drug abuse? Michael J. Meaney, et al. *Psychoneuroendocrinology* 2002:27(1-2)127-38.

21 Juvenile violence and addiction: tangled roots in childhood trauma. Van Dalen A. *Journal of Social Work Practice in the Addictions* 2001:1(1)25-40.

22 Maternal stress beginning in infancy may sensitize children to later stress exposure: effects on cortisol and behavior. Essex M, et al. *Biological Psychiatr* 2002:52(8)776-86.

23 Ibid.

24 Amygdala response to fearful faces in anxious and depressed children. Thomas KM, et al. *Archchives of General Psychiatry* 2001:58(11)1057-63

25 Ratey J. *A User's Guide to the Brain* (New York, NY: Vintage Books, 2002) p. 17.

26 The addicted human brain viewed in the light of imaging studies: brain circuits and treatment strategies. Volkow N, et al. *Neuropharmacology* 2004:47:3-13.

Chapter 2 – The Addicted Brain

1 Le Doux J. *Synaptic Self* (New York, NY: Penguin Publishing, 2002).

2 Activity-dependent structural changes during neuronal development. Hockfield S, Kalb RG. *Curr Opin Neurobiol* 1993:3(1)87-92.

3 Pinel J. *Biopsychology* (Needham Heights, MA: Pearson Allyn & Bacon, 2000).

4 Ibid., pp. 11-2.

5 Kennedy, Mary. Lab website, molecular neurochemistry, Cal Tech.

6 Why new neurons? Possible functions for adult hippocampal neurogenesis. Kempermann G. *J Neurosci* 2002:22(3)635-8.

7 Neurogenesis in the neocortex of adult primates. Gould E, et al. *Science* 1999:286:548-52.

8 AP report, Oct. 1999.

9 Ibid.

10 Neurogenesis in the adult brain. Gage F. *J Neurosci* 2002:22(3)612-3.

11 Ibid.

12 Participation in cognitively stimulating activities and risk of incident Alzheimer's disease. Wilson RS, et al. *JAMA* 2002:287(6)742-8.

13 Sticking together. Kennedy MB. *Proc Natl Acad Sci* 2000:21(97)11135-6.

14 Pinel J. *Biopsychology* (Needham Heights, MA: Pearson Allyn & Bacon, 2000).

15 Le Doux J. *Synaptic Self* (New York, NY: Penguin Publishing, 2002).

16 Ibid., p. 5.

17 Pinel J. *Biopsychology*. (Needham Heights, MA: Pearson Allyn & Bacon, 2000) p. 30.

18 Ratey J. *A User's Guide to the Brain* (New York, NY: Vintage Books, 2002) p. 34.

19 Ibid.

20 Ibid.

21 Representational plasticity in cortical area 3b paralleling tactual-motor skill acquisition in adult monkeys. Xerri C, et al. *Cereb Cortex* 1999:9:264-76.

22 Experience-dependent changes in cerebellar contributions to motor sequence learning. Doyon J, et al. *Proc Natl Acad Sci* 2002:99(2):1017-22.

23 Learning perceptual skills: behavioral probes into adult cortical plasticity. Karni A, Bertini G. *Curr Opin Neurol* 1997:7:530-5.

24 Schwartz J. *The Mind and the Brain* (New York, NY: Harper Collins, 2002) pp. 17-8.

25 Representational plasticity in cortical area 3b paralleling tactual-motor skill acquisition in adult monkeys. Xerri C, et al. *Cereb Cortex* 1999:9:264-76.

26 Schwartz J. *The Mind and the Brain* (New York, NY: Harper Collins, 2002) p. 18 (The author is quoting William James).

27 The addicted human brain viewed in the light of imaging studies: brain circuits and treatment strategies. Volkow N, et al. *Neuropharmacology* 2004:47:3-13.

28 Pinel J. *Biopsychology* (Needham Heights, MA: Pearson Allyn & Bacon, 2000).

29 Le Doux J. *Synaptic Self* (New York, NY: Penguin Publishing, 2002) pp 8, 78.

30 Ratey J. *A User's Guide to the Brain* (New York, NY: Vintage Books, 2002) pp. 54, 36.

31 Ibid., p. 36.

32 Schwartz J. *The Mind and the Brain* (New York, NY: Harper Collins, 2002) pp. 17-8.

33 Ibid., p. 19.

34 Ibid., jacket cover

Chapter 3 – Junk Food Junkie

1 *Junk Food Junkie*, Larry Groce. (Bob Adams Publishers, 1993).

2 Sheppard K. *Food Addictions: The Body Knows.* (Deerfield Beach, Florida: Health Communications, Inc., 1993) p. 3.

3 Katherine A. *Anatomy of a Food Addiction* (Carlsbad, CA: Gurze Books, 1996). Used by permission.

4 Ibid., p. iii.

5 Body mass index is a mathematical calculation to determine whether a patient is overweight. BMI is calculated by dividing a person's body weight in kilograms by their height in meters squared. This number can be misleading because some people are more muscular, and it would not apply to pregnant or lactating women. Being obese and being overweight are not the same condition. A BMI of 30 or more is considered obese and a BMI between 25 to 29.9 is considered overweight.

6 American Obesity Association Fact Sheet, 2002.

7 Shell E. *The Hungry Gene* (New York, NY: Atlantic Monthly Press, 2002).

8 Ibid.

9 Ibid.

10 World Health Assembly Report, May 1998.

11 American Obesity Association Fact Sheet, 2002.

12 World Health Assembly Report, May 1998.

13 American Obesity Association Fact Sheet, 2002.

14 Shell E. *The Hungry Gene* (New York, NY: Atlantic Monthly Press, 2002).

15 Health-related quality of life of severely obese children and adolescents. Schwimmer JB, et al. *JAMA* 2003 Apr:289(14)1813.

16 CNN.com HEALTH interview, April 8, 2003.

17 The genetics of obesity: what have genetic studies told us about the environment. Hewitt JK. *Behav Genet* 1997 Jul:27(4)353-8.

18 Ibid., p. 353.

19 Similarity between obesity and drug addiction as assessed by neurofunctional imaging: a concept review. Wang G, et al. *J Addict Dis* 2004:23(3)39-53.

20 Ibid.

21 Shell E. *The Hungry Gene.* (New York, NY: Atlantic Monthly Press, 2002) pp. 226-7.

22 Interaction of satiety and reward response to food stimulation. Gold M, et al. *J Addict Dis* 2004:23(3)23-37.

23 Chronic overeating called an addiction. Price J. *Washington Times*, 8/17/2004.

24 Interaction of satiety and reward response to food stimulation. Gold M, et al. *J Addict Dis* 2004:23(3)23-37.

25 Peripheral signals conveying metabolic information to the brain: short-term and long-term regulation of food intake and energy homeostasis. Havel P. *Exp Biol Med* 2001:226(11)963-77.

26 UPI interview, 2002.

27 Ibid.

28 'Super Size' takes a bite out of fast-food giant. Smith V. *Lansing State Journal*, May 10, 2004.

29 Burgers on the brain. Martindale D. *The New Scientist* 2003:177(2380)26-32.

30 Exessive sugar intake alters binding to dopamine and mu-opioid receptors in the brain. Colantuoni C, et al. *NeuroReport* 2001:12:3549-52.

31 Evidence that intermittent, excessive sugar intake causes endogenous opioid dependence. Colantuoni C, et al. *Obes Res* 2001:10:478.

32 Burgers on the brain. Martindale D. *The New Scientist* 2003:177(2380)28.

33 PET imaging and overeating behavior. *Addiction and Psychiatry Newsletter*. University of Florida College of Medicine, 2003.

34 *The biochemistry of human addiction*. Srivastava P. Medical Sciences Division, Office of Biological and Environmental Research April 2001.

35 Ibid., p. 29.

36 Ratey J. *A User's Guide to the Brain.* (New York, NY: Vintage Books, 2002).

37 Chronic food deprivation decreases extracellular dopamine in the nucleus accumbens: implications for a possible neurochemical link between weight loss and drug abuse. Pothos EN. *Obes Res* 1995 Nov:3(Suppl)525S-29S.

38 Ibid.

39 *CASA Conference: Food for thought: substance abuse and eating disorders*. The National Center on Addiction and Substance Abuse at Columbia University. Release; Jan. 23, 2001.

40 American Psychiatric Association. *Diagnostic and Statistical Manual of Mental Disorders, Fourth Edition (DSM-IV)*. (Washington, DC: American Psychiatric Association, 1994) p. 539.

41 Brownell K, Fairburn C. *Eating Disorders and Obesity*. (New York, New York: The Guilford Press, 1995).

42 Not his real name.

43 Sabate J, Blix G. *Vegetarian Nutrition*. (New York, NY: CRC Press, 2001) p. 103.

44 Relation between changes in intakes of dietary fiber and grain products and changes in weight and development of obesity among middle-aged women. Liu S, et al. *Am J Clin Nutr* 2003 Nov:78(5)920-7.

45 Weight loss associated with a daily intake of three apples or three pears among overweight women. Conceicao de Oliveira M, et al. *Nutrition* 2003 Mar:19(3)253-6.

46 Sabate J, Blix G. *Vegetarian Nutrition*. (New York, NY: CRC Press, 2001).

47 What is a high fiber diet? Wolever TM, Jenkins DJ. *Adv Exp Med Biol* 1997:427:35-42. Review.

48 Ibid.

49 Ibid.

50 Ibid.

51 Diet, neurochemicals, and mental energy. Fernstrom JD. *Nutrition Reviews* 2001:59(1)S22.

52 Can nutrient supplements modify brain function? Fernstrom JD. *Am J Clin* Nutr 2000:71(6)1669S.

53 Ibid.

54 Anti-stress effect of beta-carotene. Hasegawa T. *Ann NY Acad Sci* 1993:691:281-3.

55 Ibid.

56 Watson R. *Vegetables, Fruits, and Herbs in Health Promotion*. (New York, NY: CRC Press, 2000) p. 317.

57 Ibid., p. 318.

58 Ibid.

59 Dietary fat intake and the brain: a developing frontier in biological psychiatry. Greenwood C, et. al. *J Psychiatry Neurosci* 2001 May:26(3)182-4.

60 Diet and the brain. Baldwin B. *J Health Healing* 2000:22(4)3-7.

61 Somer E. *Food & Mood*. (New York, NY: Henry Holt and Co. 1999, 2nd ed.) pp. 156-7.

62 Ibid.

63 Ratey J. *A User's Guide to the Brain*. (New York, NY: Vintage Books, 2002) pp. 357-8.

Chapter 4 – Substance Addictions

1 Not his real name.

2 *2003 National Survey on Drug Use and Health*.

3 US Substance Abuse and Mental Health Services Administration. *The 2003 National Survey on Drug Use and Health*. www.oas.samhsa.gov/nhsda

4 Consumer Healthcare Products Association, Drug Topics, April 5, 1999, p. 43. *Rite Aid, GNC form and alliance*. The Washington Post, Jan 8, 1999, p. F3.

5 Limbaugh R. November 17, 2003 portion of official statement upon release from treatment center. www.rushlimbaugh.com.

6 National Center on Addiction and Substance Abuse at Columbia University. *High stress, frequent boredom, too much spending money: triple threat that hikes risk of teen substance abuse*. Report, 2003.

7 Drug addictions: cellular and molecular endpoints. Kreek MA. *Ann NY Acad Sci* 2001 Jun:937:27-49.

8 Ibid.

9 Ibid.

10 Decreased dopamine D2 receptor availability is associated with reduced frontal metabolism in cocaine abusers. Volkow ND, et al. *Synapse* 1993:14:169-77.

11 Ibid.

12 Decreased striatal dopaminergic responsiveness in detoxified cocaine-dependent subjects. Volkow N, et al. *Nature* 1997 April:386:830-3.

13 Reward deficiency syndrome: a biogenetic model for the diagnosis and treatment of impulsive, addictive, and compulsive behaviors. Blum K, et al. J *Psychoactive Drugs* 2000 Nov:32(Suppl i-iv)1-112.

14 Addiction, a disease of compulsion and drive: involvement of the obitofrontal cortex. Volkow N, Fowler J. *Cereb Cortex* 2000 Mar:10(3)318-25.

15 Not his real name.

16 Schwartz J. *The Mind and the Brain* (New York, NY: Harper Collins, 2002) p. 16.

17 Ratey J. *A User's Guide to the Brain* (New York, NY: Vintage Books, 2002) pp. 34-5.

18 Pinel J. *Biopsychology* (Needham Heights, MA: Pearson Allyn & Bacon, 2000) p. 352.

19 Drug addictions: cellular and molecular endpoints. Kreek MA. *Ann NY Acad Sci* 2001 Jun:937:27-49.

20 Ibid.

21 U.S. Dept. of Health and Human Services report. *Tenth special report to the U.S. Congress on Alcohol and Health*, 2002. (quote from the first paragraph of the 492-page book)

22 Deuteronomy 32:14, KJV.

23 John 2:1-11.

24 Isaiah 65:8, NKJV.

25 Proverbs 23:31, KJV.

26 Ibid., verse 32.

27 Pinel J. *Biopsychology* (Needham Heights, MA: Pearson Allyn & Bacon, 2000) p. 352.

28 Alcohol: a recently identified risk factor for breast cancer. Aronson K. *CMAJ* 2004 Jan:168(9)1147-51.

29 Alcohol, tobacco and breast cancer—collaborative reanalysis of individual data from 53 epidemiological studies, including 58,515 women with breast cancer and 95,067 women without the disease. Hamajima N. *Br J Cancer* 2002 Nov:87(11)1234-45.

30 Ibid.

31 Alcohol consumption impairs detection of performance errors in the mediofrontal cortex. Ridderinhof KR, et al. *Science* 2002 Dec:298(5601)2209-11.

32 Alcohol consumption and subclinical findings on magnetic resonance imaging of the brain in older adults. Mukamal KJ, et al. *Stroke* 2001:32;1939-55.

33 Canadian Press, Sept 17, 2001.

34 Effects of abstinence on the brain: quantitative magnetic resonance imaging and magnetic resonance spectroscopic imaging in chronic alcohol abuse. O'Neill J, et al. *Alcohol Clin Exp Res* 2001 Nov:25(11)1673-82.

35 Reuters Health, Nov. 14, 2001.

36 Ibid.

37 Alcohol's effects on the risk for coronary heart disease. Mukamal KJ, Rimm EB. *Alcohol Res Health* 2001:25(4)255-61.

38 Why heart disease mortality is low in France: the time lag explanation. Law M, Wald N. *BMJ* 1999:318:1471-80.

39 Ibid.

40 Red wine, dealcoholized red wine, and especially grape juice, inhibit atherosclerosis in a hamster model. Vinson JA. *Atherosclerosis* 2001:156(1)67-72.

41 Alcohol consumption and mortality from all causes, coronary heart disease, and stroke: results from a prospective cohort study of Scottish men with 21 years of follow up. Hart CL, et al. *BMJ* 1999:318:1725-9.

42 Ibid., p. 1725.

43 Alcohol-induced generation of lipid peroxidation products in humans. Meagher EA, et al. *J Clin Invest* 1999:104(6)805-13.

44 Internal Medicine News 2003 Mar:36(6) *Cardiovascular benefits of alcohol may be reflection of biased studies.* International Medical News Group.

45 Ibid.

46 Red wine, dealcoholized red wine, and especially grape juice, inhibit atherosclerosis in a hamster model. Vinson JA, et al. *Atherosclerosis* 2001:156(1)67-72.

47 Benefits of red wine may not be due to alcohol content. Vinson JA, et al. *Medical Tribune* 1999:40(1)24.

48 American Lung Association Fact Sheet: *Smoking*: January, 2004.

49 American Lung Association Fact Sheet: *Prevalence of youth tobacco use*. January, 2004.

50 Ibid.

51 Dr. Victor DeNoble, former research scientist for Philip Morris Tobacco: Smoking Awareness symposium, Andrews University, Berrien Springs, MI; 2002.

52 American Lung Association Fact Sheet: *Prevalence of youth tobacco use*. January, 2004.

53 Centers for Disease Control. Table: *Comparative causes of annual deaths in the United States*. November, 2000.

54 World Tax Database, Office of Tax Policy Research, 2002.

55 CNN news report, 1998. *Tobacco revenue drives debate as GOP champions Medicare*.

56 WHO and CDC report: *Global youth tobacco survey*, 2004.

57 Mortality and smoking in Hong Kong: case-control study of all adult deaths in 1998. Lam TH, et al. *BMJ* 2001 Aug:323(7309)361.

58 WHO and CDC report: *Global youth tobacco survey*, 2004.

59 Effects of nicotine and caffeine, separately and in combination, on EEG topography, mood, heart rate, cortisol, and vigilance. Gilbert DG. *Psychophysiology* 2000:37(5)583-95.

60 Dr. Victor DeNoble, former research scientist for Philip Morris Tobacco: Smoking Awareness symposium, Andrews University, Berrien Springs, MI; 2002.

61 A harmful way to stop smoking. Groman E, et al. *Lancet* 1999 Feb:353(9151)466-7.

62 Nicotine delivery from smoking bidis and an additive-free cigarette. Malson JL, et al. *Nicotine Tob Res* 2002 Nov:4(4)485-90.

63 Lung carcinoma trands by histologic type in Vaud and Neuchatel, Switzerland, 1974-1994. Levi F, et al. *Cancer* 1997 Mar:79(5)906-14.

64 Effect of cigar smoking on the risk of cardiovascular disease, chronic obstructive pulmonary disease, and cancer in men. Iribarren C, et al. *N Engl J Med* 1999 Jun:340(23)1829-31.

65 Effect of cigar smoking on endothelium-dependent brachial artery dilation in healthy young adults. Santo-Tomas M, et al. *Am Heart* J 2002 Jan:143(1)83-6.

66 Effect of cigar smoking on the risk of cardiovascular disease, chronic obstructive pulmonary disease, and cancer in men. Iribarren C, et al. *N Engl J Med* 1999 Jun:340(23)1829-31.

67 Bissell T. *Chewed up: a boy's rush, a man's addiction*. Reader's Digest, Oct. 2002.

68 Ratey J. *A User's Guide to the Brain* (New York, NY: Vintage Books, 2002).

69 Effect of a short bout of exercise on tobacco withdrawal symptoms and desire to smoke. Ussher M, et al. *Outcomes Management* 2001:157(4)66-72.

70 Perceived stress, quitting smoking, and smoking relapse. Cohen S, Lichtenstein E. *Health Psychol* 1990:9(4)466-78.

71 Caffeine and Health. Ashton CH. *BMJ* 1987:295(6609):1293-4.

72 Wake up and smell the coffee: caffeine, coffee and the medical consequences. Chou T. *West J Med* 1992 Nov:157(5)544-53.

73 Coffee Research Institute. Report: *Consumption in the United States*. 1999.

74 Coffee, tea and you. Greden J. *The Sciences* 1979:7:6-7.

75 Wake up and smell the coffee: caffeine, coffee and the medical consequences. Chou T. *West J Med* 1992 Nov:157(5)544-53.

76 Caffeine and Health. Ashton CH. *BMJ* 1987:295(6609)1293-4.

77 Coffee, tea, and caffeine consumption and risk of rheumatoid arthritis: results from the Iowa Women's Health Study. Mikuls TR, et al. *Arthritis Rheum* 2002 Jan:46(1)83-91.

78 Coffee acutely increases sympathetic nerve activity and blood pressure independently of caffeine content: role of habitual versus nonhabitual drinking. Corti R, et al. *Circulation* 2002 Dec:106(23)2935-40.

79 Endorsement of DSM-IV dependence criteria among caffeine users. Hurghes JR, et al. *Drug & Alcohol Dep* 1998 Oct:52(2)99-107.

80 Ibid.

81 A critical review of caffeine withdrawal: empirical validation of symptoms and signs, incidence, severity, and associated features. Juliano L, Griffiths R. *Psychopharm* 2004 Sep (Epub ahead of print).

82 UPI interview, Sept. 29, 2004.

83 A critical review of caffeine withdrawal: empirical validation of symptoms and signs, incidence, severity, and associated features. Juliano L, Griffiths R. *Psychopharm* 2004 Sep (Epub ahead of print).

84 Phelps J. *The Hidden Addiction and How to Get Free*. (Boston, MA: Little, Brown and Co, 1986) p. 3.

85 National Soft Drink Association website: www.nsda.org

86 Ibid. Secondary source: *Liquid Candy*. Jacobson M. CSPI.

87 Ibid.

88 Ibid.

89 Rice, P. *Stress and Health* (Pacific Grove, CA: Brooks/Cole Publishing, 1992).

90 Clinical and biochemical manifestations of depression. Relation to the neurobiology of stress (2). Gold PW, et al. *N Engl J Med* 1988 Nov:319(7)413-20.

91 Why stress is bad for your brain. Sapolsky RM. *Science* 1996 Aug:273(5276)749-50.

92 Chronic caffeine exposure potentiates nicotine self-administration in rats. Shoaib M, et al. *Psychopharm* 1999 Mar:142(4)327-33.

Chapter 5 – The Entertainment Trap

1 Are you stressed out? In a daze? You may be watching too much TELEVISION. Atlanta Constitution, April 30, 1990. (Review of book cited in note 5).

2 Statistics from A.C. Nielsen Co, cited on www.csun.edu and www.televisionturnoff.org.

3 Television in the home: the 1997 Annenberg Survey of Parents and Children. The Annenberg Public Policy Center of the University of Pennsylvania, June 9, 1997.

4 Healy J. *Endangered Minds: Why Children Don't Think and What We Can Do About It*. (New York, NY: Simon and Schuster, 1999) p. 196.

5 Children, adolescents, and the media in the 21st century. Strasburger V, Donnerstein F. *Adolesc Med* 2000:11(1)51-68.

6 MacNeil R. *The trouble with television. Essay.* (Englewood Cliffs, NJ: Prentice-Hall, 1989) p. 2.

7 Kubey R Csikszentmihalyi M. *Television and the Quality of Life: How Viewing Shapes Everyday Experience.* (Mahwah, NJ: Lawrence Erlbaum Assoc, 1990).

8 Ibid.

9 Ibid.

10 Ibid.

11 The most important unresolved issue in the addictions: conceptual chaos. Shaffer HJ. *Substance Use Misuse* 1997:32(11)1573.

12 Home viewers grow addicted to television. Goleman D. New York Times, 1990.

13 Gabler N. *Life, the Movie: How Entertainment Conquered Reality*. (New York: Alfred A. Knopf, 1999).

14 Television addiction is no mere metaphor. Kubey R, Csikszentmihalyi M. *Scientific American* 2002 Feb:77.

15 Ibid.

16 Neurogenesis and its implications for regeneration in the adult brain. Eriksson PS. *J Rehabil Med* 2003 May:(41 Suppl)17-9. Review.

17 Neurogenesis in the adult brain. Functional consequences. Gheusi G, Rochefort C. *J Soc Biol* 2002:196(1)67-76.

18 Victoroff J. *Saving Your Brain*. (New York, NY: Bantam Books, 2002).

19 Ratey J. *User's Guide to the Brain* (New York, NY: Vintage Books, 2002) pp. 55-6.

20 Ibid, pp. 141-2.

21 Ibid, p. 36.

22 Healy J. *Endangered Minds: Why Children Don't Think and What We Can Do About It*. (New York, NY: Simon and Schuster, 1999) p. 196.

23 Healy J. *Endangered Minds: Why Children Don't Think and What We Can Do About It*. (New York, NY: Simon and Schuster, 1999).

24 Early television exposure and subsequent attention problems in children. Healy J. *Pediatrics* 2004:113(4)917.

25 Early television exposure and subsequent attentional problems in children. Christakis D, et al. *Pediatrics* 2004:113(4)708-13.

26 Study: TELEVISION may cause attention deficit. AP news interview with Dimitri Christakis, April 2004.

27 Antonio Domasio's theory of thinking faster and faster. *Discover* 2004 May:25(5)49.

28 Ibid.

29 Packaging television news: the effects of tabloid on information processing and evaluative responses. Grabe M, et al. *Journal of Broadcasting and Electronic Media* 2000:44(4)581.

30 Ibid.

31 The psychological impact of negative TELEVISION news bulletins: the catastrophizing of personal worries. Johnston WM, Davey GC. *Br J Psychol* 1997 Feb:88(Pt 1)85-91.

32 Antonio Domasio's theory of thinking faster and faster. *Discover* 2004 May:25(5)49.

33 Ibid.

34 Healy J. *Endangered Minds: Why Children Don't Think and What We Can Do About It.* (New York, NY: Simon and Schuster, 1999) p. 199.

35 Ibid, p. 200.

36 MacNeil R. *The trouble with television. Essay.* (Englewood Cliffs, NJ: Prentice-Hall, 1989) p. 1.

37 Television addiction is no mere metaphor. Kubey R, Csikszentmihalyi M. *Scientific American* 2002 Feb:76.

38 MacNeil R. *The trouble with television. Essay.* (Englewood Cliffs, NJ: Prentice-Hall, 1989) p. 2.

39 Healy J. *Endangered Minds: Why Children Don't Think and What We Can Do About It.* (New York, NY: Simon and Schuster, 1999) pp. 201-2.

40 Influence of TELEVISION on daydreaming and creative imagination: a review of research. Valkenburg P, van der Voort T. *Psychological Bulletin* 1994:116(2)316-39.

41 Attention to television: alpha power and its relationship to image motion and emotional content. Simons R., et al. *Media Psychology* 2003:5(3)283-301.

42 MacNeil R. *The trouble with television. Essay.* (Englewood Cliffs, NJ: Prentice-Hall, 1989) p. 2.

43 Does television affect learning and school performance? Strasburger VC. *Pediatrician* 1986:13(2-3)141-7.

44 Early television exposure and subsequent attention problems in children. Healy J. *Pediatrics* 2004:113(4)917-8.

45 MacNeil R. *The trouble with television. Essay.* (Englewood Cliffs, NJ: Prentice-Hall, 1989) p. 1.

46 Brain wave measures of media involvement. Krugman H. *J Advertis Res* 1971:2(1)3.

47 Healy J. *Endangered Minds: Why Children Don't Think and What We Can Do About It.* (New York, NY: Simon and Schuster, 1999).

48 Television addiction is no mere metaphor. Kubey R, Csikszentmihalyi M. *Scientific American* 2002 Feb:76.

49 Ibid.

50 Scruton R. *An Intelligent Person's Guide to Modern Culture.* (London:Duckworth, 1998) p. 96.

51 Labalme H. *The Overwatched American.* The TELEVISION-free American, Spring, 1998.

52 Ibid., p. 1.

53 Winter R. *Still Bored in a Culture of Entertainment.* (Downer's Grove, IL: Inter Varsity Press, 2002) p. 59.

54 Labalme H. *The Overwatched American.* The TELEVISION-free American, Spring, 1998.

55 Winter R. *Still Bored in a Culture of Entertainment.* (Downer's Grove, IL: Inter Varsity Press, 2002) p. 36.

56 Guinness O. *The Call.* (Nashville, TN: Word, 1998) p. 149.

57 Labalme H. *The Overwatched American.* The TELEVISION-free American, Spring, 1998.

58 Console wars. The Economist, June 2002.

59 Winter R. *Still Bored in a Culture of Entertainment.* (Downer's Grove, IL: Inter Varsity Press, 2002) p. 52.

60 Ibid., p. 40.

61 Grossman D. *Stop Teaching our Kids to Kill.* (New York, NY: Crown Publishers, 1999) p. 68.

62 Healy J. *Endangered Minds: Why Children Don't Think and What We Can Do About It.* (New York, NY: Simon and Schuster, 1999) p. 207.

63 Measuring problem video game playing in adolescents. Tejero Salguero R, Moran R. *Addiction* 2002 Dec:97(12)1601-6.

64 Evidence for striatal dopamine release during a video game. Koepp M, et al. *Nature* 1998 May:393(6682)266-8.

65 Healy J. *Endangered Minds: Why Children Don't Think and What We Can Do About It.* (New York, NY: Simon and Schuster, 1999) p. 209.

66 Postman N. *Amusing Ourselves to Death: Public Discourse in the Age of Show Business* (New York, NY: Penguin, 1985) p. 155.

67 Report by Vincent Mathews, MD, at the 88th Scientific Assembly and Annual Meeting of the Radiological Society of North America, 2002. WebMD, 2002.

68 Ratey J. *A User's Guide to the Brain* (New York, NY: Vintage Books, 2002) pp. 237-8.

69 Grossman D. *Stop Teaching our Kids to Kill.* (New York, NY: Crown Publishers, 1999) p. 66.

70 Ibid., p. 68.

71 Ibid., pp. 67-8.

72 Exposure to violent media: the effects of songs with violent lyrics on aggressive thoughts and feelings. Anderson C, Carnagey N. *J Pers Soc Psychol* 2003:84(5)960-71.

73 Grossman D. *Stop Teaching our Kids to Kill.* (New York, NY: Crown Publishers, 1999) pp. 62-3.

74 Longitudinal relations between children's exposure to TELEVISION violence and their aggressive and violent behavior in young adulthood: 1977-1992. Huesmann L, et al. *Dev Psychol* 2003 Mar:39(2)201-21.

75 Television viewing as a cause of increasing obesity among children in the United States, 1986-1990. Gortmaker S, et al. *Arch Pediatr Adolesc Med* 1996:150:357-362.

76 Relationship of physical activity and television watching with body weight and level of fatness among children. Anderson R, et al. *JAMA* 1998:279(12)959-60.

77 Television viewing and cardiovascular risk factors in young adults: the CARDIA study. Sidney S, et al. *Ann Epidemiol* 1996 Mar:6(2)154-9.

78 Shell E. *The Hungry Gene* (New York, NY: Atlantic Monthly Press, 2002) p. 170.

79 Effects of television on metabolic rate: potential implications for childhood obesity. Klesges R, et al. *Pediatrics* 1993 Feb:91(2)281-6.

80 Does excessive television viewing contribute to the development of dementia? Aronson M. *Medical Hypothesis* 1993:41:465-6.

81 Watching TELEVISION violence can overwork your heart. Medical Tribune News Service, 1995.

82 Review of psychosocial stress and asthma: an integrated biopsychosocial approach. Wright R. *Thorax.* 1998 Dec:53(12)1066-74. Review.

83 Medical Tribune 1995:36(8)21.

84 Short-term effectiveness of anticipatory guidance to reduce early childhood risks for subsequent violence. Sege R, et al. *Arch Pediatr Adolesc Med.* 1997 Apr:151(4)392-7.

Chapter 6 – Behavioral Addictions

1 Excessive compulsive buying or "behavioral addiction"? A case study. Grusser S, et al. *Wien Klin Wochenschr* 2004 Mar:116(5-6)201-4.

2 Epidemiology of behavioral dependence: literature review and results of original studies. Lejoyeux M, et al. *Eur Psychiatry* 2000 Mar:15(2)129-34.

3 Compulsive disorders. Kuzma JM, Black, DW. *Curr Psychiatry Rep* 2004 Feb:6(1)58-65.

4 Internetworldstats.com.

5 Lost in cyberspace: the web @ work. Greenfield DN, Davis RA. *Cyberpsychol Behav* 2002 Aug:5(4)347-53.

6 U. S. News & World Report. Jan 17 2000:128(2)41.

7 Psychological characteristics of compulsive Internet use: a preliminary analysis. Greenfield (1999a) *Cyberpsychol Behav* 2(5)403-12.

8 Internet addiction: a genuine diagnosis or not? Mitchell P. *Lancet* 2000 Feb 19:355(9204)632.

9 Internet addiction: the emergence of a new clinical disorder. Young K. *Cyberpsychol Behav* 1996:1(3)237-44.

10 Psychosocial parameters of Internet addiction. Briggs R. University at Albany, New York; Dept. of Psychology.

11 Lost in cyberspace: the web @ work. Greenfield DN, Davis RA. *Cyberpsychol Behav* 2002 Aug:5(4)347-53.

12 Ibid.

13 U. S. News & World Report. Jan 17 2000:128(2)41.

14 Web addiction on the rise. Hyman G. ClickZ Stats. August 21, 2002.

15 Internet addiction associated with features of impulse control disorder: is it a real psychiatric disorder? Treuer T, et al. *J Affect Disord* 2001 Oct:66(2-3)283.

16 Psychiatric features of individuals with problematic Internet use. Shapira NA, et al. *J Affect Disord* 2000 Jan-Mar:57(1-3)267-72.

17 Young KS. *Internet addiction: the emergence of a new clinical disorder;* Presented at the annual meeting of the American Psychological Association, Toronto, Canada, Aug 1996

18 Internet over-users' psychological profiles: a behavior sampling analysis on Internet addiction. Whang LS, et al. *Cyberpsychol Behav* 2003 Apr:6(2)143-50.

19 Not his real name.

20 Ibid.

21 Pathologic gambling: America's newest addiction? Pasternak AV 4th. *Am Fam Physician* 1997 Oct 1:56(5)1293-6.

22 Ibid.

23 The neurobiology of pathological gambling. Potenza MN. *Semin Clin Neuropsychiatry* 2001 Jul:6(3)217-26. Review.

24 Psychiatric comorbidity in pathological gambling: a critical review. Crockford DN, el-Guebaly N. *Can J Psychiatry* 1998 Feb:43(1)43-50. Review.

25 Pathologic gambling: America's newest addiction? Pasternak AV 4th. *Am Fam Physician* 1997 Oct 1:56(5)1293-6.

26 Compulsion to buy lottery tickets poses a growing risk. Armstead C. *The Tennessean* 1999.

27 Video lottery addiction compared to crack cocaine. Young S. Argus Leader.com, Oct. 2000.

28 Ibid.

29 Compulsion to buy lottery tickets poses a growing risk. Armstead C. *The Tennessean* 1999.

30 Ibid.

31 Access to gambling opportunities and compulsive gambling. Lester D. *Int J Addict* 1994:29:1611-6.

32 Frontal lobe dysfunction in pathological gambling patients. Cavedini P, et al. *Biol Psychiatry* 2002 Feb 15:51(4)334-41.

33 Video lottery addiction compared to crack cocaine. Young S. *Argus Leader.com,* Oct. 2000.

34 Behavioral addictions: do they exist? Holden C. *Science Magazine* 294(5544)980.

35 The neurobiology of pathological gambling. Potenza MN. *Semin Clin Neuropsychiatry* 2001 Jul:6(3)217-26. Review.

36 Biology, addiction and gambling. *The Wager - Weekly Addiction Gambling Education Report* www.thewager.org. Harvard Medical School, Massachusetts Council on Compulsive Gambling. 2003 Jul 23:8:30.

37 Internet Filter Review website, www.Internetfilterreview.com/Internet-pornography-statistics-hmtl.

38 Child-proofing on the world wide web: a survey of webservers. *Jurimetrics* 2001. National Research Online Report, 2002.

39 Study by Standford and Duquesne Universities, *Washington Times,* 2000 Jan 26. MSNBC.

40 Leadership Survey, *Christianity Today* 2001 Dec.

41 National Research Council Report, 2002.

42 National Research Council Report, 2002.

43 The use of sexually explicit stimuli by rapists, child molesters, and non-offenders. Marshall W. *J of Sex Res* 1988 May:25(2)267-88.

44 Time/CNN 2000.

45 National Research Council, 2002.

46 Smith S. Report, *New York Post* 9/25/03.

47 Delli-Colli K. The web's dark secret. *Newsweek* March 19, 2001.

48 The use of sexually explicit stimuli by rapists, child molesters, and non-offenders. Marshall WL. *J Sex Res* 1988 May:25(2)267-88.

49 Pornography's effects: empirical and clinical evidence. Cline V. University of Utah Department of Psychology.

50 www.protectkids.com.

51 London School of Economics; Jan 2002. www.protectkids.com

52 The National Law Center for Children and Families, promoting the Child Online Protection Act (COPA), in the COPA Brief for Members of Congress.

53 Ratey J. *User's Guide to the Brain* (New York, NY: Vintage Books, 2002) pp. 54, 36.

54 Ibid., p. 36.

55 Schwartz J. *The Mind and the Brain* (New York, NY: Harper Collins, 2002) pp. 17-8.

56 Ibid., p. 19.

57 Ibid., jacket cover.

58 Hebrews 2:15, RSV. Emphasis supplied.

59 Romans 12:1-2.

60 Romans 6:16. (NKJV).

Chapter 7 – Healing the Broken Brain – Keys to Life: Connection and Community

1 Spiritual care for the critically ill. Clark C, Heidenreich T. *Am J Crit Care* 1995 Jan:4(1)77-81.

2 Religion, psychopathology, and substance use and abuse; a multimeasure, genetic-epidemiologic study. Trappler B, Endicott J. *Am J Psychiatry* 1997 Nov:154(11)1636.

3 Religious activity improves quality of life for ill elders. Reyes-Ortiz CA, et al. *J Am Geriatrics Society* 1996 Sep:44(9)S-49.

4 Religious commitment and health status: a review of the research and implications for family medicine. Matthews, DA, et al. *Arch Fam Med* 1998 Mar:7(2)118.

5 Proverbs 3:5-6.

6 A review of prayer within the role of the holistic nurse. Lewis PJ. *J Holist Nurs* 1996 Dec:14(4)308.

7 The use of prayer in spiritual care. Lo R. *Aust J Holist Nurs* 2003 Apr:100(1)22.

8 Religious practices and alcoholism in a southern adult population. Koenig HG, et al. *Hosp Community Psychiatry* 1994 Mar:45(3)225-331.

9 The relationship between a patient's spirituality and health experiences. McBride JL, et al. *Fam Med* 1998 Feb:30(2)122-6.

10 The impact of personality and religion on attitude towards substance use among 13-15 year olds. Francis LJ. *Drug Alcohol Depend* 1997 Mar 14:44(2-3)73

11 Psalm 62:8.

12 White EG. *Happiness Digest* (Silver Spring, MD: Better Living Publications, 1994) p. 44.

13 Ezekiel 36:29.

14 Ibid., verse 27.

15 Romans 8:26.

16 Philippians 4:6-7.

17 Psalm 119:130.

18 Jeremiah 15:16.

19 1 John 1:9.

20 2 Corinthians 5:17.

21 John 15:9.

22 I John 4:8.

23 Social relationships and cardiovascular disease risk factors: findings from the third national health and nutrition examination survey. Ford ES, et al. *Prev Med* 2000 Feb:30(2)83-92.

24 Social support and age-related differences in cardiovascular function: an examination of potential mediators. Uchina BN, et al. *Ann Behav Med* 1999 Spring:21(2)135-42.

25 Population based study of social and productive activities as predictors of survival among elderly Americans. Glass TA, et al. *BMJ* 1999 Aug:310(7208)478-83.

26 Merriam Webster online dictionary.

27 Quoted on *Campaign for Forgiveness Research* website, John Templeton, Ph.D.

28 Psychophysiological responses as indices of affective dimensions. Witvliet CV, Vrana SR. *Psychophysiology* 1995 Sep:32(5)436-43.

29 Forgiveness in response to interpersonal conflict. Lawler K, et al. *J Behavioral Med* 2003 Oct:26(5)373-93.

30 Religion and the forgiving personality. McCullough ME, Worthington EL. *J Pers* 1999 Dec:67(6):1141-64.

31 Ibid.

32 Is the glass half empty or half full? A prospective study of optimism and coronary heart disease in the normative aging study. Kubzansky LD, et al. *Psychosom Med* 2001:63(6)910-6.

33 CNN report, 1999.

34 Meyer J. *Beauty for Ashes* (Tulsa, OK: Harrison House, 1994) p.101.

35 Ibid., p. 109.

36 Ibid., p. 108.

Chapter 8 – Healing the Broken Brain – Keys to Life: Lifestyle and Environment

1 Ratey J. A *User's Guide to the Brain* (New York, NY: Vintage Books, 2001) p. 17.

2 Proverbs 23:7.

3 Somer E. *Food and Mood* (New York, NY: Henry Holt Reference Books, 1995) p. 4.

4 Phelps J. *The Hidden Addiction and How to Get Free* (Boston, MA: Little, Brown and Co, 1986) p. 73.

5 A replication study of violent and nonviolent subjects: cerebrospinal fluid metabolites of serotonin and dopamine are predicted by plasma essential fatty acids. Hibbeln JR, et. al. *Biol Psychiatry* 1998 Aug 15:44(4)243-9.

6 Mood changes during exercise. Lane AM, et al. *Precept Mot Skills* 2002 Jun:94 (3 Pt 1)732-4.

7 Energy, tiredness, and tension effects of a sugar snack versus moderate exercise. Thayer RE. *J Pers Soc Psychol* 1987 Jan:52(1)119-25.

8 Fitness effects on the cognitive function of older adults: a meta-analytic study. Colcombe S, Kramer AF. *Psychol Sci* 2003 Mar:14(2)125-30.

9 A randomized controlled trial of the effect of exercise on sleep. Singh NA, et al. *Sleep* 1997 Feb:20(20)95-101.

10 Hare E. *Make God First* (Washington DC: Review and Herald Publishing, 1960).

11 Reactivation of hippocampal ensemble memories during sleep. Wilson MA, McNaughton BL. *Science* 1994 Jul:265(5172)676-9.

12 Sleep loss results in an elevation of cortisol levels the next evening. Leproult R. *Sleep* 1997:20(10)865-70.

13 Effects of sleep deprivation and exercise on glucose tolerance. VanHelder T, et al. *Aviat Space Environ Med* 1993:64(6)487-92.

14 Partial sleep deprivation reduces natural killer cell activity in humans. Irwin M, et al. *Psychosom Med* 1994:56:493-8.

15 Mark 6:31.

16 Genesis 2:2-3.

17 Hebrews 4:11.

18 Deuteronomy 7:26.

19 Ratey J. A *User's Guide to the Brain* (New York, NY: Vintage Books, 2001) p. 191.

20 Psalm 46:1.

21 Dean William Ralph Inge.

22 Katz N, MD, Ph.D. *The Aging Brain* Seminar, 2003. Institute for Natural Resources. Held in Detroit, MI.

23 Mathew 6:27.

24 Philippians 4:6-7.

25 Matthew 11:28.

26 Merriam Webster online dictionary.

27 Ratey J. *A User's Guide to the Brain* (New York, NY: Vintage Books, 2001) p. 239.

28 Ibid.

29 Ibid, p. 241.

30 State anxiety reduction and exercise: does hemispheric activation reflect such changes? Petruzullo S, Landers D. *Med Sci Sports Exerc* 1994 Aug:26(8)1028-35

[31] Ratey J. *A User's Guide to the Brain* (New York, NY: Vintage Books, 2001) p. 229.

[32] The Duchenne smile: emotional expression and brain physiology II. Ekman P, Davidson R. J *Pers Soc Psychol* 1990:4(5)342-5.

[33] Alterations in brain and immune function produced by mindfulness meditation. Davidson RJ, et al. *Psychosom Med* 2003 Jul-Aug:65(4)564-70.

[34] Psalm 119:59.

[35] Proverbs 4:26.

[36] Optimism is associated with mood, coping, and immune change response to stress. Segerstron SC, et al. *J Pers Soc Psychol* 1998 Jun:74(6)1646-55.

Chapter 9 – The Attitude Factor – Spiritual and Emotional Healing

[1] Isaiah 61:1.

[2] Psalm 113:7.

[3] Hebrews 2:15.

[4] John 5:6.

[5] I Peter 3:3.

[6] Ratey J. *A User's Guide to the Brain* (New York, NY: Vintage Books, 2002) p. 356.

[7] James 3:5-6.

[8] Schwartz J. *The Mind and the Brain* (New York, NY: Harper Collins, 2002) pp. 17-8.

[9] Ibid., p. 384.

Notes:

Notes:

Want to learn more?

What you've learned in this book could be changing your life already! But if you want to learn more, or to see the interviews from the *Delivered* sections of this book, go to LifestyleMatters.com and order the *Living Free* DVD. It also contains tips on healthy eating while you're traveling, exercise tips, menu planning tips, graphics-rich interviews, and much more. And while you're at our website, check out the other publications from Lifestyle Matters® including:

Diet & Stress: Simple Solutions — Food choices can either help or hinder your stress sensitivity and how intensely you respond to stress. That's why eating right is an important part of stress management. The book and DVD will show you how to implement smart, healthful, simple lifestyle changes that will help you tame stress in your life—and boost your ability to fight disease!

Foods for Thought — Research is now confirming that a healthful diet can improve your mood, help you think better, and lower your risk for dementia. The *Foods for Thought* book and DVD are filled with practical tips, helpful charts, and lots of delicious recipes to help your mental engine purr instead of ping. If you have children or grandchildren, this book and DVD are a must!

Presenter's materials, including planning sections, nightly schedules and handouts, a fully-scripted multimedia presentation, a comprehensive training DVD, and advertising ideas are available for all three topics.

Lifestyle Matters™
Changing Lives...for Good!

For more information, or to place an order for any of the Lifestyle Matters® materials, visit www.LifestyleMatters.com or call 1-866-624-5433.